W9-AGV-492

THE

COMPLETE AND UNALTERED

TOTEM

# ALSO BY DAVID MORRELL

## FICTION

First Blood (1972)

Testament (1975)

Last Reveille (1977)

The Totem (1979)

Blood Oath (1982)

The Hundred-Year Christmas (1983)

The Brotherhood of the Rose (1984)

Rambo (First Blood Part II) (1985)

The Fraternity of the Stone (1985)

The League of Night and Fog (1987)

Rambo III (1988)

The Fifth Profession (1990)

The Covenant of the Flame (1991)

Assumed Identity (1993)

## NONFICTION

John Barth: An Introduction (1976)

Fireflies (1988)

# THE

## David Morrell

# TOTEM

COMPLETE AND UNALTERED

THE TOTEM *(COMPLETE AND UNALTERED)*

Copyright © 1979,1994 by David Morrell

 Illustrations Copyright © 1994 by Thomas Canty

Book design by Thomas Canty and Robert K. Wiener

Printed in the United States of America

**Library of Congress Catalog Number  94-76568**

ISBN - 1-880418-26-6 Trade Edition

❖

FIRST EDITION

DONALD M. GRANT, PUBLISHER, INC.
HAMPTON FALLS, NEW HAMPSHIRE 03844

# I NTRODUCTION

One of the first things I learned as a writer was when in doubt don't throw any pages away. That rule has frequently been of help, especially when due to over-familiarity with a manuscript in progress I edited a book too stringently, taking out scenes that shouldn't have been omitted, needing to go back and reinsert them, grateful that I'd saved the original versions. My filing cabinets became crammed with material that I eliminated from various works. Even after those works were published, I continued to save the files.

As a consequence, this is what you might call a "found book." In 1991, the British publisher, Headline, decided to reissue my only (to date) out-and-out horror novel, *The Totem*. It had first been released in hardback by the American publisher, M. Evans, in 1979 and had subsequently been reprinted by Fawcett in paperback one year later. The hardback was eventually discontinued. By the end of the eighties, so was the paperback. My memory of the story dimmed.

Thus when Headline suggested that it might be interesting for me to write an introduction to its new edition, I decided that I'd better reacquaint myself with the text so I'd be accurate about what I was introducing. But when I pulled *The Totem* off the shelf and studied it, I discovered to my dismay that the book I remembered was not the book that had been published. So much was different. So much was missing. Where was *this* scene, and where was *that?* I asked myself with increasing shock.

Abruptly a barrier in my memory fractured. I suddenly recalled that when I'd submitted *The Totem* in the late seventies, my editor had not been pleased. "It's too big, too sprawling," he'd said. "Where's the love interest? How come it takes so long to introduce your main character? Why isn't this about the military as in *First Blood?*" Given the ultimatum that if the novel wasn't changed it wouldn't be accepted, I reluctantly produced an alternate version of *The Totem,* half as long, twice as fast, with my main character appearing on the first page, and yes, with a love interest.

Not that I feel uncomfortable about that version. I think it's effective, and I'm gratified that it has acquired a reputation among horror fans. Critics have described it as one of the best horror novels of the seventies. It's been cited in *Horror: 100 Best Books,* and Denver's *Rocky Mountain News* in 1989 placed it on that newspaper's Halloween list of "10 Scariest Books." But it's not the book that I wanted published, and after I reread *The Totem* in preparation for writing the Headline introduction, I couldn't resist the impulse to search through my files, and with delight, I discovered the original version that the turmoil of my negotiations with the book's 1979 publisher had forced me to forget.

The manuscript was dusty, dogeared, and yellowed, written on a typewriter, not a word processor. I felt as if I'd opened one of those metal boxes that are sometimes placed in the cornerstones of buildings so that historians from a later age can open them and study the once-contemporary objects sealed within them. I can't emphasize sufficiently how much I'd repressed my memory of the first version of *The Totem*. It's no exaggeration to say that I truly couldn't remember having written it. As I said, a found book. A time capsule from and about the sixties and the seventies. And having found it, I couldn't help smiling. There were the scenes that I'd subconsciously been missing. There were the length and scope and texture that I'd wanted. An expansive alternate style. A new beginning. A quite different ending. And as for the middle . . . well, let's put it this way: the story is twice as long and two-thirds dissimilar. There isn't just *more* plot—the extra material gives the plot a different twist. So what you're about to read is the intended version of this novel. If you're familiar with *The Totem* in its previously published form, you're about to enter its alternate universe. I think you'll find some pleasantly scary surprises.

David Morrell

Santa Fe, 1994

For Geoffrey Household,

1900-1988,
the thriller writer beyond compare.

# C ONTENTS

# ILLUSTRATIONS

——| *totem*, noun:

1. among primitive peoples, an

animal or natural object

considered as being related by

blood to a given family or clan

and taken as its symbol.

2. an image of this.

The power of the moon on animals and people is well known. Passing over the parallel between a woman's monthly cycle and the phases of the moon, we note the predominance of industrial accidents when the moon is at its fullest, the tendency of dogs and other canine animals to bay at it, of lunatics to do the same. Perpetuating ancient myth, we link the moon with love and with fertility. We speak of harvest moon. We speak of someone's being moonstruck. The very motion of the earth, its tides and shifting subzones, are related to the moon. We even set aside one day in worship of it, Monday, what in ancient times was Moon day.

Jacob Steiger,

*The Pathology of Madness*

# POTTER'S

## PART ONE

# FIELD

SOLITARY RIDER ON A RIDGE. THAT WAS THE BEGINNING. HE'D BEEN OUT FOR HALF A day now, checking the borders of his ranch, and coming from the high ground, he stopped to look down past the pine trees toward the sweeping grassland.

It was something that he never failed to marvel at. Sitting up here at the farthest reach of what he owned, staring down at all that rich wide ground, the abundant grass, the dots of sagebrush, he remembered how his father had used to take him here and point to it and tell him how his father's father had to fight for it and how the land would one day soon be his. He hadn't known that his father was then dying. He wasn't sure that his father even knew. But six months later he had seen his father buried—death had been both quick and painful—and then all the land was his.

That had happened twenty years ago. Now at thirty-eight

he still came out here on the anniversary of when his father had died, and looked down at the valley from where his father once had pointed to it, and was proud. Pride of ownership. And something else: of knowing who his father had been. No, not who but what. The kindest, gentlest, and yet strongest man he'd ever met. Still after all these years he loved the man. And loved the land because of him.

He sat there, his reins tight on his horse, and stared out at the pasture stretching off as far as he could see and rubbed his weathered face and shook his head. He knew that he should go. The sun was fierce upon his back, his head protected by his cowman's hat. The horse would need some water soon; he still had lots of range to check. All the same, he didn't want to leave. He waited, his boots pressed into the stirrups, leather creaking, admiring the land his father had shown to him, and then the moment passed. He loosened the reins, nudging with his heels, and he was leaving.

The ridge led to a gametrail that wound down through shade beneath the pine trees. There was water at the bottom, and he felt the horse increase its gait, the cool smell evidently reaching it. He held back on the reins, working past a sharp turn in the trail, then easing farther down, the angle so steep now that he was forced to lean back. In the shade, his sweat-soaked shirt was cool against his sticky back. He reached behind to tug at it. Then he was working past another sharp turn, angling farther down, and he could see the stream below him glinting in the sunlight. His horse's hoofs plodded on the fallen pine needles.

He looked and saw another carcass, this one wedged between two trees. Another deer. Or possibly an antelope. From this far away, he couldn't tell. He likely couldn't tell regardless. The winter had been so severe, the snow so deep, the storms so frequent and intense, that many animals who normally survived up in the mountains had come down here for food. But the winter had been just as bad down here, so they had wandered, becoming thin and weak and cold until they dropped and maybe tried to stand up once or twice and dropped again and died. Sometimes scavengers would find them and, when finished, would leave only bits of bone and skin. Other times, like this, the carcass hadn't been discovered; it had dried and shrunk till just the empty hulk remained. The positions they assumed were on occasion fascinating. Like this one that was wedged between the two trees. An outsider might think that it had tried to squeeze between the trees, had gotten stuck, and there had died. But then of course the ground had not been visible in the winter. The animal had walked upon a floor of ice-impacted snow. The snow had been quite deep, at least ten feet and likely more. The two trees veered apart at that height. The animal had lots of room. It walked between, and died, and with the thaw, it settled toward the ground and wedged.

He rode down near it, passing it, and he was right. Deer or antelope. He couldn't tell. It was the fifth such carcass he had seen today, and he was sure that if he looked around more intently, he'd find several others. He couldn't take the time. It didn't matter anyhow. He wasn't out here just to admire the land, to commemorate an anniversary; he was checking on his stock. He heard the low of cattle off to his right now, and he stopped beside the stream, sunlight angling through the trees and glinting off it, long enough to let the horse lean its head down and take a drink. Just enough to give it strength, but not enough to make it sick. Then he was pulling on the reins and angling off, emerging from the trees to the grassland, turning right.

The low of cattle was much louder now. He guessed that they were just below the coming rise. He reached the top and saw them spread out across from him, a gully between, and he was riding toward the gully, looking for an easy place to dip down, up, and then across to them. At first he thought the carcass in the gully was another deer. It had the same tawny color. But then he saw that it was one of his stock, and frowning, he was pulling up and getting off. He looked around to tie the horse but couldn't find a place, holding tightly to its reins as he walked slowly down among the open earth and rocks. The steer was lying on an angle with the slope, its back to him, and he was thinking that it had fallen and snapped its neck. But coming toward it, he saw nothing strange about the neck, and none of the legs looked broken, and he was thinking, afraid now, of disease. He shifted toward its head, peering at its mouth, but there wasn't any froth on its lips, and he was thinking of a dozen diseases that could kill a steer and leave no trace when

suddenly he came around and saw its midriff and was nearly sick. He stumbled back and dropped the reins. The horse began to bolt.

TWO

The old man in the chair was tired. He'd been out and making rounds all day, from just after dawn till well past sup- pertime, checking on some newborn calves, giving shots, a dozen other things, once even coming on a case of founder. Odd how people who had worked with horses all their lives could still forget the basic rules and get their stock in trouble. He had needed just one look to know that the case was classic. Take a hot day and a tired, hungry, thirsty horse. Give it too much grain and water. Something happened to the horse's blood. The veins within the hoofs swelled. The horse went lame. He'd helped to get the horse to stand in water. That would cool the veins and possibly reduce the swelling. But not much. The horse would never be the same. The swelling would leave scars and, more, would change the horse's gait. He'd cut away part of the outside crusted nails, had given purgatives to get the horse's stomach and its bloodstream back to normal. But he didn't have much confidence. Most cases like this ended with the horse dead on its own or else destroyed. On rare occasions when the horse recovered, it almost never worked well after that and ended as a family pet. If the rancher had the toler- ance. Livestock out here was a business after all, and anything that didn't earn its way was hardly welcome.

The old man sat in the rocking chair and glanced out at the setting sun. Its stark, red, swollen disc was very close now to the mountains. Shortly it would touch and disappear behind them. From the kitchen he heard cupboards being opened, dishes rattled, knives and forks selected. Supper had been heated and *re*heated, he'd been told. His wife had been mad about it. Not because she'd had to do more work. God knows, she never let that bother her. But she'd been mad that he had let himself go on so long. A man his age should be retired. At the very least he ought to cut back on his hours. But at a time when he should take things easy, he was working more than ever, more than any other vet in town, and she was angry, claiming that his system couldn't take it.

"I'm a doctor. I know what I'm doing."

"Sure. Of animals. Not people."

"What's the difference?"

"Don't be smart," she said. "A doctor doesn't treat himself."

"You've got me there. I'd best sit down and take it easy."

He'd smiled then as he left her in the kitchen, sitting, glancing out the window, hearing pot lids being lifted and replaced. No point in telling her that she had not slowed down much either, going out to see the sick, the orphaned, and the poor, cooking for them, mending clothes or making them. There was a phrase they used to have for that. What was it called? The corporal works of mercy. The truth was that he was more tired than she guessed, short of breath and feeling dizzy. There had been a time when he would come in after making rounds all day and smoke and make a drink and sip it, eat, and go out with her for a walk or maybe to a movie. Then he'd read till one or two o'clock. Now he couldn't stay awake. The cigarettes and whisky were long gone. The walk was too much, the movie something on the TV while he slept. It was more than feeling tired. He was feeling sick. His appetite was less each day, his stomach faintly queasy. He told himself it was the heat, but he knew better. It was something with his heart. No pains yet in his chest or down his arm. Just a vague discomfort that would shortly be much worse.

All the same, he didn't know what he could do. It was in his nature to deny himself, to make of weakness strength. Besides, he didn't know how he would fill the time. He'd been a vet now forty years. He couldn't just forget all that and sit around the house. He joked about that to his wife. "You wouldn't want me under foot all day. Be grateful." But the joke was very poor. A man whose occupation was his life, he didn't have much choice. He had to work.

And one thing more: the ranchers who depended on him. He had worked with many of them all their lives, all his own life. He had seen their fortunes rise and fall, or fall and rise, their families grow, their ranches go through all the good times and the bad. He had measured out the seasons with them. Now they were a part of him, the rhythm of his life. He couldn't any more restrain himself from going out to work with them than he could stop the racing in his blood each April when the warm winds first began the long slow thawing of the snow. Maybe he was wrong. Maybe they didn't depend on him so much as *he* depended on *them*. Or maybe it was both together. There were vets enough to go around. That was sure. But he was part of their lives too. They'd had him with them through so many times that maybe they felt incomplete without his presence in their common rituals. Maybe. It was hard to say. He'd never ask. But ranchers had their superstitions. They had patience only with what worked, and what worked best was often very old.

Like himself, he thought. But really, he knew what the truth was. He was getting older than he liked to think, and he was damned if he would sit around and let death come to him. What was the greatest disappointment in the world? That of feeling useless. If he didn't work, he didn't see that he was justified. Still, he guessed his wife was right. He didn't have a reason to put in this kind of day. Maybe he would cut back, work just mornings, spend some time around the house. His wife was aging too, and maybe they should find out more about each other. While they still had the opportunity.

He sat and thought, his breath now coming easier, glancing out the window while he listened to his wife reheating supper, and the phone rang.

"Don't get up," she told him, and he understood. This likely would be business. Most calls at this hour were, and she was bound to see he wasn't bothered. He sat, waiting while it rang. He heard her put a lid down on a pot, then saw her walk across the entrance to the kitchen, disappearing toward the phone that hung against the cupboard wall. She got there halfway through another ring.

"Hello. . . . No, I'm sorry he's not in right now. I'll take a message. . . . What? How are you, Sam? I didn't recognize your voice. How's the. . . ? No, I don't know where he is. . . . Well, is it serious? If you'll tell me what it is, I'll have him call. . . . You're sure? All right, then, Sam, I'll have him call you first thing he comes in. . . . No, I won't forget. . . . Right, Sam. Yes, I will. . . . Right. Goodbye."

And that was that. He heard her hang the phone up and

then saw her walk across the doorway toward the stove. He knew three Sams, but he didn't dare ask which it was. If she wanted to, she'd tell him, but he knew that if he asked her he would only make her mad. So he waited. He sat, smelling supper as it cooked. Then she told him it was ready. He went in and ate. Slowly as she wanted him. Pork chops, string beans, and potatoes, boiled, then stirred with butter and crushed parsley, as he liked them. Then she had a pie for him, apple with brown sugar and no upper crust. Again, the way he liked it. Then there was some tea, Chinese black, light and smooth and mellow. And he waited. He sat back and looked at her and tapped his fingers on the table.

And she told him. "That was Sam Bodine."

He nodded.

"Best get over there."

He had to laugh. "I thought you didn't want me to."

"I've changed my mind."

"What is it?"

"That's the point. He wouldn't say."

The old man looked at her.

"You should have heard his voice. I think you'd better go."

He looked at her a moment longer and then stood to get his bag.

### THREE

The old man's house was on the edge of town, the side that faced the western mountains. He got in the car and backed out of the driveway, aiming toward the setting sun. It was almost down behind the mountains now. Its topmost swollen rim was barely showing.

Rocky Mountains. Tall and jagged, capped with snow although June was oddly warm. In August, some would be rock bare, but most would be snow-covered all year round. That was one nice thing about this kind of country: the difference in the weather. In the valley, it might be one hundred, but five hours drive up there and you could dig snow caves and wear a jacket. Plus, the sun did strange things with its color. It might be white with heat from nine to five, but after that, as it came closer to the mountains, dipping down behind them, the sun changed first to red and then to orange, bathing everything in alpenglow, a rich warm golden tone that made the countryside seem magical. It was like that now, everything the same calm soothing color. Even trees were tinted by it, the green of leaves now more like yellow, the range grass all around reminding him of grain and honey.

The old man drove down the road past fence posts stretching off as far as he could see, past ranch homes nestled in their hollows, cattle feeding, windmills turning in the evening breeze. The supper had been very good. He had eaten more than was his custom. Indeed he felt much better now, his breath more easy, his legs more steady. That was why he drove the kind of car he did: to help him with his legs. The effort of a clutch had lately been too much for him, and he had traded to an automatic, which was bad for hills and snow, but he was forced to pace himself. In little ways he had to compensate. He sat back in the seat, his foot relaxed on the pedal, his hand light on the steering wheel, and glanced at all the country as he passed, the isolated trees, the sweep of rangeland stretching off, the fences, and the cattle, and he thought of Sam Bodine. No, of Bodine's father. At one time, the old man had been just about his closest friend, although they hadn't been old back then, thirty, forty years ago, hunting, fishing, working. No, not just about his closest friend. His only friend. They had been like brothers. He had loved the man, and still he missed him dearly. After twenty years, he marveled at how constant was his grief. He had seen the son grow to a man and seen him marry and have children. He had helped him every bit as much as he was able. But the son was not the father. He had different interests and concerns, and things were never quite the same.

Now he drove out toward the ranch as he had done so many times before. He passed the tree that he had seen grow from a seedling to a giant and then start to crumble. He passed the ditches he had helped to dig, the fences he had helped to set. He came around the curve that led down toward the entrance, slowing, turning left to rattle across the grate that lay over a gully and that kept the cattle off the highway, its metal gaps so wide that cattle couldn't walk across them. Next he was on gravel, gaining speed again, spinning up a swirl of dust behind him as he drove on toward the house and barn, their structures now in dusk, the alpenglow abruptly gone, the sun behind the mountains.

Then he saw him standing by the gravel parking space beside the house, big and tall, dressed in denim shirt and jeans, cowman's hat and boots, hands gripped on his thighs. His face was strong and solid, leathered, at the same time almost chiseled. He was walking forward even as the old man pulled in on the gravel.

"Thanks for coming."

The old man nodded. "What's the trouble?"

"I don't want to say. I'd rather have you look."

The old man glanced at him a moment and then got out with his bag. In all his years he'd never heard a rancher talk that way. They almost always had a thought of what the problem was and told him right away. Whatever was the matter out here surely wasn't ordinary.

Bodine was already walking. "How you feeling?"

"Pretty good," the old man said.

"We're going to be a while." Bodine said that with his head turned as he walked, angling toward the big garage.

"It isn't in the barn?"

Bodine shook his head and pointed. "Out there on the edge of the foothills. My boy's there watching now. We'd best take the truck."

And that was that. Bodine was already climbing into the truck to start the engine.

The old man climbed in the other side and set his bag between his legs. "But what's the mystery?"

"I don't want to say. A thing like this, if I tell you, you'll get preconceptions. Have a look, then you tell me."

And they were driving out the open doorway, turning west beside the barn, and heading off across the range.

FOUR

They headed toward the spot of light. The darkness was all around them now, the truck's lights on, and they were jouncing across the open bumpy ground, the old man with his hands

27

braced on the dashboard. Bodine glanced at him and then ahead. The spot of light was flickering. A fire, and Bodine had to smile. He hadn't thought to tell his boy to build one, but then he had talked to him when it was day, and clearly they would need a thing to aim for.

Bodine saw a patch of smooth ground up ahead and gathered speed, but then he hit a bump he hadn't seen that jounced the old man very hard, and had to slow. The headlights showed the rangeland stretching off beneath them. Up ahead, a rabbit was paralyzed by them. Bodine veered to miss it. Then he picked up speed again.

The light was now distinctly flames, growing as he neared. He saw his boy stand up and walk in front of the fire, his body silhouetted by it. He saw the motorcycle parked beside the fire. The fire was very close before him as he pulled up and he stopped.

He kept the lights on, then stepped down onto the ground. The old man was already out.

The boy walked toward them.

"Anything?" Bodine asked.

The boy just shook his head.

"No animals? No tearing at the carcass?"

"It's been pretty quiet."

"Well, that's something anyhow. You stayed up here the way I told you? You didn't go down, messing any tracks?"

The boy just shook his head again.

"Okay, then. Doc, it's down there in the gully. Careful of the slope."

The old man walked across the glare of the headlights, standing at the edge of the gully. "I can't see much without more light."

Bodine reached beneath the seat to get a high-powered flashlight. He held it, long and heavy, walking toward the old man as he flicked the switch. The light shot out across the range. He dipped it toward the gully, sweeping back and forth until he found the carcass.

"There."

Its back was toward them, just the way it had been when Bodine had come upon it. As much as he could tell, it looked the same.

The old man started down, and Bodine stopped him.

"I don't know. I think the way to do this is to walk up here a ways, then cut across and come down looking on the other side. I want to keep from messing any tracks."

The old man hesitated, looked at him, and nodded. They went where the gully was more narrow, climbing down, the old man needing help to get up on the other side. The ground was hard and rocky. The old man's breath was forced as he got up and straightened.

"You all right?"

"It's nothing. I'm not used to this."

"You sure?"

"I said I'll be all right."

"Okay then."

And they waited. Then the old man had his breath back, and they walked along the top until they stood across from where the headlights and the fire were. Bodine aimed the flashlight into the ditch. The old man didn't speak.

He didn't speak for quite a while.

"All right, now tell me what the hell it was that did that," Bodine said.

"I don't know." The old man cleared his throat. "Right now I couldn't say."

It wasn't that the sight was shocking. He'd seen worse too many times. But the thing just didn't make much sense. Whatever had disemboweled this steer had done so from below and ravaged at the guts. But nothing seemed to have been eaten. The guts were mashed together, chewed and mangled, but the point was they were here. Whatever did this hadn't eaten at the flesh, had only chewed at organs and then left them. He had never seen this—he had never heard about a thing like this before.

The old man saw the flies that crawled upon the guts, smelled the stench that was coming from the gully, shook his head, and turned away. "I just don't get it."

"You're the expert," Bodine said. "Take a guess."

"Well, process of elimination. What would prey upon a steer?"

"I already thought of that. Bobcats. But they don't come down here. Wolves, the same. Coyotes maybe. I even thought it was a cougar. They don't single out the guts, though. Not when they've got flesh to eat."

"And one thing more. It doesn't look like anything's been eaten," the old man said. "What about those tracks you mentioned? Were they any help?"

"I never found them. If they were around, I didn't want them messed before somebody good came out to have a look."

The old man turned, again toward the gully, and he pointed. "Well, I don't know if I'd mess the tracks, but I should go down and have a look."

"You're the expert."

So the old man slowly worked his way down into the gully, Bodine close behind. But there was nothing he could tell.

"The only thing I notice is the blood."

"Or lack of it."

"That's what I mean. A thing like this, there should be lots of blood." The old man thought a moment. "Could be something spooked whatever did this, and it didn't get a chance to eat. It just licked all the blood."

"Could be. I don't know."

The old man looked around. "Well, I can't tell out here. I'd like to get this into town where I can have it on a table and dissect it. If there's a way for us to move it. What about your herd? There's nothing strange about it?"

"You were out two weeks ago. You said that it was fine."

"Well, something might have happened in the meantime. What I'm getting at is if this steer was sick, whatever tried to eat it might have felt the taste was off and left it."

"Maybe. But I hardly think it's likely," Bodine said.

"I don't think so, either. What about the truck? Can we get this in there?" the old man asked.

"That's no problem. We'll rig a line."

So they climbed up from the ditch, the old man breathing hard, and Bodine got a rope and tied it around the head of the carcass and hitched the rope to the truck and used the truck to drag the steer up onto the level. Then he opened the back and pulled out a ramp and this time hitched the rope around the motorcycle. His boy was working with the bike while Bodine pulled and guided on the rope, and slowly, motorcycle revving hard, the steer was dragged up onto the ramp and then pulled into the back. They stood and frowned at the carcass.

"Well, the guts stayed pretty much the same," the old man said, and Bodine flashed the light around to see if any had been left behind.

The old man walked back toward the gully. "Nothing down there either. But the swath the steer made sure played hell on any tracks."

Bodine turned and studied the old man. "There's one other thing I'd like to show you." He walked toward the woods, the flashlight in his hand, its wide beam sweeping through the trees.

They came to where the stream flowed through the trees, and found a narrow spot to step across and walked up onto the gametrail. Bodine led the way about a hundred yards, then stopped to let the old man come up close to him. He shone the flashlight in among the trees.

The carcass of a deer.

"All right. So what's the point?" the old man asked.

"Well, I saw a lot of these when I came through here just before I saw the steer. I figured, what the hell, the winter was a bad one. Then I didn't know. I came back up and checked on this one." Bodine poked with a stick where he had pushed the carcass from between the trees. "There. See where all the stomach skin's been eaten. Otherwise it isn't touched."

"But it's been dead for several months. Hell, anything could have caused that. Maybe insects."

"Even so."

The old man looked at Bodine and wondered what he must be thinking.


### FIVE


The old man drove while Bodine followed in the truck. The boy stayed back at home. They rattled across the grate and then turned right and headed toward town. It was after midnight, the car and truck the only traffic on the road. All around, the countryside was dark, no lights on in ranches, the stars clear, a few clouds across the moon. Isolated trees were black against the murky gray of night. The old man heard a coyote howling in the hills.

He was tired. This was late for him, and he was worn out from climbing into the ditch, then walking through the woods. He was feeling sick again as well, the good meal he had eaten now gone bad on him and rising in his stomach. He could taste the undigested pork. What did he expect? He knew he shouldn't eat so large a meal and one that was so heavy. But then he had been hungrier than was common for him, and besides his wife had gone to so much trouble that he couldn't very well refuse.

Now he paid. He squirmed in his seat, wishing he would throw up and be done with it. His foot was heavy on the pedal, not because he wanted to get quickly into town, but he was so tired now that he could hardly move his feet. They were like a separate part of him. He felt that they were swollen. Water filling up, he thought. He'd have to take another pill for that.

He suffered, glancing at the darkened country as the car sped down the road. One curve, then another, and he almost missed the third. Better take things easy, better get control, he told himself, and gripped the wheel more tightly, tensing muscles in his leg to get life in his foot. He glanced at Bodine's headlights in his rearview mirror. He looked ahead and saw a car approach him, its headlights growing larger as it neared. He glanced away as it flashed past, the headlights hurting his eyes, and then the car was gone, and he was staring at his own lights and the dark. Up ahead the carcass of a badger had been flattened on the road. At least he thought it was a badger. He had only one quick look before he was upon it and had passed. He thought about it and then had to concentrate on going around another curve. He shook his head to clear it and then squinted down the headlight-flooded road.

Twenty miles. In terms of effort, they felt more like eighty. He was thinking he was getting closer, thinking of his bed. He blinked his eyes to clear them now, staring down the road. And then he saw the first light in a house, another one closeby, and he was at the outskirts, coming around another bend and starting down the hill, and there the town was spread out wide before him, its streetlights sending up a glow that in the cool of night was like a yellow mist. Traffic lights and lights on in some houses, lights on in the diner and the first bar that he passed and then the all-night service station. After staying up so late, climbing in that ditch, walking through those woods, after this long drive, tired as he was, the warmth of all these lights, he felt that he was home.

The town was Potter's Field, so-called not because of any graveyard that was near it, although there were a lot of those from the old days. Farmers passing through. Trappers, ranchers, sheepmen, range wars. And the miners. At one time the hills around had all been rich with gold. But that was ninety years ago, and the gold had soon been gone. There had been two towns back then, one high in the hills that they'd called Motherlode, the other down here where the miners came from work to get supplies and drink and rest and often die. Like the farmers, trappers, ranchers, and the sheepmen. All passed on and laid to rest in graveyards that were like a page from history.

The town up there had long since gone to ruin, but the one down here had grown and prospered, twenty thousand people in it now and growing bigger, better, all the time. There were rumors about oil, ski resorts, and breweries, but the main trade here was cattle, and a lot of people didn't want those other things. The town was in a rich wide valley, mountains all around it, and the first man who'd come through here, back in 1850, was named Potter. He had been a farmer, and he'd liked the country so much that he'd tried to work it. But the soil was wrong for farming, and at last he'd given up, staying on nonetheless, hunting, fishing, living out his days here just because he liked the place. His shack had been rebuilt several times since then, set apart beside the courthouse with a plaque explaining who Potter had been and telling all about his field.

The field was where he'd tried to farm, about the size of what was now the city limits. The town was built exactly where he'd lived. It was the property he'd still retained after all the farmers and the cattlemen had come through here and bought up any land he'd sell them. At first he didn't want to sell, but Potter had anticipated what was coming, and he didn't see much point in holding out. Either he would sell or else they'd take it, and so he'd sold and seen the farmers leave, the ranchers stay, had seen the cattle business grow around him. Then he had a store, and then a bar, a hotel and a restaurant, and soon the town was on its way.

Still Potter had tried a bit of farming, marking off a plot of ground beside his shack which he refused to leave and where he died, growing corn and lettuce and potatoes. The ranchers thought him funny, but he prospered, and he still was going out to plant his corn the day he died that spring in 1890. So the field was both the city limits and that plot of ground he tended, the latter set aside behind the shack, a little park and flower garden.

POTTER'S FIELD. A PLACE WHERE YOU CAN GROW. So the sign said as the old man passed it, heading down the hill and driving farther into town. Below him, he could see the main street cutting through from right to left, one long row of double-story buildings, feed stores, hardware stores, bars and shops and restaurants, a movie theater, the police station, and the courthouse. The last two were beside each other, surrounded by great elms, sent in from the east donated by a rancher. Indeed the other trees through town were all sent in from other places too, maple, ash and oak, a dozen others, the color of their leaves in autumn stark against the fir green of the mountains.

Down the hill now, farther into town, he reached the stoplight where the two main roads intersected, waiting until the red changed to green and angling right, driving down two blocks and turning left to pull in at the wide two-story building made of cinder blocks and painted white that was his office. Not just his, but everybody's. Every vet in town. There were eight of them, and they had long ago decided that instead of each one having a separate office it was better, at least cheaper, more efficient, if they all combined to build a place that would be better equipped than each could ever manage alone. In addition to the offices, there were operating rooms, a storehouse, and a kennel. It had been expensive, but the ranchers out here paid to keep their livestock healthy, and besides there hadn't been much choice. To operate on bulls and stallions, you just had to have the space.

Headlights arcing, the old man went down the driveway toward the back, stopping by the double doors that led in to one operating room. The parking lot was walled with concrete, and he sat there, cut his motor and his lights, waiting in the dark, flexing his hands and kneading his legs to get more life back into them. He wondered how long it would be before he got to bed. He'd never felt so tired.

Then he heard the motor, saw the headlights flashing up the drive, and stepped from the car as Bodine's truck pulled into view. The old man lost his balance, put his hands against the car, then waited, took his keys, and opened the double doors. He went inside and switched on all the lights. The room was suddenly like day, brighter, like the starkest hottest day he'd ever seen, fierce overhead lights stabbing down at him. He had to turn away, barely glancing at the long wide metal table in the middle, at the white walls and the cabinets and rows of medical supplies. He sought out comfort in the darkness, waiting for Bodine to back the truck up to the entrance. Bodine came up almost into the room, then shut off his lights and motor, and stepped down onto the concrete parking lot.

The old man didn't move.

"What is it? Something wrong?" Bodine asked.

The old man shook his head. "You'll have to help me."

Bodine nodded, walking past him toward the glare that spilled from the entrance to the room. He'd helped with this before, heading toward the pulley that was on a bar up on the ceiling, grabbing at the straps that hung down from it, tugging at them so the pulley rolled along the bar up there and stopped above the back bin of the truck. He climbed up into the back and hitched the straps around the midriff of the carcass, just inside the legs. It was heavy work. Even though the steer was not full-sized, he still had lots of trouble heaving at its bulk so he could slip the straps beneath and slide them into position. Once the stench of all those open guts, left out in the sun all day, became too much for him, and he was forced to turn away. Then he had the straps in place, and he secured them, pulling downward on the chain to work the pulley until the steer was slowly rising, its hoofs dangling above the floor of the truck. A hunk of guts dropped out and plopped near Bodine. He didn't even look at them, just climbed down from the truck, tugging at the straps to slide the carcass from the truck, across the room and then above the table. Another hunk of guts dropped. He grabbed the chain and yanked down on it in the opposite direction, the pulley in reverse so the steer was slowly settling onto the table. Next Bodine slid the straps from beneath it, heaving at the carcass, and he moved the pulley toward the entrance to the room.

The old man was inside, his hand above his eyes to shield them from the light.

"You're sure that you're okay?" Bodine asked.

"I'm fine."

"All right then. Guess it's up to you now. What about those guts that fell?"

The old man looked around. "Take these forceps and that plastic bag. Put them in it."

Bodine did what he was told. He set the bag on the table. "How soon till I hear?"

"I don't know yet. I can't tell yet what I'm looking for. Tomorrow afternoon."

Bodine nodded, walking toward the truck. "I'll be waiting."

"Yes, I know you will."


SIX

Then, truck gone, it was quiet. No, the lights up in the ceiling made a buzz. Funny how he'd never noticed that before. But then he hadn't been here this late in some while. In the daytime, there were always sounds and people. He just wasn't used to being here alone.

The old man kept his hand near his eyes to shield them from the light, staring at the carcass on the table. What to do? What he'd said was true. He didn't know what he was looking for. He needed rest, a chance to think and sleep. He needed to sit. And then he realized. He hadn't even thought to ask Bodine to help him slide the carcass into the cooler. He didn't have the strength to do it on his own. He could put the bag of guts in there. But not the carcass. It would simply be too much for him. He wondered what to do.

The phone rang. He almost didn't answer. But he thought about it, and he guessed it would be his wife, and so he walked with effort toward the door that led down to his office, reaching for the phone beside the counter by the door.

"Doctor Markle here. . . . Hi. How are you? . . . I'm just

about to leave. . . . I don't know yet. Something got a steer. . . . We're not sure. We brought the carcass in to see. Listen, don't wait up. I might be half an hour or so. Go to bed. I'll tell you all about it in a while. . . . No, I won't be long. I promise. . . . Right. Goodbye."

And he hung up. She'd told him that she loved him, and he'd smiled. With his hand above his eyes again, he turned to face the carcass, and he realized that he had lied. He would not go home directly. He would stay and work a little on the steer. Either that or let it stay out all night decomposing more until he couldn't do the proper tests. A few slides for the microscope. Maybe take a portion of the brain and cool it for tomorrow. Test the feces. Take a sample of the blood, the little that there was and in such poor condition. He winced from the sickness in his stomach, and he almost changed his mind. Then he braced himself. Nothing for it but to go ahead. His legs heavy, he went over to the sink and washed his hands and put on rubber gloves, a gown and face mask, out of habit really, and to keep his clothes clean, and to bear the stench. He didn't think his samples would be clean. All the same he liked to do things right and not contaminate anything.

So he stumbled toward the carcass, and he wondered what he'd tripped on and then realized it was himself. His legs weren't working properly; he'd have to do this soon and rest. There were three facts that he needed to learn right away. Whether the steer had been dead before the animal had gotten at it. Whether the organs were all there. Whether the predator had left some sign of what it was. The first he thought he knew. If the steer had been dead, especially for some time, the blood would not have flowed. No matter that they hadn't found the blood, it clearly wasn't here. The predator had maybe drunk it, but that still meant that the steer was freshly killed. The only sure test was to open up the heart. A lot of blood would mean the steer was long dead when the animal had gotten at it. Little meant the steer had still been living when attacked. The point was that a dead steer meant a scavenger, and that would help identify the animal that had picked at it.

The fact about the organs, whether all of them were present, was related to the first. If some of them were missing, the assumption was that they'd been eaten, and that would help eliminate a good deal of the mystery. The steer had been attacked for food. On the other hand, if all the organs were still present, he'd have to figure why. The extensive damage meant that the animal had lots of time to eat. Even if it had been scared away, there had to be a reason why it didn't take advantage and eat something at the start. Could be that the steer was dead, and something, not a scavenger, instead an animal that preferred fresh kills, had tried to eat and given up. Could be too the steer was dead, and something, a disease perhaps, had made the meat taste bad. Could be, but the only way to tell that was by checking on the cause and time of death.

The other fact he needed, a sign to help identify what kind of animal had done this, he was hoping he would find as he examined the organs. Something like a piece of fur, a tooth-mark, anything. But that would come as he went through the process. First he'd get a sample of the heart, the brain, the feces. Since the carcass was already open, he would start in on the heart.

But as he went around the table, looking at the open guts, at first he couldn't find the heart. Then he did, mashed in with the lungs and upper stomach. It was more complete than he had hoped, and he was cutting carefully around it, reaching in to pull it out and slice it into quarters. He was taken up with interest now, breathing fast and hard, staring at the sectioned heart. It was almost empty. That was that. The steer had died from the attack. Of course it might have been diseased as well, and he would tell that as he checked the other organs. But at least he knew that what had done this was no scavenger. It had been a full-scale hunter, on the prowl for food.

His legs gave out, and he was forced to grip the table. This was wrong. He had to get away, get home, and get to bed. But he couldn't make his legs move. Then he had them working, and he straightened. He tried to go but couldn't take his mind off all those organs, sorting through them. Liver, bladder, kidneys, all those stomachs. He couldn't understand it. Even shredded as they were, it seemed that nothing was missing. But that shouldn't be. He cut deeply into the abdomen to where the bowels were still intact and took a sample of the feces. The stench, on top of what was in his stomach, made him almost retch. He had to find a reason. If the animal had been a hunter, then it should have eaten. But it hadn't, and he didn't understand.

His legs gave out again. His chest constricted. The pain shot through his left arm, and he was praying. He thought about his wife. He thought about how she had said she loved him, and he wished that he had said it back. He thought about so many things. Just before he fell, he singled in on one small portion of the guts, staring at them, disappearing into them, and noticed a detail so horrible that in his death at last he understood.

SEVEN

They found him in the morning where he lay on the floor by the table, one fist full of guts that he had taken with him as he fell. That was shortly after seven. The men who found him phoned a doctor, but it wasn't any use. The doctor came and knelt and checked him and just shook his head.

By then the old man's wife was there. She had waited up for him, but then, in spite of all her good intentions, she had gone to sleep. She had wakened early and had missed him, searching through the house. She'd seen that the car was gone and phoned the office, but there wasn't any answer. She had waited half an hour before going into town.

She came around the corner and started running when she saw the ambulance. The double doors were open, and she saw a crowd in there, and she was pushing through, stopping as she saw him, and she gasped. She ran across to him, kneeling down to cradle him, then yelling at him, pushing, shouting that he was a fool. No one understood. The doctor had been just about to leave. He tried to calm her, to lead her carefully away, but she kept screaming. Then she started hitting the body, and the doctor had somebody hold her while he opened his bag and swabbed her arm and filled a hypodermic, giving her a sedative. It didn't calm her right away. She kept screaming, began to sob, crouched beside her husband once again, and finally it seemed all right to try to make her go. They led her down the hallway to the office.

The medical examiner was there to see the last of it. He

waited while they led her down the hallway. Then he checked
the body, doing more or less the same as what the doctor had,
but taking more time, making notes. He straightened, putting
pad and pen together, turning toward the open double doors as
behind the people there he saw the police car pulling up. He
waited while the driver's door was opened and the big man got
out, putting on his hat. The uniform was tan, the hat a Stetson.
Even with the people there the policeman's face could be seen
above the crowd, burly, craggy, strong-boned with high cheeks,
just a little puffy near the eyes, the medical examiner assumed
from too much beer. What the hell, if you worked the hours he
did, you'd be puffy near the eyes as well, never mind the beer.

The policeman's name was Slaughter, and that had meant
he almost didn't get the job. He had settled here five years ago,
and when the old chief had died, Slaughter had asked the town
council for the job. At first the council was reluctant, but
Slaughter had showed them his credentials, and they couldn't
pass him by. Twenty years a policeman and detective in Detroit,
trained in every manner of investigation, tired of living in the
city, wanting to come out and live in peace, he had tried his
hand at raising horses but then realized he wasn't any good.
The only thing he knew was being on the force; he did it well.
The council needed him. He needed them. They finally worked
it out. Some had feared, thinking of his name, that he would
be too tough for them, that coming from the East he would
treat them as if he were in the city, breaking heads as if this
were Detroit. But they had phoned Detroit, and reports about
him there were even better than he claimed. He had never had
a complaint against him. He was never one to push. So they
had tried him on condition, and they had kept him ever since.
At least in terms of lack of crime, the town had never had things
better.

As the medical examiner kept watching, Slaughter
started, big and solid, through the crowd, talking to them, his
hand pressed down around his gunbelt, bullets showing, that
was shoved a little low around his waist. Then the crowd was in
back of him, and he released the hand from his holstered gun.
Instincts from the city. Among the few that Slaughter still
retained. Standing there in cowboy boots and cowman's hat, a
toothpick in his mouth, he looked about as local as a person

could become. Not because he wore them, but because he wore them with a certain pride and made the townsfolk proud to see him and to speak with him. That faint inflection in his voice that he had picked up since he'd come. To see him grow to meet the town had made the town aware of what it was. He had added to it.

Now he paused and glanced around. Taking the toothpick from his mouth, he walked across and frowned down at the body. "Old Doc Markle?"

"Yes, I'm sorry. I know how you felt about him."

Slaughter didn't answer.

"Heart attack," the medical examiner said. "His wife was here to see him. She's just down the hall."

Slaughter looked at him.

"She had to be sedated."

Slaughter shook his head. "She'll have it rough from now on." His voice dropped with sorrow. He tried to distract himself by paying attention to details. "What time did he die?"

"I don't know yet. Rigor's set in. That means several hours."

"Some time in the night?"

"It had to be. Otherwise somebody from the office would have seen him."

"Maybe. Let's find out for certain." Slaughter glanced around. He saw the people by the open double doors and went across to talk to them. They listened, saying something back to him. He spoke again. They nodded, slowly breaking up to go away. He turned and saw the people in the green lab coats standing by the wall. He waved to them to follow him as he walked back toward the table.

"You all work here. Anybody see him just before you closed?"

They shook their heads. There were six men and two women. One, the youngest woman, twenty, maybe slightly more, began to cry. It was clear, the way her face and eyes were red, that she'd been crying earlier as well. They were looking at the body, then away, then in a moment back again.

"No," one man was saying. He was red-haired, freckled, maybe thirty-five, thin and going bald. "I came through to lock the place, and Markle wasn't here."

"You check all the rooms?"

"Yes. In case someone forgot to lock them."

"What time did you check?"

"Shortly after six."

"Were you the last to leave?"

The red-haired man nodded.

"Anybody else? You've got kennels. Anybody come in after that to check the animals?

"I did." The older woman, maybe thirty-five as well, short but solid, her hair cut to just below her ears. "A little after ten. The doctor wasn't here then, either."

Slaughter looked at her. "The doctor? *He* said Markle," pointing to the first man.

"He's a vet. I just work here."

"That means Markle came in after ten," the first man said, "and died a little after."

Slaughter glanced at him and shook his head. "I don't know. You're the one who found him?"

"That's right."

"Did you change anything?"

"I turned the lights off."

"What about the doors?"

"Well, they were open."

"Then it wasn't after ten," Slaughter said. "When I sent all those people home, I found a man who's got a room in a building that looks down on here. He was out till well past midnight. He came home and checked his window, and he's sure that everything was dark down here. If the doors were open and the lights were on, he surely would have seen it. No, the doctor came here after one. Now I know you people put in heavy hours the same as all the rest of us, but one o'clock, I can't believe that's normal."

No one answered.

"What about this steer? Tell me what's the story on it."

"I don't know." The vet came around the table, looking at it. "You can see that it was dead before he brought it in."

"You're sure of that?"

"It had to be with all that damage. You can see that he was doing tests on it. There isn't any record why."

"You don't know whose it is?"

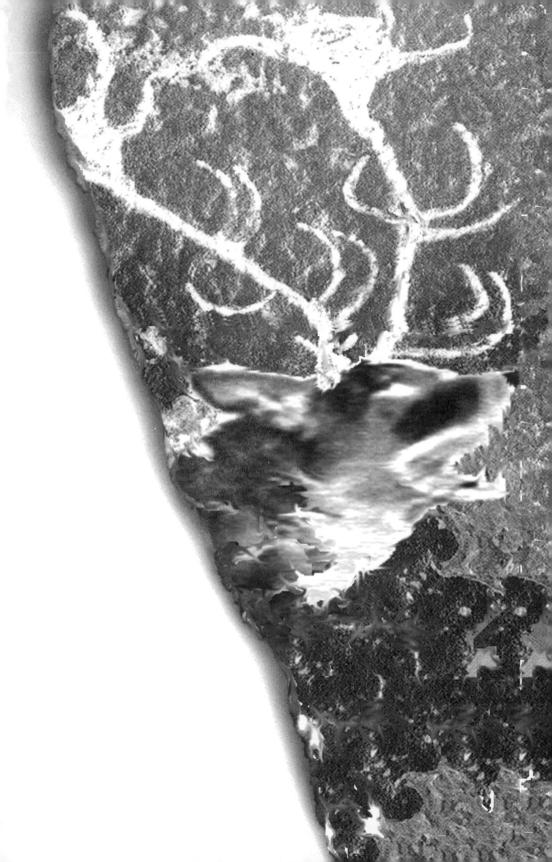

No answer.

Slaughter looked at him, then at the steer and at the body, and he turned to face the medical examiner. "Heart attack, well, maybe. All the same, I think we'd better run some tests."

"Again?"

But Slaughter only frowned at him. Then hearing someone coming through the hallway door, Slaughter turned and saw the doctor. He went over to him. "How is Mrs. Markle?"

The doctor shook his head.

"Can I speak to her?"

"She won't understand."

"How soon till she does?"

"Maybe after supper. She'll be at the hospital. I'll check on her and let you know."

"Thanks." Slaughter stared at the floor. "It's too bad. A woman that age. Now she's all alone." He sighed, then walked toward the double doors.

The medical examiner was waiting for him. "What about the body? Can I move it?"

"I'll have pictures taken. Then it's yours." Again he tried to distract himself. "Is everything all right for tomorrow?"

"As near as I can tell."

"Okay. I'll see you then."

Tomorrow was the weekend, and they always got together out at Slaughter's. That was Slaughter's way of keeping everybody friendly. Everyone he worked with had an open invitation to the ranch—although "ranch" wasn't quite the word, just five acres with a house and barn. But he had two horses, and the house was very nice, and he liked to have the people whom he worked with out, the only friends he had. He'd been married once. His wife, though, had divorced him, which was common with policemen who were married to their work. She had kept the children, one boy and a girl, and now he hardly ever heard from them except when he insisted that they come out for a visit. That had been a month ago, and since then he'd been distant. It was obvious that he was looking forward to have people with him for tomorrow.

Now he walked to the cruiser, glanced around, opened the driver's door and slid inside. He sat there for a moment, then reached to grab the microphone from the two-way radio on the dash.

He pressed the button. "Marge, it's Slaughter. Any news?"
He released the button.

Hiss of static. "Nothing, Chief. What about Doc Markle at
the vet's?"

Slaughter didn't answer.

"Chief?"

He swallowed. "It's too late. He's dead."

"Oh." Hiss of static. "Lord, I'm sorry."

"Yeah, well. . . . Guess his time just came." The words were
like stones in his throat. "Damn it," he murmured.

"Say that again, Chief. I didn't understand you."

"Nothing. I'll be back to the office shortly." Slaughter
returned the microphone to the radio, grabbed the key and
twisted it, starting the car.

He had tried his best to be objective in there. Really it was
hard. The doctor and the medical examiner both knew the way
he felt. So did Marge. That was what she'd meant when she had
said that she was sorry. Not for Markle, but for him.

Markle was the man he'd known out here the longest. It
was Markle who had come out showing him about the horses he
had tried to raise, explaining his mistakes. Markle had told him
that a vet should come out twice a year at least, checking, giving shots and worming. Just when Slaughter got so he had one
thing right, though, he would screw up on another, and soon
Markle had to come out nearly every day. In the end, the old
man had asked him why he wanted in this business in the first
place, and then Slaughter had told him of his ideal image, living
in the country, raising horses, selling them, sitting on the porch
and watching all the animals run free. Markle shook his head.
The word he'd used was "business," and he meant it. If you
wanted horses just to ride and look at, that was one thing. Raising them and selling them, that was something else. People out
here bred their own. Anyway, you needed decent stock. Good
brood mares, a winning stallion. It took years to build a proper
herd. Not to mention all the care and work. Days and nights of
making sure that they were healthy, taking pains that they stayed
out of trouble. You needed to watch them all the time.

Slaughter had listened, nodding, but he'd persisted, and
only when the herd—not one horse or a couple, but the whole

damned herd—came down with colic, did he know enough to stop. It was Markle who had told him of the old chief's death and how the town council needed a replacement. Markle was a member of the council, and that had helped, of course. Plus, Markle felt close to Slaughter by that time, at first just full of pity and exasperation toward him but then growing to admire his determination and the way he liked the country and the people and the style of life. Indeed, they'd gotten to be good friends, sitting on the porch each time Markle had come out, discussing each new set of problems, Slaughter drinking beer, the old man drinking Coke. The old man sensed in him a gentleness that went beyond Slaughter's name and strong, tough manner. The old man had told him so, and while there were some members of the force who stood in line to get the job, the old man had felt that since Slaughter had singled out this place in which to live and since he had a sympathy for ranchers, since he had the best credentials, he ought to have a good chance for the job.

So the two of them had done their best, the old man working on the members of the council, especially those who felt that big-time tactics weren't exactly what the town required, Slaughter coming in to say that big-time tactics were exactly what he didn't want, that they had been the reason he had left Detroit. He made a good impression. The issue was—even those who didn't want him had to say—he knew so much about this kind of work. They couldn't help but be convinced. And Markle was the cause of it. That night Slaughter took the old man on a celebration. Markle even drank some beer.

And now Markle was dead. Slaughter pulled up at a stoplight, waited, thinking, shook his head, and when the light turned green, he angled left. He thought of how he'd never spent the time he planned to with him. There had always been a thing to do, some aspect of the job to keep him occupied. Oh, sure, he'd gone around to see him and his wife from time to time. But not enough and not for long, and now he'd never have the chance again.

EIGHT

The door was thick wood, rich and solid, and Slaughter swung it open, stepping into the shadowy coolness of the stairway. The cells were down the stairs to the right, connected to the courthouse by a tunnel. Above and straight ahead, a wide square vestibule led into the offices. The floor was wood. The vestibule was rimmed by treelike plants. The ceiling, two floors up, was domed with glass.

He climbed the stairs and stood in the middle of the vestibule, looking at the ceiling and the glass. The sun was not yet high enough to gleam in. Where he stood was in halflight. He felt the halflight match his mood, thinking of the old man, and then shaking off his mood, he turned abruptly left to enter his office.

"Morning, Marge."

"Morning, Chief. Your coffee's on the desk. The night sheet's right beside it."

"Thanks."

But he'd already known she would say that. It was what she told him every morning, reduced now almost to a ritual. In spite of what had happened, he was forced to smile, walking past her toward his glassed-in section of the office in the far right corner. Marge was forty-five, gray-haired, heavy-set. She had been here briefly with the old chief just before he died, and wanting to keep everything efficient, the change as smooth as he could manage, Slaughter had kept her on. It was the best move he could have made. Marge was widowed with two full-grown children, and she had gone to work to get some order in her life. She had helped Slaughter ease in to his job, telling him which man was good at what he did and which was faking. She organized things so he could find out quickly what was going on. It had been her notion that they move the two-way radio unit from the room across the hall and put it in here with him. That way Slaughter could overhear whatever messages were coming through and maybe save some time. Certainly that saved the town some money. Rather Marge did, taking on two jobs instead of one, freeing one man who had always worked the radio (now he could go out on the street), at the same time taking Slaughter's calls and acting as his secretary.

She had the unit on the desk beside the entrance to the office, typing at another desk and waiting for the cruisers to start checking in with her. Behind her, desks were set in rows where officers would come in for debriefing after finishing their shift. The desks were empty now. There wasn't any point in having men here waiting for some trouble; best to keep them on the street and have Marge call to tell them where to go if they were needed. Slaughter barely glanced around the quiet room as he entered the glass-partitioned section of the office, sitting at the desk. He reached to swing the door shut, peered out the window at the cars and trucks that went by past the trees out there. Then sipping at his coffee—cool; he hadn't drunk it soon enough—he took the night sheet, leaning back until his chair was braced against the metal filing cabinet.

There were ten notes on the sheet. Last night hadn't been busy. A break-in at the hardware store. He saw that two men from the day crew were already working on that. They would check the manner of the break-in, find out what was taken. Chances were by Monday they would catch whoever did it. Strangers didn't come to steal here very often. When they did, they surely didn't try the hardware store. Most likely these were locals. Even though the town had a population of twenty thousand, it was small enough that there would be no problem discovering who'd suddenly gotten his hands on lots of hardware store equipment.

Two drunk driving, one assault (that was at a truckers' bar—an argument during a pool game), one dog that kept barking all night, and one prowler. That was on the other side of town, and Slaughter would have a cruiser checking there tonight. He scanned the other items on the sheet. Two car accidents, no injuries. A broken window at the high school. A missing person. Well, not really missing. That was Clifford who had left his wife three times already. He kept going out and getting drunk and then not coming home. Clifford's wife would phone to say that he was missing, and they'd find him two days later at a friend's. Well, Slaughter would have a man check all the friends and this time tell the guy at least to phone his wife when he got sober. They had better things to do than run a marriage-counseling service.

That was that. Nothing pressing. Although he didn't want to, Slaughter would have to work some more on organizing traffic control for the Junior Ranchers meeting that was coming up next week. He would have to make a speech there too, and for sure he was going to have to work more on what he planned to say to them. He thought about the old man. Might as well get started. He was reaching into his desk for a pencil and some paper when the buzzer sounded on his desk.

Slaughter pressed the button on the intercom. "What is it, Marge?"

"A call for you. It's Doctor Reed."

Reed had helped calm Mrs. Markle. "Put him through." Slaughter straightened, reaching for the phone. "How are you, Doc?" And then he frowned and listened.

Mrs. Markle was still unconscious from the sedative. She kept talking anyhow. Babbling was more like it. Mixing things like Sam Bodine, the steer, the old man, several other things as jumbled. Mostly, though, she just kept saying Sam Bodine. The doctor thought that Slaughter ought to know.

"You think Bodine owns the steer Doc Markle had on the table?" Slaughter asked.

"I don't know. It's hard to tell. I thought I'd better call you, though."

"I'm glad you did." Slaughter set down the phone, scratched his chin, and peered out the window.

"Marge," he said and opened the door.

She looked at him.

"Sam Bodine and old Doc Markle. Weren't they friends?"

"The father and the doctor were. I don't know much about the son."

Slaughter didn't either. He had heard the old man talk vaguely about him, but he'd never understood the story.

"Guess it's time I took a drive. Anybody calls, I won't be back till after lunch."


NINE

It was a place he'd never been. Slaughter had made a point of getting close to nearly all the ranchers around town, but Bodine was a loner, and except for once or twice a year, at ranchers' meetings or in passing on the street, Slaughter almost never saw him. Strictly speaking, Slaughter had jurisdiction only in the town. The state police had power in the valley, so it wasn't strange that Slaughter barely knew him. All the same, the town and valley were related, and he liked to keep on top of what was going on out there.

He meant to tell Bodine what had happened, to find out if the steer the old man had been working on was his. Slaughter could have phoned to do that, but really it was better that he drive out and do it in person. This way, he had a chance to be alone and think, mulling through the times that he and Markle had shared together, facing up to what had happened so he could adjust to it and keep his feelings separate from his work. That was just about the only value that he had, the largest one at any rate. Of course, that value was a mix of several others, but they all combined to just one thing—the need to keep his life as straight and simple as he could. Since his work was really all that mattered to him (so he told himself at least; he wished he had his children with him), that meant keeping his work as straight and simple as he could as well. He couldn't be two people, feeling one way, acting some way else. He had to bring them both together, which was why he liked to have the crew he worked with out at his place on the weekends. Seeing all those people was a way of merging leisure with his work.

So the old man had passed on now. Never mind "passed on." The old man was plain dead. Three days later, Monday, he'd be underneath the dirt. There wasn't anything that Slaughter could do about it. Feeling bad was just a distraction. Anyway, he told himself, how come you're feeling bad to start with? For the old man, for his wife, or for yourself? Is that sorrow or regret? You owed him things. You didn't go around to see him. Now he's dead, and you start wishing that you'd gone. Some friend you turned out to be. All right, hey, get control. Get it straight that next time you've got dues to pay, you pay them. Next time you make friends, you understand the obligations.

Right, he told himself and then repeated. Right, he thought and shook his head. And then because he didn't like the way his mind was working, he did his best to switch it off, to concentrate on driving, to look at the fields around him, at the mountains. The sky was almost white now. He could feel the stark sun burning through the rear glass of the car. Today would be the hottest yet, and he was thinking of the ranchers who'd be working in the parched grass of the range. The cattle wouldn't breathe well. Some would die. Then, because the thought of death was going through him, he began to notice all the carcasses of animals that were here and there beside the road. Five of them in just one mile. A raccoon and a porcupine, a field squirrel, and a rabbit, then a skunk, stiff and bloating in the sun. He thought of old Doc Markle, shook his head, and didn't bother counting anymore.

He turned left, rattling across the grate, heading down the dusty road between the fields, seeing cattle, coming up a rise, then seeing where the house and barn were down there in a hollow. He saw trees and sheds, a wood pile, a big corrugated metal building that looked like it would serve as a garage. The house itself was newly painted, white with gray around the windows and the eaves, fresh and clean and bright against the summer sun. It was big and getting bigger as he neared, wider than he'd thought, a porch that faced off to the left, a gravel parking space on this side of the house. He pulled up, and he cut his motor, getting out, putting on his hat, walking toward the porch.

The thing was, no one seemed to be around. The windows all were open. Anyone inside could not have helped but hear him. All the same, there wasn't any sign of anyone. Slaughter knocked, but no one answered. Then he turned and looked out toward the barn, toward the corrugated metal structure which he saw now had one door open, nothing in there on this side except a motorcycle. Well, that helped explain it. They were on the range and seeing to the stock. Either that or gone to town. Even so, you'd think that someone would have stayed. The wife perhaps. He'd met her once in town. Nice hands. She didn't seem the type to go out working with the stock.

He put his hand down on his holster, stepping off the porch and walking toward the barn. He saw where posts and boards were rigged to form a horse pen, a nice looking appaloosa in there underneath the shelter of a cottonwood. He saw a water trough, a salt lick, and a feed pail. That reminded him to get another salt lick for his horses. He turned, facing toward the house again, the flowers on one side, the well-kept strip of lawn around the house and porch. He scanned the sheds, the barn, the open space between them, nothing out of place, nothing dirty or run-down, everything as freshly painted as the house, and thought that this must be among the best-kept ranches that he'd seen.

He stood between the house and barn and shouted. No one answered. The horse was looking at him. Slaughter went over, leaned on the fence, and snapped his fingers at it. "What's the matter? No one home?"

The sun glared down on him. The horse moved its hoofs as if to come across to him and then stopped, its head cocked toward the house. Slaughter sensed before he heard it. A constant, high, shrill whistle. It was coming from the back of the house. He walked along the side, looked through a kitchen window in the back, and saw it. There upon the stove. A kettle with a flame beneath it, steam escaping through the whistle on the spout. He found a door in back that led in to the kitchen, knocked but no one answered, went in and shut off the stove. He didn't understand. He searched through all the downstairs rooms and then the bedrooms up on top. He thought that someone might have turned the kettle on and then lain down to rest a moment and then gone to sleep. But there was no one anywhere. The well-kept grounds, the freshly painted house. It wasn't like the people here to go off with a kettle on the stove. Slaughter went out, checking through the barn, the sheds, and the garage, but there was no one, and he didn't understand. What would make them leave a kettle like that? Why had they forgotten? Where in hell had they gone anyhow? The kettle had started shrieking only a while ago. They must have turned it on just before he came, so where in God's name were they?

TEN

Dunlap was hungover. He was slumped across the back seat of the bus. He had made connections with the nearest airport and had thought that he would take a taxi to the town. He hadn't remembered to check his map, though, and was told that Potter's Field was fifty miles away. No one would agree to drive him. It wasn't just the distance. It was that the town was on the other side of all those mountains. Getting there was several hours. Better take a bus. "But I want to go there in a taxi." They just shook their heads. This was something new to Dunlap. In New York where he came from, taxi drivers would grab the chance to go that kind of distance, picking up another fare and coming back. That was just the trouble. No one would be coming back. People took the bus. "But I'll pay to have you go both ways," he told them. They just shook their heads again. "All that driving through the mountains. We'll stay here and save the cars."

So Dunlap took the bus. He'd stayed up drinking late the night before in Denver, waking almost too late for his morning flight to here. The plane had propellers. It hit some rough air just above the northern mountains, jolting up and down, and sick already, Dunlap had barely kept his stomach down. He'd tried some coffee. That didn't help. He tried some Alka-Seltzer, and it almost worked. Then he made a joke about a little of the dog that bit him, asking for a drink. At first the flight attendant was reluctant, early in the morning like that, but Dunlap made a point of it, and in the end he convinced her to sell him a Jim Beam on the rocks. That was just the trick. It went down sharp and made him gag, but it stayed down, and it seemed to settle his stomach. Two more sips, and he was fine. At least he thought he was, returning to his stupor of the night before. Another drink, and then his stomach let him have it. He was in the washroom, throwing up.

He washed his face, looked in the mirror at his gray wrinkled skin, walked back, and slumped, but he was glad to have it out of him at least, and he was sleeping, even through the turbulence, as the plane struggled through the clouds and jounced down for a landing. Waiting for the bus, Dunlap went in to the men's room, washed his face again, opened up his travel bag, took out a bottle, and had another drink. He knew that he was classic: drinking all night, sick and yet in need of still another drink. All the same, he needed it, and if he did his job right, who could tell the difference? Just as long as he could function. That's what you do? Function? Just about. He had another drink. He had another on the bus, his pint bottle hidden in his jacket pocket. He sprawled, feeling sick again, staring at the seat before him, and then sitting up, he glanced at all the grassland going past. It was flat at first, but then it started rising, sloping up to foothills and then mountains, fir trees angling off as far as he could see now, rocks among them, and at one point, looking out, he saw the guardrail and a straight drop down to boulders and a section of the road that curved around a ridge down there. An object came around the lower bend. He knew it was a car, but down that far it resembled a toy, and suddenly aware of just how high he was, Dunlap felt a spinning in his brain, a rising in his stomach, and he had to look away. Either that or throw up again.

He settled back in his seat, glancing at the people who were near him. Men in cowboy hats, women wearing gingham dresses (gingham—Lord, he thought that had gone out of style fifty years ago), old men in suspenders, all with sun-creased skin that looked a bit like leather. Two seats ahead of him, an Indian was looking at a magazine. The Indian's dark hair hung to his shoulders. He wore a pair of faded jeans, a red shirt and a beaded necklace, his boots stuck in the aisle, showing cracked seams, run-down heels, and something on one side that looked distinctly like a piece of horseshit. Dunlap watched him as he turned the page. There was something strange about the photograph. It showed a naked woman, braced, her crotch against a tree. Dunlap peered a little closer. She was dark-haired, ruddy-skinned, exactly like the man who read it. And the language, as he leaned a little closer, wasn't English. Christ, a pornographic magazine for Indians. He'd have to make a note about that. Clearly he could use it. Local color and all that. He squinted at the pear-shaped breasts upon the naked woman. Then the page was turned, and he was looking at a beaver shot. Dunlap thought of Indians and made a joke about a Little Beaver, shook his head, and took another drink.

What kind of place was this to build a commune anyhow? he thought. Why not east or maybe on the coast? At least he had some friends there. Well, there had been many communes in those places, but none had ever been like this. Besides, he didn't choose his assignments. His bosses told him what to do, and he went out and did it. Maybe that was how they got at him for all the drinking that he did. Maybe. Still, he did his job. Or so he told himself at least. He'd have to clean the act up. That was sure. After this job, he would dry out, and he'd show them. Sure. Just as soon as this was over. He slumped so no one could see and had another drink.

#### ELEVEN

The sign said POTTER'S FIELD GAZETTE. Of course, Dunlap thought. That almost slipped my mind. Gazette, for God sake. What else could it be? At least the building had a little class. It was mostly windows on both stories, shiny metal strips connecting all the panes. And clean at that, he told himself, thinking of the bus depot he had left. There were like-new imitation marble steps that led up to the all-glass door, shiny metal all around it, a shiny handle on the door. Dunlap waited for a truck to pass, then stepped off the curb, and started across the street toward the entrance.

The door turned out to be electrically controlled, swinging open with a hiss. The reception area was spotless, bright lights in the decorator ceiling, all-white walls, shiny imitation marble on the floor. What was better, the building was air conditioned, sweat already cooling on Dunlap's forehead. He thought that this might work out, after all.

He glanced at polished metal counters on his right and left, desks and people typing at them.

"Yes, sir. May I help?"

Turning, he saw a woman on his left, early twenties, thin-faced, attractive, her hair combed straight back in a pony tail. He smiled and leaned against the counter.

"Yes, I'm looking for a—" Lord, he couldn't remember the name. Parsons. That was it. "I'm looking for Mr. Parsons."

She stared at his wrinkled sport coat, at the sweat marks underneath its arms. Something shut off in her eyes. "Yes, and may I have your name?"

"Dunlap. Gordon Dunlap. I'm from New York on a story."

Then the eyes were bright again. "Of course. He's been expecting you. Take these stairs. The first door on the right."

She pointed toward a flight of stairs beyond the counter, and Dunlap smiled, nodding, walking toward them. She wore a silk blouse, her bra quite clear beneath it, the two top buttons of her blouse spread open. Dunlap thought about that all the time he climbed the stairs. After all the women he was used to seeing with no bra, their nipples almost poking through their tops, this was exotic. He stopped and took out a handkerchief and wiped his face. To the left he saw a corridor of offices, their doors open, people typing, talking on the phone. To the right, he noticed a wooden door, the first wood in here that he'd seen. MR. PARSONS. EDITOR. Dunlap knocked and entered.

Another woman, older, sat at a desk and studied him. "Yes, sir?" When Dunlap told her, she said, "Of course." She went out through another door, this one wooden like the first, although the desk and chair and cabinets were metal. He waited. Everything was just as clean and shiny as downstairs. Through the windows, he could see the stores across the street. The woman came back, smiling, saying he should go in. Dunlap nodded, walking through.

Everything was wood in there, bookshelves, desk and chairs and tables, even the walls. No, not everything. A thick rug occupied a large part of the floor, and two of the chairs were leather. The difference was the same. This was more a study than an office. More than that, a sanctum. People summoned here would be impressed. Whoever summoned them understood the principles of power.

Parsons. He was smiling, getting up from where he sat behind the desk, coming around to shake hands. "Hello there. We expected you the middle of the week."

"Yeah, well, something came up at the office. They wouldn't let me go till yesterday at noon." And then because he knew he'd sounded rude, "I hope I didn't inconvenience you."

"No, not at all." Smiling again, Parsons pointed toward one of the well-stuffed leather chairs before the desk. "Have a seat. Can I get you something?"

"Coffee would be nice."

Parsons pressed a button on the intercom and looked at him.

"Cream and sugar. Lots of it," Dunlap said.

And Parsons put the order through. Then still smiling, Parsons sat back, his hands upon his lap, and waited. He was maybe fifty-five, husky, almost fat, but not exactly. Mostly he was just big-boned: massive chest and shoulders, hands as big as a heavyweight boxer's. His head seemed extra large as well. Even with his bulging stomach, he seemed very much in shape, though, his skin as fresh and smooth as athletes in their twenties. When he'd come around to shake hands with Dunlap, he had moved as if he were a dancer or a man of half his size and weight. Dunlap was impressed. This man had a presence. More than that, he knew what he was doing. He had never once appeared to notice Dunlap's wrinkled coat and ravaged face and eyes. Clearly, though, he'd been aware of them from the start. He was not a man who did things without thinking. The way he'd fixed this office so it stood out from the others. The way he sat, his expensive suit conspicuous in a town where everyone wore cowboy clothes, his blue shirt crisp and clean, his striped tie meticulously knotted, his hands upon his lap, leaning back and smiling, as if he were at his leisure (but he wasn't). Dunlap knew he'd have to watch him.

"Yes, well, tell me," Parsons said, still leaning back and smiling. "I know you told me on the phone. But just to help me understand, why not tell me once again?"

Dunlap lit a cigarette. "Well, we're doing retrospectives."

Parsons leaned ahead abruptly, pointing. "No, not here."

Dunlap wondered what he meant. He looked around. He saw that there were no ashtrays and understood, standing up to crush the cigarette against the inside of a refuse can. "Sorry."

"Quite all right. You couldn't know."

"Sure." And now you're up on me, you bastard, Dunlap thought, sitting back and going on. "Like I said, we're doing retrospectives—"

"*Newsworld* magazine?"

"That's right."

And Parsons nodded. "Quite a thing. A man from *Newsworld* magazine to come here."

"Yes, well—"

"Must be quite a story."

Then the door opened, and the woman came in with the coffee.

"Thank you."

"Certainly." And she was gone.

Dunlap tried to continue his explanation. "We've been—"

"How's the coffee?"

"Just the way I like it."

"Fine."

And Dunlap had lost count of how much Parsons was ahead of him. "The commune," he was saying.

Parsons looked at him. He evidently hadn't figured they would get so quickly to the point. His eyes narrowed. "That's right. I remember now. You're checking on the commune."

"The commune twenty years after it was founded."

"Twenty-three."

"How's that?"

"*Twenty-three* years since it was founded."

"Yeah, we figured that might make a point."

Parsons shook his head and frowned. "I don't quite understand."

"Well, the difference between then and now. Nineteen seventy. Dope and acid. Vietnam. Young people either going into politics or dropping out of society."

"But what about the commune?"

"Well, we figured we would check on how it went."

"I still don't understand."

"It's a way to measure how the country changed. All those fine young good intentions."

Parsons made a face. "The new republic. That's the thing they called it. Free love, free food, and free spirit." Parsons made another face.

"Yes, but never mind the 'free love' business. That's the part that people always pick at. What we want to know is what came out of all that."

"You could have saved yourself a trip. I'll tell you what came out of all that. Nothing. That's what came of it."

"Well, that's a statement in itself."

"Hey, wait a minute," Parsons said. "Do you have that tape recorder on?"

Dunlap nodded.

"Turn if off."

"But what's the matter?"

"Turn the damned thing off, I said."

Dunlap obeyed. "But what's the matter? Listen, radicals back then are running corporations now. Either that or writing books about how wrong they were. Entertainers who dropped out and went to China are out hoofing on the stage again. Everything has changed. It's a different world. What's so wrong to talk about that? All the communes are long gone as well. But then none of them was quite like this. None of them had so much money, so much talent and ambition, coming out here from the coast, buying all that land and setting up to start a brand new country: Brook Farm in our century."

"Yes, and Brook Farm went to bust, and so did this," Parsons said.

"But what's so wrong to talk about it?"

"Look, you didn't come here just to see the difference. You came here to start that trouble once again."

Dunlap didn't understand.

"It's common knowledge how the town put pressure on them," Parsons said. "How the freaks came through here in their long hair and their costumes, dressed as Superman and God knows what all, turning kids to dope, standing on the corner, howling, blowing kisses. How the town refused to tolerate them, wouldn't sell them food or clothing or supplies, wouldn't even let them in the city limits, tried to find a way to get them off that land. How one rancher had his boy run off and went up there to get him, went a little crazy, pulled a gun and shot a guy. There's a lot of memory yet in town about that. There's a lot of feeling. I don't want you going around and making people ugly once again. Either that or guilty. I don't want you writing so this town looks like the nation's asshole. We had lots of that before. Writers coming in and making trouble, sympathizing with those freaks. You tell me how things have changed. Well, one thing hasn't. Reporters like an underdog, and the way the town reacted to those freaks, there wasn't any question who the reporters sided with. My guess is you'll be doing just the same."

"But really I'm not here for that," Dunlap said. "I just want to see the difference."

"Will you mention what went on back then? How the town reacted?"

"Sure. I guess so. That's a part of how things changed as well."

Parsons shrugged. "All right, then, there you have it."

And they looked at one another, and they waited.

The buzzer sounded on the intercom. Parsons touched a button.

"Don't forget you chair a council meeting in an hour," a woman's voice said.

"Thank you."

Parsons took his hand off the intercom, leaning back.

Christ, Dunlap thought. He isn't just the newspaper's owner and the editor and maybe owner of a half a dozen other places too. He's the god-damned mayor. Dunlap tried to think of how to smooth things. "Look," he told him. "You know just as well as I, there are two sides to a story. Back in nineteen seventy, everything was polarized. The straights and the longhairs. The hawks and the doves. One group acted one way, and the other did the opposite. The thing to do is talk to people in the town and get their version of the story, then to talk to people in the commune and get their version too."

Parsons shrugged. "There's no one out there now."

"What?" Dunlap straightened in surprise. "Nobody told me."

"Maybe two or three are still there. If they are, it's news to me."

Dunlap stared at him.

"Of course, there are ways to track the others down," Parsons said. "The names are all on file. If you've got the time."

Dunlap went on staring at him.

"Look, I'll tell you what," Parsons said. "You may have gathered from that message that I don't just run this paper. I'm on the town council. If I wanted, I could make things tough for you, see that people didn't talk to you, deny you access to the paper's files, other things."

It was the "other things" that Dunlap didn't like the sound of.

"But I won't. For one thing, that would show up in your story too. For another, you'd just work a little harder, and you'd get your story anyhow. All the same, if I wanted, I could make things tough. Now the point is, I don't want you thinking I'm against you. The fact is that I'm not. In your place, I'd act the same as you. What I do want is a simple understanding. Anything you need is yours. Ask and I'll arrange it. You go out and do your story. Then you come back to this office, and we talk. I want the chance to make this town look good to you. These people here are fine. I'm anxious that they don't get hurt."

Dunlap squinted.

"No, I'm not afraid of business being hurt," Parsons said. "People out there don't stop buying cattle just because a story makes a town look bad. What I said was true. I just don't want these people hurt."

Dunlap took a breath. "Fair enough."

"What do you need?"

"Well, for starters, let me in your paper's morgue. Then I'd like to see the records the police kept."

"That's no problem. What else?"

"Courthouse records. Trials and transcripts."

"That's no problem either."

"Then I'd like to talk to people in the town. I'll go out to the commune, too, of course."

"Of course. I'll see that someone goes out with you."

Dunlap shrugged. "That's all I can think of for now."

"Well, you'd best get at it then. Just remember. Anything you need."

"Don't worry. I'll get back to you."

"I know you will." And Parsons stared at him as Dunlap stood to leave. One thing now was certain, Dunlap thought. This was going to be a whole lot harder than he'd expected.


### TWELVE

Ken Kesey was the cause of it. The Merry Pranksters and that bus. That was back in 1964. Kesey had already finished *One Flew Over the Cuckoo's Nest* and *Sometimes a Great Notion*. With his money, he had bought some land near Palo Alto, California, gathered freaks around him, and started on a trip. That was back when LSD was legal, and the trip of course was only in his mind. Then the trip was real. He had bought a bus, had sprayed it every color of the rainbow, and then dressing like a comic strip, he had shooed his freaks on board and started for New York. *On the Road* a decade later, Neal Cassidy as driver, that same Cassidy who'd been with Kerouac. They had ballyhooed across the country, music blaring out of speakers on the top, channeled in upon itself so that it echoed and then echoed yet again, police cars stopping them while Pranksters jumped down—Day-Glo-colored costumes, Captain Marvel, Mandrake the Magician—setting up their movie cameras. "Yes, sir! Yes, sir! What's the trouble? Speak right toward this microphone." Well, the policemen didn't stay long, and the Pranksters got few traffic tickets, roaring on across the country, popping acid, blaring music, acting out the movie of their lives. They reached New York and headed back, and by now they were noticed, not just by the strangers they were passing but the press as well. There were numerous stories about their odyssey, acid rock and Day-Glo paint, so that when they got back to the commune, others of their kind were waiting for them, and the movie went on, only larger, more extreme. From the commune, they went to the cities, starting what they called their acid tests, light shows, flashing pictures, music coming from each corner of a hall they rented, speakers blaring, all matched with the flashing in their minds from all those Kool-Aid pitchers spiked with acid. Then Kesey was arrested for possession, not of acid but of marijuana. That took place in 1965. In 1966 he was arrested yet again, same charge, but convicted by now on the first offense and out while sentence was appealed, he had fled his second trial, heading south toward Mexico. Unlawful flight. Rumors where he was. Then back in California where he was arrested once again. In 1967 he was serving time. That was how the acid culture got its start, from Kesey and his life style bigger than his books.

But there were other ways, those who said that Kesey had been wrong, that with a good thing going he'd been foolish to be so in sight. Better to do it on the sly, keep things quiet, keep them truly out of sight. Like the commune, some were saying. That had been a good idea. The trouble was that Kesey ventured out. He had been his own undoing. Better find a place where no one went, stay there, do your thing. Well, they did it, and where they chose to do it was near Potter's Field, Wyoming. All it took was one rich kid whose parents had both died. He'd been with Kesey. He had seen the trouble that was coming, and he'd split. Twenty-one, he had complete control of all the money he'd inherited. He'd found a spot where no one ever went, fifty acres of thick timber in the mountains far across the valley from the town. He had bought it, paid the taxes for ten years, set up buildings, and moved in. It wasn't just a place for freaking out. He had notions of a kind of ideal way of life. Those who marched against the Vietnam war but felt they weren't accomplishing anything, those who tried to change society from within the system but found that the politicians they worked for betrayed them, these and others like them he would welcome to his arms. The new republic. Free love, free food, and free spirit. Everything was on his tab. Not an orgy, not the kind of free love everyone was thinking of. But something else. Simple freedom that permitted love, love in any form, physical, emotional, as long as no one would be harmed, the kind of freedom those who were attracted to him hadn't seen before. First there were the freaks, imitation Pranksters, some who had indeed been Pranksters. Then there were the drop-outs, those who couldn't stand things anymore, who couldn't even bear to watch the television news. Queers and junkies, cowards, troublemakers, traitors and more, that was how the straight world saw them, but in Quiller's fifty acres, they were just themselves.

Quiller, twenty-one and rich and leader of his version of a country. Photographs of him were not at all what a conservative would expect. No long hair and beard and ragged jeans. No beads, guru shirts, or Captain Marvel costume. Quiller looked just as straight as those who spoke against him. Short hair reminiscent of the fifties, sideburns even with the middle of his ears, fair-skinned to begin with so his clean face looked like it was always shaved. He wore custom-tailored shirts and designer slacks and hand-sewn patent-leather shoes. Tall and thin. No, that didn't quite describe him. Tall was far too relative. He stood six-foot-eight, a star in basketball in college, but that still did not convey his seeming height. Think of what he weighed. One hundred and sixty, sometimes less, just sinew, bone, and muscle, running ten miles in the morning and another ten at night. He looked as if someone had put him on a rack and stretched him, long legs, long arms, neck and body, stark thin hips and chest and waist. His face was in proportion, high and narrow, slight jaw, small lips, thin nose. Mostly what you noticed were his eyes, though. Even in the photographs. Bright and clear and gleaming, almost piercing. In color photos, they were blue.

Some who were against him said his eyes were bright like that because of all the speed and acid he was popping. Others, more inclined toward him, maintained that they were bright like that because he was so god-damned smart, his I.Q. close to genius, up there near one hundred and eighty.

All that Dunlap had already checked on, going through old *Newsworld* files back in New York at his office. There were photographs of Quiller talking to reporters, of the conference that he had called, using all the power of his wealth, to tell them what he planned. Reporters had been glad to come, promised champagne, pheasant under glass, and caviar, eager too to find another Kesey. They had written many stories based on Kesey. Now they hoped to write a lot more like them based on Quiller, disappointed when they saw how straight he seemed. Quiller had them writing soon enough, however. First he told them how disgusted he was that he couldn't get attention without bribing them to come, how he hoped the caviar would choke them and remind them of the sickness in the country. He explained his views about the nation, and he told them to go out and spread the word. They, of course, refused. Some were standing up to leave. But he had something yet in store for them. "The Exodus," he called it. Two months further on, July 4, Independence Day, he would free his people from their bondage. Starting out from San Francisco, he would lead a caravan of misfits, malcontents, and dispossessed from City Hall at nine a.m. and take them to the promised land. He told reporters of the fifty acres, told them what he planned to do there, told them of the kind of ideal life he hoped to lead. Because he couldn't change the nature of the world, he would turn his back on it and make his own. No hate, no wars, no repression. Only peace and mutual respect and harmony. He invited all the reporters in the room to join him. Mostly, though, he let them in on what amounted to a newsman's holiday. Two months from now, they'd have stories all right, more than they could handle, visions of those photogenic hippies, traffic jams and confrontations, Day-Glo buses, vans and motorcycles, God knows what all, heading down the road. Local color and events. That was it: events. This had the feel of something major. Quiller got what he had wanted. They went out and spread the word.

It was a media-created happening. Later, many would maintain that nothing would have taken place if reporters had been silent. But the media said that it would happen, and of course it did. Five thousand freaks of all descriptions, half as many vehicles. It wasn't just a traffic jam. It amounted almost to a riot, police attacking the freaks, claiming the assembly was unlawful, dragging hippies off. Quiller put a stop to that. He'd used his money there as well, buying various permits from officials.

And they started away, Quiller at the lead in a bright red classic 1959 Corvette, heading across the country. They went through Nevada and then Utah, others joining in along the way, a five-mile caravan of cars and trucks and bikes and buses, straight or twisted, some plain, others Day-Gloed, orange and green and purple, every color you could think of. It was something else, they said. It was also Quiller's last cooperation with reporters. He had broken his first rule—don't let people know what you're doing. He'd been forced to. Without newsmen, he had no publicity. But now he had no need for them, and he ignored them all along the way. He reached Wyoming, moving close to home. He crossed the rangeland, worked up through the mountains, crossed more rangeland, then more mountains. Then he reached the valley, coming through the western pass, never getting close to town, simply heading north within the valley until he reached the loggers' road and going up, and that was where the story ended. No reporter ever saw the compound. Lord knows, many tried. Quiller, though, was adamant. Echoing a famous Kesey slogan that a person's either on or off the bus, he said that newsmen too were free to join. The catch was, they would have to stay. "You're either in or out of the compound. There's no in-between." Many newsmen tried to fake it, but he wouldn't have them. He wouldn't accept a lot of freaks who'd come with him as well. He wanted only those who sensed a mission. Those who wanted nothing but parties he ordered to leave. There were thugs he had hired who took care of forcing them to leave and many of the chosen who took care of forcing them as well. At last he had a thousand. Then he cut them down to half, and all the gates were closed.

From all accounts, there wasn't much to see, regardless: just an open space within the trees, wooden buildings set out into streets and sections, not like houses, more like barracks, just as if this were the Army. That had turned a lot of people off, helping to thin the ranks. The place itself was far off in the forest. Quiller hadn't bought land near the highway. He had bought it away up in the mountains, also buying a strip of land to get to it. That was why you couldn't see the compound. Walking up the loggers' road, you came to where a gate was closed and members of the commune watched it. You could work across and come in from the side. That took several hours, though. The woods were thick and slashed with ravines. But the borders there were guarded too, and anyway the woods were still so thick you couldn't see the commune. For a picture of it, you would have to walk right to the forest's edge, and someone surely would have spotted you. There were rumors that one man had gone there, been discovered, had his camera taken from him, and been chased. But no one ever found the man to talk to him, and no one ever knew.

And anyway, so what? The story by then wasn't at the compound. It was in the town. All the freaks who'd been rejected or had lost their interest showed up in Potter's Field. That was when the trouble started, when the town rejected all those crazy perverts, wouldn't sell them food or even gasoline, and called in the state police to have them sent away. There were fights and broken windows, shattered heads, Day-Gloed buildings, litter, obscene gestures, and a lot of dope. It was two weeks that the town wished hadn't been. In the end, the freaks were all evicted, but the town looked on the compound as the cause of all the trouble. Indeed the town drew no distinction between Quiller's people and those others, and it wouldn't sell the compound food.

Dunlap knew that from the files in New York too. He had seen the photos of the San Francisco riot, policemen dragging hippies off, kicking, swinging clubs and pushing, a great mass of pained and twisted faces, bodies trampled underfoot—photos that reminded him of others like them from the previous decade, especially the march on the Pentagon and the Chicago Democratic convention. He had read about the sudden permits that came through, suspecting that Quiller could have had them sooner but that Quiller held off until he made a point, binding all those people to him. Dunlap saw photos of the

Corvette heading out of San Francisco, the long procession following; of locals by the road who even in still pictures seemed to shake their heads and turn and frown and ask each other what the hell was going on. State patrol cars waiting for a traffic violation. Restaurants that wouldn't serve them. By the time they got to Utah, the photos began to seem ordinary. Editors enlivened them, juxtaposing Brigham Young, the Mormon trek, and Quiller's ragged motorcade. The point was obvious, Day-Gloed buses against covered wagons, this new trek a parody of what had once been dignified and meaningful. Even layouts like that soon lost their effectiveness, however, so that by the time the column reached Wyoming, there was little new to show. Oh, sure, there were the mountains and the valley, the road up to the compound, and the gate. But all those pictures didn't have much drama to them. Editors rejected them in favor of what was happening in town.

As near as Dunlap could remember from the photos he had studied in New York, there didn't seem much difference between how the town had looked back then and what it looked like now. A few new buildings maybe, and of course the slogans had been erased from the walls, but really nothing much was changed. The same wide central street, the same two-story buildings that went straight down on both sides, their clapboard walls painted white. A pocket of tradition. Continuity. The place had likely looked the same back in the fifties too. Dunlap had seen pictures of the confrontation in the town, beaded hippies face-to-face with stern-eyed men in cowboy hats, state policemen standing by patrol cars waiting for trouble; fights and local people jeering; flying stones and bottles, broken windows, tents and garbage through the park—and more fights, further confrontations, each day worse than the one before until the roundup in the park, patrol cars all around it while the troopers went in from all sides and pushed the hippies toward the center, county buses waiting for them, those on foot at least, others forced to start their cars and trucks and vans and get the hell out from the town. The state police cars stayed with them right through the town and valley, up the pass, and only left them when they reached the other side. There were some who, stubborn, came back, but they didn't last long, forced to leave again, and then that part of everything was over. The story idled.

There was nothing doing. Newsmen and photographers soon left. Potter's Field was by itself again, except for Quiller and the compound.

So much for the files that Dunlap had gone through in New York. Parsons had been right, of course. The press had sided with the hippies. Civil rights and freedom of expression, not to mention that the hippies were the underdogs. All the same, Dunlap couldn't blame the town. It really hadn't been prepared for several thousand strung-out, West-coast freaks descending on them. There was just too little understanding. It didn't matter anyhow. That wasn't what he'd come for, although he'd have to note it for perspective in his story. What he wanted was the story of what happened next, the story no one else had covered, the subtle many-year changes that when isolated didn't have much drama but when put together and compressed might make a dramatic point.

Quiller and the compound, what went on up there behind those sentries and that gate? Dunlap was guessing that the new republic failed, all that wealth and innocence not good enough to make a difference. Lofty ideals compromised, gold turned into lead. Not that Quiller's ideals had been very deep or complicated. Regardless of the I.Q. they had come from, they were mostly well-phrased slogans. Sure, there was the paradox of using wealth to make a way of life that didn't need it. There was, too, the paradox of Quiller, straight and clean-cut, leading all those hippies, his classic Corvette at the head of all those music-blaring buses. Nonetheless, for all that Dunlap knew, Quiller had just made himself look straight so he could use the system to create his enterprise. The only way to know that was to talk to Quiller, and as much as Dunlap was aware, no one from the outside had heard news of Quiller since he'd closed the gates and gone back in the wood-enshrouded compound back in 1970. It was almost twenty-three years ago exactly. Parsons had been right. Next month, the middle of July, would be about the time the trouble had reached its worst within the town. Dunlap guessed that if the compound went to hell, its members simply drifted off, Quiller with them, so dejected no one wished to talk about it. Could be Quiller lost his wealth and disappeared, no longer powerful, only disillusioned and anonymous. Could be. All the same, you'd think that someone would have told.

Well, the only way to know was to do the research, get the facts, and get out of here. Dunlap sat before a microfilm machine. He was in the newspaper's basement, in a small room at the far end of a corridor. His coat was on a chair, the only light the one that glowed from the microfilm machine. It was pleasant down here in the half-dark, cool and faintly soothing, even with the sound of a fan that blew air past the film to keep the reading light in there from burning through it. He had asked the man in charge down here to give him all the reels for summer, 1970. Actually he'd been surprised that Parsons had the Gazette's morgue on microfilm. Most town papers like this just had issues put in storage, destroying many when they needed room. Parsons, though, was up on things. Dunlap hated reading microfilm. All the same, he was impressed.

He sat there, fooling with a reel, adjusting it. He turned the reel until he got an image on the screen before him, centered it, and started reading. What he wanted was some aspect of the story that the files he'd read had not included. Some small detail that would tell him what had happened in the compound while the troubles in the town upstaged it. For a time, the microfilm before him and the files he'd read in New York were the same. Different writers handled them. There were different slants, one in favor of the town and one against it, but the information was the same. Then he came across an item that he'd never seen before. The cars and trucks and vans that went up in the compound. Quiller had them sold. Some he sent down to the local dealers, trading at a loss for cash. Then the trouble in the town intensified so much that angry dealers wouldn't any longer trade with him, and emissaries from the compound had to leave the valley for the dealers in the nearest other towns. Emissaries. That was it. Quiller wasn't ever with them. What was more, the emissaries wouldn't ever mention what was going on up there. That was no surprise, of course, although Dunlap thought that it was subtle. Good religious precepts. Swear your followers to secrecy; have them give up all unnecessary worldly goods. The money they earned from the sale would have been nothing when compared to Quiller's wealth, but this way they were adding to the enterprise, giving, not just taking. The thing that puzzled Dunlap, however, was the sports car. In all the local items that described the way they traded all their vehicles for cash, there wasn't any mention of the classic red Corvette. Even back in 1970, a 1959 Corvette was special. Chevrolet had switched designs, and many buyers felt the earlier was better. Surely some reporter would have made a note if it were sold. Dunlap told himself that, when he had the time, he'd have to call the other papers in the area. In the meanwhile, though, and on a chance, he scanned the used-car advertisements on the microfilm. He knew that, if a dealer had his hands on that Corvette, he'd surely want to advertise. There wasn't any mention, though.

Dunlap looked ahead for several weeks, and still there wasn't any mention. He would have to check the other newspapers, of course. But could it be, was it possible that Quiller had ordered his members to sell their vehicles and, while they did it, had kept his own? What the hell was going on?

Dunlap turned the reel and read more of the microfilm. Once again, except for how events were slanted, this was much the same as what he'd read in files back in his New York office. The roundup, the expulsion, and the slowly settling peace. Then there was a difference, local items on how much it cost the town to clean the garbage from the park, to put in new windows, and to scrape the slogans off the walls. There were letters praising how authorities had handled things, attempts to understand a strange and changing world, confusion and bewilderment. Only one dissent, no name, saying that the town had been too hasty, that "instead of beating on those kids we should have tried to understand them." Maybe so, but if there had been others who agreed with that, there was no published sign of it. The overwhelming sense was of a town that still had not recovered from its shock. Weird beaded costumes, long hair, beards and what all, they were one thing, although Dunlap guessed that local people with their cowboy clothes and gingham dresses had seemed just as strange to all those West-coast hippies as the hippies seemed to them. Dope and shiftlessness and filth, though, they were something else, something that the town could neither understand nor tolerate. A woman wrote in, angered by two infants she had seen, dirty-faced and crying, diapers unchanged, while the mother stretched out on the grass and looked away. Another woman wrote that all she'd seen some children eat was half-cooked rice and moldy cheese and milk which with the specks of straw inside had clearly not been pasteurized, and where on earth they'd got that kind of milk she didn't know, but what was going on? The dope had really done the trick, though. They had evidently smoked it clear out in the open, almost flaunting it, and Dunlap, going through the items in the paper, was surprised that no one was arrested. Sure, he understood that too, he guessed. To pick up one, you'd have to take them all. Otherwise you punished one and let the others get away. The jail was likely far too small, the trouble just not worth the cost of feeding them. Better just to clear out the lot of them. Which is what they did.

Then Dunlap read some issues of the paper where there wasn't any mention of what happened. Things were getting back to normal. So the townsfolk were pretending. That was just about the time the newsmen and photographers decided that the story was played out and started leaving. They weren't present for what happened next, the murder, headlines straight across the page. At last.

### THIRTEEN

The door creaked open. Dunlap swung. A man stepped into view, outlined by the hallway light that spilled in. He was tall and gangly, wearing suspenders, his shirt sleeves rolled up, his white hair haloed by the light behind him, the man in charge of microfilm whom Dunlap had talked to earlier. "I'm sorry, sir. We close at five." The words were hushed as if this truly were a morgue, the almost-empty room echoing.

Dunlap stared at him and breathed. Then he leaned back in his chair and rubbed his temples. He looked at his watch. Ten to five. He'd started shortly after two, so taken up by what he read that he hadn't realized how quickly the time was going.

Abruptly he felt tired.

"What time do you open in the morning?"

"Eight o'clock. We close at noon." The room echoed again.

Dunlap lit a cigarette and nodded. "Thanks." He'd been afraid that the newspaper's office wouldn't be open on Saturday. He stood and put his jacket on, glancing at the notes he'd made, surprised that there were so many of them, unaware he'd made them. He put the microfilm back into its box, stacked it on the other boxes, snapped the light off on the reader, picked the boxes up, and walked across the room to hand them over. "Thanks," he repeated, and with his camera, tape recorder, and his notes, he went out past the man and down the hall.

On the street, Dunlap had to squint again. The sun was low, descending toward the mountains, but the glare was as bad as earlier. In contrast with the air-conditioned building he'd just left, the air out here was close and humid, and he started sweating almost immediately. There were people going past, walking home from work, lots more traffic on the street. He glanced at several women, young and tall with soft, loose-fitting dresses that nonetheless suggested hips and breasts, and shook his head. He turned and walked up toward the right. As much as he remembered, that was where the two big buildings with all the trees had been when he'd arrived on the bus at noon. He looked and saw the trees in the distance, and he kept walking. The trees seemed five blocks away at least, and he was wondering if the effort would be worth it. Mostly he was hot and tired, and his hands shook so bad that he knew he'd have to stop soon for a drink. But reading through that microfilm had perked his interest, and he didn't want to stay here any longer than he had to, so he'd take a chance, and if the office up there were still open, maybe he could save some time. Maybe, but the trees seemed just as far away, the more he walked, and several times he almost weakened, glancing at the bars.

Then he stood across from all those trees, the big, stone, pillared courthouse, and the brick, three-story building that he guessed would be the police station. He crossed the street toward them, reaching the shadow of the trees and feeling cool beneath them as the siren started wailing and a cruiser shot out from the corner of the building, racing down a side street, emergency lights flashing, barely stopping at the main street as the big man in there swerved the cruiser sharply to the left and, tires squealing, rushed down through the center of the town.

Dunlap watched him go. This was more like home. There were people all along the sidewalk stopped and watching. There were cars that pulled close to the sidewalk while the cruiser wailed quickly past. Then the cruiser was so far along that Dunlap couldn't see it anymore. He heard the siren rising, falling, becoming fainter. Then he couldn't hear it, and after he noticed that the traffic and pedestrians were going on about their business, he started up the sidewalk toward the police station's entrance.

There was rich, well-tended lawn on each side of the walkway. From the shadow of the trees, he guessed. The sun could not get in and scorch it. He was thinking of the brown grass on the rangeland, thinking of the cruiser, what in this small town would merit such commotion. Probably an accident, he thought. A bad one, rush hour and all that. He reached the stairs that led up to the entrance, brick just like the portico and walls, old and dark and weathered. He went in. There were stairs that led down to the basement, stairs that led up to a vestibule, wide and tall and spacious, treelike plants in pots along the walls, doors that led off on each side. The place gave off the not-unpleasant must that comes with many years. He saw a door wide open, saw the sign on top, POLICE CHIEF, NATHAN SLAUGHTER, and he entered.

The room was bright: white walls, lights across the ceiling. To the left, he saw a heavy, gray-haired woman at a desk that supported a bulky, two-way radio. At first, she didn't notice him. All she did was sit there, staring at the radio. He moved, and then she turned to him.

"Yes, sir, may I help?"

Dunlap glanced across the empty room and doubted it. "I'm looking for the chief."

"Sorry. He's not in." The woman stared at the radio again.

"Well, my name's Dunlap. Mr. Parsons sent me over."

"You're the reporter from New York?"

He nodded.

"Mr. Slaughter had a call about you, but he couldn't wait. Something came up, and he had to get there."

Sure, the cop who raced out in that cruiser, Dunlap thought. As the woman stared at the radio yet again, he couldn't tell if she was being rude or was merely preoccupied. "I don't suppose you know when he'll be back."

The woman shook her head. "Tomorrow morning."

Swell, Dunlap thought. "Then maybe you can do something for me."

"That depends."

"I need to see some files."

The woman shook her head again. "You'll have to ask the chief about that."

Swell, Dunlap mentally repeated, and abruptly a call crackled from the radio.

"Christ, he's dead, all right," a man blurted, his frenzied voice distorted by static. "Lord, he hasn't got a—"

FOURTEEN

Slaughter skidded to a stop behind the other cruisers. He was getting out and putting on his hat even as he reached to turn the motor off. His siren faded. Over to his right, he saw them standing in a circle in the middle of the field, staring down toward what appeared to be a hollow: several members of his force, a few civilians, and the medical examiner. They looked at him as he hurried around the cruiser. Then they turned and went on staring. He was stepping onto the curb, rushing through the stiff brown grass, looking at the stockbarns over to his left, smelling cattle droppings, mounds and mounds of them, the one thing out here that he still wasn't used to, cattle milling in the pens, brought in to be force fed and then shipped. He was almost running as he came up to them and looked down in the hollow. No one spoke.

"Jesus," he said and turned away and then looked back again. "You're sure that this is him?"

Someone nodded to his right, the husky blond policeman who was Rettig.

Rettig handed him a wallet. Slaughter opened it and read the driver's license. *Clifford, Robert B.* It was him all right, unless somebody had made a substitution. All those times his wife had called and said that he was missing, afraid that something had happened to him, when in fact he'd just gone out to have some drinks and get away from her. And this time, damn it anyhow, her fear was justified.

What made Slaughter think about a substitution, what made him read the license, was the body splayed out stiffly in the hollow. The body had no face. Its eyes and lips and nose and cheeks and chin and forehead, everything was ripped and mangled, as if somebody had shoved the face into a wood shredder. There were bits of chin and cheekbone showing, sockets where the eyes had been, but mostly what was shocking were the teeth, bared, no flesh around them, white against the dark, dirty, scab-covered flesh. The ears were gone as well. No, not gone exactly. They were mixed in, bits and pieces, with the other mangled flesh, tufts of hair stuck where his eyes had been, the illusion that the hair had grown in the sockets. Slaughter was almost sick and had to turn away.

He took a breath. "Okay, what have you got so far?"

Rettig stepped a little closer. "Well, he was drinking last night at that bar down on the corner."

Slaughter squinted down the street. The Railhead. Where the stockyard workers went for lunch and after five. He nodded.

"He was drinking quite a bit. He stayed till closing, bitched a lot because they wouldn't serve him. Then he left."

"Was he alone?"

"That's what the bartender says."

"No one saw him after that?"

"Nobody I can find."

Slaughter glanced once more at the wallet in his hand, searching through it. "Two fives and a one. We know he wasn't robbed, at least." He brooded and turned to the medical examiner. "So tell me what your guess is."

"I won't know until I get him on the table."

"Hell, it's obvious," a man nearby them said.

Slaughter turned. He saw a young policeman. Red-haired, bothered by what he was staring at. His name was Hammel. Slaughter had hired him several months before, and now he guessed he'd have to start to teach him. "No, it isn't obvious. There are just three ways this could have happened. One: he was already dead when something came and ripped at him. Two: he fell unconscious, and it happened. Three: he got attacked while he was walking. Now if he'd been dead already, then we have to know what killed him. Someone might have slit his throat, and then an animal came by and smelled the blood." Slaughter kept staring at the young policeman who was red-faced, blinking, looking one way, then the other. Slaughter knew that he had shamed him, that he shouldn't press it any-more, but he was powerless to stop. "In case you haven't noticed, there's a difference between a dog attack and homi-cide. If that's what kind of animal to blame." He turned toward the medical examiner again. "Is that what you think did this?"

"I don't know. I'll have to measure all those lacerations. You can see there aren't any claw marks on the body. That rules out a cat or something like that."

"Cat? You mean a cougar?"

"That's right. Sometimes mountain lions come down here to the stockpens where the cattle are. But not too often. And certainly not lately. Not in twenty years. There aren't many cats around here anymore."

"You think it was a dog then?"

"That's my guess. I'll have to check to see, though, as I said. One thing that I want to look at are those pant cuffs. You can see where they've been torn. It could be something nipped at him and brought him down."

"Could be. On the other hand, they could be old pants that he didn't bother changing when he left the house. I'll send them to the state-police lab and in the meantime go around and see his wife about them." Slaughter was thinking that he'd have to go and see her anyhow, and then he didn't feel like talking anymore. He turned and saw the young policeman who con-tinued to look flustered, his cheeks red, blinking.

"—never saw a thing to beat it."

"I did," Slaughter told him, trying to make up for how he'd spoken to him. "Back in Detroit, working homicide. Bod-ies one and two days old, bite marks all over their arms and legs, their faces and their necks. Rats in tenements. We got so we expected them. If we weren't out there fast enough, we some-times didn't find too much. Just take it easy. A thing like this can throw you. Come to think of it, a thing like this can throw me too."

The young man nodded.

Slaughter nodded back. He turned to Rettig. "Go down to those houses on the corner. See what people know. Screams. A dog that's loose. Any thing they might have noticed."

"Right." Rettig hurried away.

Slaughter faced the medical examiner again. "We'd better

call and have the ambulance brought out." He paused and watched as Rettig moved across the barren lot. "You know what I've been thinking?"

"I'm not sure."

"I'm thinking of that chewed-up steer we found by old Doc Markle."

"Some connection?"

"I don't know. But I can't shake the feeling something's wrong."

# THE
## PART TWO
# COMPOUND

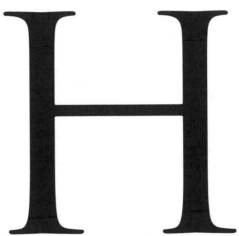

IS NAME WAS
WARREN. HE WAS NINE, OLD ENOUGH TO SNEAK OUT FROM THE
house when it was night, but too young for the trouble he might
get in. Now he waited for his mother and his father to stop talking in their bedroom. He crouched beside his partly open door,
watching for the light to go off underneath the door across the
hall. Once he almost panicked when his father came out toward
the bathroom, walking back and stopping as if he might look
in and check on him. Warren knew he couldn't make it to the
bed in time. He crouched and trembled, but his father
shrugged and went in to his mother, and the light went off, and
Warren was fine.

   He waited quite a while, or so it seemed to him, at least.
He heard no noises in the room across there, and he guessed
that they were both asleep. Cramped from crouching, he gently closed the door and straightened, his legs stiff, groping

through the darkness toward the window. It was open, crickets sounding out there in the grass and among the bushes. He was just about to free the catches on the screen and set it to one side when he remembered. Here he'd gone to all the trouble making up a plan, and now he'd almost climbed out and forgotten. He turned to the right to touch his bed and pull the covers back and slip a pillow under there to make it look as if he was sleeping. He'd seen that trick several times on TV, and it seemed a good idea in case his mother or father peered in to check on him. Then he reached beneath the bed and felt around to grab the sack of crackers. He moved toward the window, took off the screen, and crawled out, his legs still feeling cramped as he eased down onto the porch and put the screen back in the window.

But it kept falling off, and he was forced to tilt it so the bottom angled out, the top part leaning on the frame. He studied it a moment. Then he turned and walked across the porch, climbing onto the rail and hanging down, fearful that his parents might still find him, letting loose and dropping, his stomach scraping against the wood that stuck out from the porch. He huddled in the bushes, rubbing his stomach. He wore the pirate top his mother had slipped on him when she brought him in to bed, him waiting until she left, then taking off the pirate bottoms, putting on his jeans and running shoes. He felt beneath the top and touched the welted skin across his stomach, tensing from the sharp, biting pain. That's all he would need is for his mother to see marks across his stomach in the morning. Well, he couldn't do a thing about it. He was out, and he might just as well keep going.

All the same, he crouched among the bushes several moments longer. He groped for the sack where he had dropped it when he'd slipped down from the rail. Then he had it, paper crackling beneath his fingers, and he froze. He glanced around to see if any lights came on inside the house, but nothing changed in there, and he was certain he was being foolish. If they hadn't heard him climbing off the rail and landing in the bushes, then they surely wouldn't have heard the noise when he touched his sack of crackers. What had really bothered him, he knew now, were the crickets. They had stopped their squeaking. That was how his mother had explained their noises to him.

Crickets made that sound by squeaking one leg across the other, and they'd stopped as soon as he had landed. In the darkness, every noise seemed extra loud, and now the silence frightened him. Well, if that was how this expedition would turn out, then maybe he should go back in the house. He'd been brave enough when he was planning this. Now that he was outside in the dark, he started getting scared. Maybe he should go back. No, he told himself. He mustered his resolve and straightened, the sack bunched in his hand as he stepped from the bushes.

Where he lived was in the older section of the town— between the business district and the new homes along the outskirts. There were trees and shrubs for cover and a shaded lane that stretched behind the houses. Wary of the streetlights in the front, he crept toward the murky lane, his sneakers soaked with dew from the grass as he reached the lane's rough, dusty gravel. Back in here, away from all the streetlights, it was blacker than he had expected. He moved slowly, working up his nerve. Over to his left, he saw an object huddled by a shed. He froze again and almost turned to run before he realized that it was a garbage can. His eyes adjusted, and he recognized what in the daylight would have been familiar sights, the swing set in the backyard of the house next door, the old well that was filled in and that he sometimes hid behind, the wooden wheelbarrow from the old days that the man in back put flowers in. He took a breath. The moon emerged from clouds, and he started walking again.

The moon made quite a difference, almost full but not exactly, lighting the darkness around him with a pale, silver glow. There were stars out, too, he saw, and he felt better with each step, passing trees and bushes, cars and gardens, sheds, garages, and more garbage cans, all lit dimly by the silver of the moon. He heard an owl; instead of being frightened, he pretended that the owl was cheering him on. The lane came to a side street, where he waited in the bushes until the headlights of a car went past, and when it was safely up the street, he ran across to where the lane continued. He knew this section of the lane about as well as that part down behind his house, looking at the flower garden up ahead, the tree house, and the old-time water trough and hitching post, watching for the dog the people down here kept out on a chain.

The dog was not around, it seemed, although he could see the chain quite clearly, stretched out from the dog house, lying in the grass, reflecting moonlight. No dog barking, nothing coming after him. He held his breath and hurried past it. Then he felt relieved. Maybe they had let the dog in. Maybe they had taken it away. He didn't know, but he was feeling even better as he passed the last few houses on the lane. He had never been out on his own this late before, and with his fear now gone, he felt exactly as he'd thought he would, happy and excited, thrilled to be out doing this. He came to where the lane stopped and the park loomed up before him. There were trees that shut away the moon, a few thin silver streaks that filtered down upon the grass. He didn't mind the darkness, though. This was one place where he always felt at home. He played here often, coming here with his mother nearly every day. Over to his left would be the swing sets, although he couldn't see them. Down there straight ahead would be the swimming pool and tennis courts. And over to his right would be the stream that wound its way through town and then through here to meet up with the lake. There were ducks and fish and turtles in the lake, and sometimes he would walk there with his mother, eating lunch beside it.

That was where he went, not directly toward the lake, but toward the stream that met up with it, toward a bend that they had walked along. They had gone there Wednesday and then yesterday, and each time they had seen it, the little animal that lived down in the reeds beside the stream. He had been the one who'd noticed it first. "Look, there, Mother, at the cat down by the water." She'd gazed where he had pointed, and she'd said that it wasn't a cat. "The bushy tail and pointed face and mask around the eyes. That's a raccoon." It stood there in the water, staring at them, and then slowly walked up on the bank and disappeared within the reeds. They waited, but it didn't show itself again. It looked so soft he wished that he could touch it. "Better stay away from it," his mother had said. "It might be wild. It likely is." That night they had told his father what they'd seen, and he had nodded. "Sure, there might be coons still living in the city. Look at all the rabbits, moles, and possums. There's no reason why it couldn't. But they hardly come out in the daylight. Chances are nobody else has even seen it." That had been exciting, the only ones who'd ever seen it. Warren had thought about it all night, and the next day he had made his mother take him there again.

And he had seen it again. It was standing high up on the bank this time and staring at them like before, its head cocked, sitting on one hip. It had stayed there quite a while. Then it had crawled back into the reeds. His mother said there was a hole in there. That was why they always found it in this place. And Warren was even more excited, thinking he had come upon a secret. But today when he had walked there with his mother, it was gone. It hadn't shown itself at least, and he'd been disappointed. He remembered what his father had said, that raccoons didn't like the daylight, and he guessed that, if he'd ever have a chance to touch it, he would have to go at night. Even if he saw it in the day again, he knew that his mother would never let him touch it. So he'd have to wait until dark and go there on his own.

At first, the thought was scary. After all, he'd never gone out by himself like that, and what was more, he knew his parents would be angry. But the thought kept working on him. He remembered what the raccoon looked like, how he'd wanted to reach down and touch it. He remembered how he'd often been tempted to sneak out when things were dark and learn what happened in the night.

Soon the thought quit being scary. He would go on his adventure and one day announce, "Mother, by the way, do you remember that raccoon we saw? Well, one night I went down and touched it." She would look at him, and he would smile, and then she'd know that he was bigger than she thought.

Maybe he would even catch it. That was what really made him go ahead with this. To catch it, bring it home, and train it as a pet. Then his Mom and Dad would surely know how big he was. But even as he thought of that, he knew that he was wrong. His parents wouldn't let him keep it. They would just be mad at him. The thing to do was catch it and then let it go. Later when he'd grown a bit, he'd tell them what he did, and they'd be proud. For now, though, he would only hold it and then let it go. That would be almost the same as having it for a pet. Plus, he'd be out on his own at night, and thinking of that prospect, he was so excited that he started making preparations. All through supper, he'd been half-scared, half-eager, his heart-beat so loud he couldn't believe that his parents didn't hear it. After eating, he had tried to play a game of catch with his father, but he kept dropping almost every pitch his father threw him, fearful that his father would ask him why he was so nervous. He had fidgeted through several shows on television. Then at last the sun had gone down. His mother took him in to bed.

Now, his sack of crackers in his hand, Warren walked among the dark, looming trees, sometimes coming on a silver strip of moonlight and then moving into darkness again. He felt more nervous than when he'd left the house. As much as he was used to coming here, the park at night was quite a different thing. Shapes that should be friendly he could hardly recognize. Others even scared him. That dark object over there. Was that something lurking for him? He didn't think he'd ever seen it. What about that crouching shadow by that tree? Looking toward it, Warren bumped past the water fountain, stumbling back before he realized what he had hit. Then he looked to see the shadow, and it wasn't there now, and he didn't know which way to go. Sometimes he heard noises far behind him, and he turned to figure what they were. Other times the noises were quite close, and he was forced to run. Then he slowed. Then he ran again. And then he heard the trickling of the water, came around a clump of trees, and saw the silver pool of moonlight on the lake, and knew that he was too far to the left. Even so, he'd managed to get here, and the light was better, and he felt a little more at ease. He stopped to eat a cracker, but the brittle, biting noise he made unnerved him, and he dropped it. Then he took a breath and left the lake to walk along the stream's edge, looking for the bend.

There it was, directly ahead. He saw the wide curve in the stream, the reed tops sticking up from down there on the bank, and he was walking closer. The moon was gone a moment, off behind a cloud, making him stop. Then the moon was back, and he started walking again. He was almost there. He looked down at the reeds and hoped that he would see the animal, but he didn't. He strained to notice some sign of movement, but there wasn't any. Then he glanced around him, up and down the stream. There was just the silver-tinted water, shallow, rippling on the stones. For sure if the raccoon were here, he would have seen it. Then it must be hiding in the reeds.

But how to go about this? First Warren walked a distance back and scrambled down the bank. The slope was steeper than it looked. He ended with one sneaker in the stream. The water shocked him, and he lurched back onto the shore. He had no socks on, and the water sloshed within his sneaker, cold and faintly greasy, draining out. He shook his foot, and then his skin adjusted, and he put the foot down on the shore. It sank into mud as had the other. He revolted, and the sneakers made a sucking noise as he stepped onto firmer ground. Now he'd really fixed things. He had mud upon his sneakers, and his mother couldn't help but see that. Surely she would know. He almost panicked. Then he thought of water—he could wash them—and the image of that drinking fountain came to him, and he knew that he could wash them there. He began to feel relieved.

He stepped a little closer to the reeds, worried that the noise he'd made had scared the raccoon into its hole. He had almost dropped the bag of crackers, and now he clutched it to him, drops of water on it and on his hand. He crouched, peering in through the reeds, but there was nothing he could see. The reeds were thick and dark, and he would never find the hole. All the same, he peered as close as he could manage, his face up even with the reeds. Still, he couldn't see. For all he knew, the raccoon was right there in front of him, and if it didn't move, there wasn't any way for him to know. Then he thought that where the raccoon went down into the stream and then turned back and went up to its hole, there had to be a little path, a kind of tunnel within the reeds. He stood and looked down at the stream and made his choice. Bracing himself against the shock, he stepped with both feet into the stream, waded, then turned to face the reeds.

At first, Warren didn't notice it. Then he did. A little burrow in the reeds, a kind of channel where the raccoon came and went. Somewhere up inside would be the hole. He stooped and opened the sack of crackers, reaching in to grab a few. "Here, coon," he was saying softly, but he didn't like the noise, and so he switched to whistling, short and low. He didn't like that either, but he liked it better than his voice, and so he kept on whistling, pulling out the crackers, throwing them. They rattled up the passage in the reeds. "Here, coon," he was saying and then caught himself and started whistling once again. He threw a few more crackers, listened harder, but there wasn't any movement.

What to do? Warren crouched a good deal closer, the crackers in his hand. He thought that he would throw them like the others. Then he thought that he would reach in with them. Maybe it would take the crackers from his hand. He held them at the entrance. He reached his hand up in there, watching the hand disappear,

And that was when he heard it over to his right. He looked. It was coming down the bank. It seemed to be off balance. "Hi, coon," he was saying. "Here's some crackers for you." But it didn't stop. It just kept coming, and it made a hiss. He had never heard a sound quite like it, something like a cat, but not exactly, and it kept on coming, hissing, and he had his hand out with the cracker, thinking it was going to eat, already knowing how he'd reach to grab it firmly behind the ears, just the way his father had shown him how to grab a cat, and it was past the cracker, its teeth sunk into his hand.

"Aaiieee!" Warren jumped up, stumbling into the stream. The raccoon was attached to him, its mouth sunk into his hand, its weight suspended so it dragged him downward, almost falling into the stream. He couldn't bear the pain, the sharp teeth biting, tearing, scraping on a bone, his flesh now ripping from the weight of what was hanging on him. He was struggling for his balance, flailing, grabbing at the raccoon to free it, swinging, jerking with his arm, and then he swept around and flung the arm, and he was free of all that weight, the raccoon flipping through the air, thudding on the other bank. Warren didn't have a chance to marvel at his strength. The animal was bigger than he'd thought, almost half his size. And heavy—he'd expected he could lift it like it was a cat, and here it felt like someone he was wrestling with.

The force of flinging it away had toppled him against the bank, and he was scrambling to his feet now as the raccoon came for him again. It must have hurt itself when it had landed. It was limping, listing to one side as it surged across the stream. It hissed, and Warren was scrambling with his back against the slope, staring down and kicking with both shoes. The raccoon snapped and bit and got one shoe and wrenched its head from side to side as if to tear a piece away, and Warren felt its teeth go into his foot, and he was kicking at it with his other shoe, ramming down against the raccoon's nose, and then Warren's foot was free, and he was scrambling farther up the slope. That pointed nose, those bandit eyes, he had thought that they were cute, and now he couldn't stop from screaming at the terror of them. He was at the top now, feeling where its breath was at his ankles, jumping up to run, and he could hear it hissing there behind him as he ran with all the power of his fright. He had never run so fast before, his legs stretched out beneath him, his chest on fire, gasping, choking, crying, and the thing kept on behind him, and he kept on running, and he turned to see how close it was and rammed against a tree.

He fell back, his shoulder smarting, and sprawled across the grass. He didn't know how long he'd been there, blinking, straining to move. He fumbled to his hands and knees. The thing was very close. He couldn't see it, but he sensed that it was near, and he was stumbling to his feet. He turned and lost his balance, reaching for the tree. He shook his head and heard the hissing behind him, turned to kick at it, and there it was, but it was nowhere close, out there in the moonlight, turning in a circle, limping, lurching in a circle. He had never seen any animal behave like that. But he didn't stay to watch.

He suddenly was running again, his legs unsteady, his breath an effort, stumbling, his arms out to keep balance, and he didn't stop until he was almost to the lane. He limped along it, his hand on fire. Then he started running once more. He didn't even think to watch out for that family's dog down there. He just kept running. Then he crossed the side street toward the last part of the lane, and he was limping again, looking back to see if it was after him. It wasn't, and he looked down toward his house now, walking slowly toward it, his injured hand oozing blood, warm and sticky, making him wince from the pain. He realized that he had dropped his sack of crackers at the stream. He didn't know why that should seem important, but it was, and he couldn't help sobbing. Then he started across the backyard toward his house.

He worried, not just because his wound hurt and he didn't know if it was bad but as well because his mother couldn't help seeing it. She'd be angry, knowing what he'd done. I have to hide it, he thought. How he didn't know. Keep his hand in his pocket. Stay away from her. Even if she didn't find out until tomorrow night, that would give him time to say it had happened in the afternoon. A dog perhaps. A cat. He couldn't decide. But for sure, he couldn't let her know the truth. He reached the porch, thinking he would climb up, but he didn't have the strength, so he walked around the front and went up softly onto the porch. In the glow of streetlights, he saw his hand, and it was ugly, caked with dirt and blood, the flesh all torn and jagged. He was frightened by it, put his good hand over it, and quickly looked away.

He came around to where the screen was leaning against his window, took it off, and crawled through into his room. Now he feared that he would get blood on the carpet and the drapes, leaning swiftly out to put the screen back in and snap it shut. With one hand underneath the other, catching drops of blood, he fumbled at the doorknob to his room and tiptoed down the hall to close the door behind him in the bathroom. When he switched the light on, he was shocked. The hand looked worse than he had thought, the bite deep down to the bone, and wide, and swollen, oozing blood, covered with grit, a mass of ugly, bulging, ragged flesh. He gripped the sink to keep from dropping to his knees. He had never felt a pain like this, made worse by the sight of what was causing it. In the mirror, he saw the sweat on his face, the dirt and blood across his pirate top, his skin as white as the towels that hung by the sink. His pallor really scared him. He was trembling. He couldn't stop. He turned on the tap to wash his hand, understanding that he'd have to wash the pirate top as well. After reaching down to take it off, he rinsed it, then squeezed it to get the water out. He checked to make sure that all the blood was off, and then he went back to his hand. The more he washed, the more it continued bleeding. But at least the wound was clean now, and he grabbed a rag beneath the sink to bind the wound and keep the blood from dripping. Nothing more to do. He thought about some first-aid cream, but he had bound the wound already, and he didn't feel like doing that again. Indeed he felt sick, and he was thinking only of his bed. He took the pirate top and shut the lights off, turned the knob and went out down the hall.

"Is that you, Warren? What's the matter?"

He froze and waited.

"Warren?"

"Nothing, Mother. Going to the bathroom."

"All right, dear."

Warren tiptoed into his room, closed the door, and leaned against it, breathing hard, sweating. He bit his lip to ease the pain. He waited, but his mother didn't come. He hung the pirate top within his closet, limped to the bed, and sat there, taking off his shoes. The mud. He hadn't thought to wash the mud off, and he'd have to hide his sneakers. Somewhere in his closet. Far in back. He didn't want to, barely had the strength, and had the feeling that this would never end. He took his pants off, put on his pirate bottoms, and crawled into bed. He wished that he had never gone out. He wished that he had stayed at home and gone to sleep. He tried to sleep. His hand kept throbbing. He stared at the moonlight on his wall.

TWO

"It was a dog, all right. There isn't any question."

"That's what ripped his face, or that's what killed him?" Slaughter asked.

"Both. The cause of death was loss of blood from massive wounds around the face and neck."

Slaughter put his beer can down. "You mean there really is a chance his throat was slit?"

The medical examiner just shook his head. "No, I remembered what you said back in that field. I checked the throat especially. The jugular was ripped, not cut. Oh sure, some nut might still have gone at Clifford with a hand rake, something that would tear, but *that* would leave a different set of marks than all those bites you saw on him."

The medical examiner reached for his own beer can, and Slaughter shrugged.

"Okay then," Slaughter told him. "How about this? The nut rips Clifford's throat and runs away. A dog finds Clifford and starts chewing. That way all the first marks are obliterated."

The medical examiner just shook his head again.

"Well, why not?" Slaughter asked.

"All the wounds showed evidence of bleeding."

"Oh." And Slaughter leaned back in the chair and studied his beer can. That was final. Only living bodies bleed, so Clifford must have been alive when he was mangled. If some nut had ripped his throat, Clifford might have lived for half a minute longer, but not long enough to bleed from what a dog might later do.

It was half-past two at night, and they were in the medical examiner's office. Slaughter had stayed near the stockpens, helping Rettig and the new man ask the neighbors if they'd heard some trouble in the night. He had asked about a prowler or a stray dog that was barking. Then he'd met with Rettig and the new man, but they hadn't learned a thing. The trouble was, the field was too far from the houses. Near the noisy stockpens and the highway over there, a sound from a dog would not have carried very well. Slaughter told his men to write their report and go home but in the morning to search the field.

"What for?"

"I'm not quite sure yet. Do it, though."

Then he'd looked at the setting sun and known he couldn't put it off much longer: he would have to go see Clifford's widow. In Detroit, he'd on occasion had to tell someone that a wife or child or husband had been killed, but he'd never known the people he was telling. By contrast, here those he told were always people he knew, and some days it was worse than being the chief of police was worth.

Like today. To see his friend Doc Markle dead beside that mangled steer. To hear about his friend's wife so distraught that she was in the hospital (Slaughter planned to visit her as well). And then to go out and explain to Clifford's wife what had happened. It was bad enough to have to say that Clifford had been killed. But not to know why he'd been killed or how, that made Slaughter feel inept and worthless. He had held Clifford's widow, let her keep on crying, and helped her sit down on the sofa. He had brought her coffee, waited until her son arrived from the other side of town, and finally decided that he'd earned the right to leave. He told her that he'd let her know when she could have the body, that he'd pass on any news the minute he received it. Then he'd said good-bye and went outside and nearly lost his balance on the porch.

By then the sun was gone, and he was looking at the stars, the rising moon, thinking that he ought to go see Mrs. Markle, but he couldn't make himself. The scene with Clifford's widow had been just too much. The only thing Slaughter wanted was to get away from this, to get inside his car and roll the windows down and drive. To his place out in the country where he fed and watered both his horses—he'd forgotten when he last had ridden them—and then because the things he'd seen today had ruined any appetite he might have had, he put off supper, driving back to town.

He parked, lights off, in the shadows by the stockpens, looking toward the field in case he saw some movement. But there wasn't anything, and after all, he couldn't spend the night like this, so he drove to the station. The lights were on along the hall. The night man was on duty by the two-way radio. Tall and thin. An Adam's apple that bobbed whenever he spoke. "Hi, Chief. I wondered who was out there."

"Much doing?"

"Quiet."

"For a change today."

Slaughter walked toward his glassed-in section of the office. He sat and thought a moment, looking at the night sheet he had read in the morning. He tapped a pencil on his desk and reached to open the phone book. First, the hospital. Mrs. Markle? She's asleep now, resting better. Thank you. Then a number in the valley. Sam Bodine. But no one answered. Then the state police.

"It's Slaughter here. I wondered if you'd check on someone for me. Sam Bodine. . . . That's right. He's got a ranch on Route 43, twenty miles north of town. I wonder if you'd look in on him for me. . . . No, there's nothing wrong, at least not that I know of. But I went out there today, and no one was around. It seemed like they had left in quite a hurry. I phoned later this afternoon and then again just now, but both times no one answered, and I thought if you had a man out that way, he could maybe have a look. . . . Thanks. I appreciate it."

Slaughter hung up and again tapped his pencil on his desk.

Too much in one day, he thought. Fifteen minutes later,

the night man told him that the medical examiner was on the line.

Slaughter picked up the phone. "So how'd you know I was working?"

"Well, I called your house, and no one answered. Where else would you be? You mean you've got a lady friend shacked up that I don't know about?"

"You would have wakened me at this hour?"

"Why not? All the rest of us are working. Actually I knew you'd be waiting, and I phoned this number first. You care to visit?"

"You're finished?"

"Just this minute."

"On my way."

"Hey, hold it. Don't forget—"

"I have it in my trunk."

Slaughter stood and left the office. "I'll be at the medical examiner's," he told the night man. He was moving down the hall. What he'd put inside his trunk were two six-packs of Coors that he'd picked up at a convenience store as he was heading toward the office. It was now a ritual with them. Whenever Slaughter made the medical examiner work late, he always dropped in at the hospital and offered beer and talked with him a while. The gesture was a small one but appreciated, and besides, the chance to talk, to get to know the people whom he worked with, that was part of Slaughter's reason for his move out here. In fact, he'd even started looking forward to their chats, as if a corpse were not the reason for their late-night conversations. Not this time, however. No, not this time.

Slaughter got there in five minutes. In a town this size, there wasn't any place he couldn't get to quickly. He parked in back beside the spaces for the doctors and went in through the Emergency ward. The hospital was small by big-city standards: two stories made of brick and glass with wings off to the right and left, and one wing down the middle. But though small, it served the town quite well, and thinking of the nightmares of Detroit, Slaughter was grateful that he seldom saw a bleeding, groaning patient who'd been brought in from a knife fight or a shooting. He walked along the corridor and reached the section marked PATHOLOGY where, without knocking, he turned the office doorknob, and the medical examiner was in there, sitting, waiting.

As they sipped their beer, Slaughter shifted in his chair to face the darkness beyond the open window where a dog began to bark. A frenzied howl came shortly afterward, then some sounds that Slaughter couldn't identify. He listened, strangely fascinated, at the same time apprehensive.

"You know," he said and turned and paused because he saw that the medical examiner was looking toward the window too and evidently concentrating on the sounds out there. "You know," he said again. "Since we saw Clifford in that hollow in that field, I kept remembering the night sheet that I read this morning. There's a mention about Clifford being missing. Something bothered me about it. I went back tonight and read it through once more. A couple lines above where Clifford's missing, there's a note about a dog that howled all night, another note about a prowler."

"So?"

"Both complaints were from that neighborhood."

The medical examiner glanced from the window, looking at him.

"Not quite near the field, but close enough." Slaughter squinted. "How drunk was he anyhow?"

The medical examiner just shrugged, not even checking through the papers before him. "Point-two-eight percent, and he'd been drinking like that several years. His liver looked like suet."

"Could he walk, though?"

"I see what you mean. Did someone drag him to that field, or did he walk? I found no evidence of a struggle. It could be you'll find something different in the field. I did find some bruises on his right forearm that are compatible with his position in that hollow. Also bruises on his shoulder."

"So?"

"Well, think about it. All those bruises were fresh, so fresh in fact that he incurred them just before he died."

"Not after? Someone kicking at him once he'd died?"

"No, bruises are just localized internal bleeding. If you strike a corpse, you'll cause some damage, but not bruises in the sense we mean them. Only living bodies bleed, hence only living bodies can develop bruises. Now a bruise will take a little time before it starts to color. Half an hour as an average. . ."

Slaughter stared at him. "You mean he landed in that hollow at least half an hour before he was attacked?"

"That's right. But bear in mind the words I used. I said the bruises were compatible with his position in that hollow. Could be he received them earlier some other place. But it's my educated guess that they're from where he fell down in that hollow. Now it's possible that someone pushed him. If so, I don't know what point there would have been, because the cause of death was dog bites at least half an hour later."

"What time?"

"Three o'clock. Three-thirty at the latest."

"Yeah, the people at the bar said Clifford left a little after two when they closed. Fifteen minutes walk up to that field. Half an hour or so beyond that. Yeah, it brings him pretty close to three o'clock."

"You're understanding then?"

"I'm getting it. There wasn't any other person, as the untouched wallet more or less suggested. He came lurching from that bar and stumbled up the street. He had to piss, he tried a shortcut, or maybe he was just confused. We'll never know exactly why he tried that field. But halfway through, he passed out from the booze. That's how he got the bruises. Then he slept a little, and at last the dog came on him."

"That's the way I reconstruct it."

"But how many?"

"What?"

"How many dogs? One? Or several?"

"Oh. Just one."

"You're sure about that?"

"You know how the language goes. My educated guess."

"Sure, but on what basis?"

"Well, the teeth marks were all uniform. But let's assume for argument that we've got two dogs with the same sized teeth. Their enzymes would be different, though."

"Their what?"

"Their enzymes. Their saliva. Hell, the crud inside their mouths. A dog can't plant its teeth in something and not leave saliva. All the enzymes in those wounds were uniform. They came from just one dog."

"Not a coyote, or a wolf?" Slaughter asked.

"No, the teeth were too big for a coyote's. Yes, all right, a wolf, I'll give you that. A wolf would be a possibility. No more than that, however. No one's seen a wolf down here in twenty years. It's hardly worth considering."

"All right, a dog, then," Slaughter said, abruptly exhausted. "Tell me why."

"You've been living here—what?—five years?"

"Just about."

"Well, I was born and raised here. Dogs are something to be frightened of. People take them into the mountains, camping. They lose them or abandon them. The weak and spoiled ones die. The others turn more wild than many animals who live up there. You see a dog up in those mountains, get away from it. You might as well have stumbled on a she-bear with a cub. I've heard about some vicious maulings. Hell, I've seen some victims with an arm chewed off."

"But this is in the town."

"No difference. Sure, they live up in the mountains, but they come down here for food. The winter was a bad one, don't forget. You know yourself, the stockpens put on guards at night to make sure that the steers are safe from predators. The field is near the stockpens. Some dog from the mountains came down near the stockpens and found Clifford."

"But nothing tried to eat him. He was just attacked."

"Without a reason. That's the point. We're dealing here with totally perverted animal behavior. They just like to kill. They'll sometimes come down here and chase a steer for several miles just to get some exercise. They'll bring the steer down, kill it, and then leave it. In a human, we would call that kind of behavior 'psychopathic.'"

Slaughter put his beer can, vaguely cold yet, up against his forehead. He was thinking of old Doc Markle. "In the morning, I want you to go over to the Animal Clinic. I want you to examine that steer we saw this morning."

"What?"

Slaughter's eyes became stern. "I know it sounds a little crazy. All the same, just do it. Look for similarities. Something's going on here." He managed to stand.

"Slaughter, you don't look too good."

"I need a few hours sleep is all." Slaughter headed toward the door.

"Hey, what about the beer? There's still a six-pack left."

"You keep it. Hell, you've earned it. What you did on Clifford. Just make sure you do that steer. Let me know when you're finished." Slaughter reached for the doorknob.

"Something's going on, you said?"

"That's right, and what, I wish to God I knew."


### THREE

The corridor was empty, and the sound the door made when Slaughter closed it echoed. Like a mausoleum, he was thinking, looking at the imitation marble floor. He paused beneath the harsh neon lights in the ceiling, trying to decide if he had finally accomplished everything he'd meant to do tonight, and still not certain, vaguely troubled, he walked down the hallway. One turn to the right, he nodded to the nurse on duty at Emergency, and then, the automatic doors hissing open, he stepped out to face the night.

The parking lot was rimmed by darkness. There were floodlights just above him, though, illuminating the lot itself, and he was walking toward the cruiser, noticing the countless insects that were swirling around those lights. The swarm of insects bothered him, making him scratch at a tingle that inched down his neck. The air at least was cool, pleasant after the heat of the day, and fresh as well in contrast with the cloying sick-sweet smell of the formaldehyde which, because he liked the man, he never mentioned to the medical examiner. He reached the cruiser and glanced in the back seat before sliding into the front, a habit that he retained from when he'd worked nightshifts in Detroit. Then he sat there, thinking once again, not prepared to go home, but still uncertain what it was a part of him intended he should do. He was tired, that was certain, but he couldn't keep from feeling that his work was not yet complete. No, it wasn't even duty. Something strong out there was drawing him.

He turned on the engine and backed the cruiser from

between two cars. After glancing one last time at all those swirling insects, he drove along the side of the hospital and out the front to reach the street. The night was darker here. He swung left without thinking, merely following his inclination, and when he steered right at the next intersection, he was guessing that he meant to go back to the station. But he reached a stoplight, and when it changed to green, he didn't go straight through but instead veered left, and now he found that he was driving toward the outskirts, toward the northeast section of the city, and he finally knew where he was going.

There was little traffic. The lights were out in most of the houses. A few streetlights were out as well, and he came around the corner, driving slowly, glancing around, stopping by the Railhead tavern. It was closed by now. This late it had better be, he thought. He got out, his flashlight in his hand, and walked up to check the doors. But they were locked as he'd expected, although it would have been a pleasant joke to come here for a different reason and then as an accidental extra find that they were serving liquor after hours. To be certain, he checked all the windows, too, and then the back. He even checked the garbage bin to see that all the bottles had been broken as the law required. Now you're getting mean, he told himself, and switching off his light, he walked back to the cruiser.

It was three o'clock now, just about when Clifford had been killed. Of course, Clifford had entered that field at least a half hour earlier, and maybe if he'd fallen, sleeping, closer to an hour. But now was when the attack had occurred, and Slaughter stood by the cruiser, staring up the street toward the field. There were houses all along the far side of the street, rundown mostly since this section was the closest that the town had to a slum: listing porches, dirt instead of grass, cardboard here and there in place of windows. But the people, although poor, were peaceful, and he'd never had much trouble with them. From the bar, of course, but that was mostly workers from the stockpens, and Slaughter stared up past the field toward the vague silhouettes of buildings at the stockpens. Three of them. The cattle stayed outside except for special auctions, and there wasn't any need for more than just an office and two arenas. In the stillness, Slaughter heard cattle lowing faintly from the far side of the field. He hesitated, then started up the sidewalk toward them.

In the open like this, he had no need for his flashlight. There were stars, a nearly full moon. They gave the night a glow that made it almost magical. So Clifford would have thought, he guessed. He himself was trying hard to think like Clifford. Last night had been bright like this, and Clifford had come from the bar and walked up this way toward the field. Clifford had been drunk, of course. With that much alcohol inside him—point-two-eight percent—the glow would have been just about the only thing he noticed. And he wouldn't have been walking. He'd have *staggered*, lurching slowly up the street, and maybe that was why he'd tried the awkward shortcut through the field instead of going twice the distance around the block. Because Clifford knew that in his condition he would never otherwise have managed to get home. He had stumbled slowly toward the field, and anything that might have hidden low in the weeds there would have seen he was an easy target. No, the timing was all wrong, Slaughter thought. Keep remembering those thirty minutes between when he fell and when he was attacked. Anything that saw him come and knew he was an easy target would have tried him right away. There wasn't any reason for the animal to put off lunging. Unless the thing had not been interested. Unless it tried the cattle next and didn't like the men on guard there and then came back, killing Clifford. Why? It didn't eat him. Out of anger? And the thought was strangely chilling now as Slaughter left the sidewalk, stepping into the rustling grass and weeds and crunchy gravel of the field.

Slaughter told himself that this was crazy. He was tired. He should be home and asleep by now. But if there were some kind of wild dog coming into town, it would return to where it was successful at its killing, and the next night was as good a time as any to expect it. Slaughter was ten steps through the field, moving up from the corner in a vague line toward the center and the hollow there and Clifford's house up near the far end of the other block. This route would have been close to the direction Clifford followed, although Slaughter wouldn't know for sure until the two men he'd assigned to this had come here in the morning and investigated. Oh, that's fine, that's really great, he told himself and understood now just how tired he must be, shuffling through here, marring any tracks that they might find. That's great police work. Like a bad joke. Thinking that the criminal will come back to the crime scene, our investigator scuffs out any evidence that might be left. That's really great. Just what the hell must you be thinking? Well, I've done the damage now, he told himself, and he was too committed to his purpose to go back without some satisfaction. He might just as well keep going.

Which he did reluctantly. Because in spite of his determination, he felt really, unaccountably, disturbed. Not the vague uneasiness that he had been experiencing since finding old Doc Markle. This was something different, more precise, some visceral reaction to this place and hour. Part of it was no doubt caused by Slaughter's fatigue, by memories of Clifford's shredded face, by thoughts of what the medical examiner had called "psychopathic" animal behavior. Mere Pavlovian suggestion that he understood and could make compensation for. And part of it was no doubt too the stillness of the night, Slaughter all alone here in the silence that by contrast emphasized each brush of his pantlegs through the weeds and grass, each crunch of his boots upon the gravel. He was knee-deep in the grass now, moving slowly, the flashlight in his left hand ready to be switched on if he needed it, his right hand near his revolver in its holster, and he told himself that he was being silly. He had gone through worse than this when he had worked on nightshift in Detroit, checking through an unlocked warehouse, chasing someone down a mazelike alley, walking into that grocery store, those two kids. That was quite a while ago, he told himself, heart pounding. You're just not used to this the last few years. It didn't help as well that now a rustling wind had started blowing through the weeds and tall grass, making sounds as if there were movement in them. Once Slaughter turned, but he saw nothing, fighting the impulse to switch on his flashlight. No, save it until you're absolutely certain, he was thinking. Don't scare off some thing before it's close enough for you to see it.

So Slaughter continued walking. He had thought that with the night light from the stars and moon he'd have no trouble seeing. But the silver glow distorted things. Indeed it made objects seem much nearer, and it obscured details so that everything seemed blurred. He glanced toward the stockpens with their shadows and their faintly moving shapes of cattle and the buildings behind them. He was thinking that he'd better not get too close to the pens, or some guard might mistake him for a thief and pull out his gun. Slaughter was halfway through the field now, and he couldn't find the hollow. He'd been glancing so much all around that he had angled from his course, and now he didn't know if left or right was where he ought to go. The hollow had been rimmed by long grass, he remembered, and he maybe wouldn't find it even if he stood ten feet away. He told himself he should have kept his eyes toward Clifford's house across there, keeping in a line with it, but now that he considered, there was no way drunken Clifford would have staggered in a straight line anyhow. He'd have veered off one way, then the other, so this was still a replication of what had happened, and Slaughter figured that he'd shifted too much toward the stockpens. Moving now the other way, he suddenly was conscious of the wind. Or rather the absence of it. But the rustling through the grass had still continued, coming nearer.

He turned, startled, ready with his flashlight, lurching back to gain some distance, and the tangled strand of broken wire must have been there all along for him to see when he first came here, staring down at Clifford. It was snagged against his heels now, and his arms flew out, his head jerked up to face the moon, and he was falling. He was braced to hit the ground, already calculating how he'd have to roll to break his fall, but he kept dropping, surging heavily past the level of the ground, and then his head struck something hard that set off shockwaves through his brain and left him sightless for a moment. He was rolling. That was all the motive he retained, just reflex and his training, pure adrenaline that scalded him into motion. He was reaching for his gun. He'd lost it. He was in the hollow. Panicked thoughts that he was powerless to order. Christ, the hollow. It had happened just like this to Clifford. Slaughter groped for his flashlight, but he couldn't find it. He heard rustling coming toward him. Scrambling from the hollow toward the open ground where he at least would have the chance to run, he felt the claws flick down his face, and he was screaming, falling backward, landing breathless on another object which was so hard that it seemed to rupture his right kidney. He was fumbling for it, Jesus, and he saw up there the thing as it was crouching now to leap at him, its fur puffed up to make it even larger, hissing, its eyes wild, mouth wide, teeth bare, leaping toward him, and he had the gun from underneath him now. He raised it toward the hissing fury diving toward him, squeezing the trigger, blinded this time by the muzzle flash, knocked flat by the recoil as the fury blew apart above him, thudding on his stomach, and he didn't think the blood would ever stop its shower upon him.

### FOUR

The hotel room was small and musty, space enough for a narrow bed, a desk and chair, a TV on the desk, and that was that. The desk was scratched, its finish cracked by years of drinks spilled across it, plus the television had no channel dial. You had to grip a tiny metal post and turn until your fingers ached, and even then that didn't do much good because the television only got one channel. The image kept flipping, black and white. The window had no screen. You had to leave it closed to shut the insects out, which partly was the reason for the mustiness in here, but mostly, Dunlap knew, the must was from the aging wooden walls. The place had been erected back in 1922. Dunlap knew that from a plaque that he had seen embedded in the bar downstairs, as if a hotel so outdated were something the town was proud of. Threadbare carpet, creaky bed, a common toilet at the far end of each hall. He'd had to get up in the night to urinate, had made a wrong turn coming back, and almost hadn't found his room, so involuted were the halls, one merging in a T with others and those others merging yet again with others, like a rabbit's den, a gigantic maze that kept twisting inward. Dunlap was fearful about what he'd do in case of a fire, which considering the tinderlike walls was overdue for several years now, and he didn't like the thought of jumping toward the alley from the second story.

Plus, he didn't have much strength to do it. He was sick again. He tried to think back to a night when he had not been sick, and with his lack of memory, he was doubly fearful. How much longer could he keep doing this? He'd sat and watched the reruns on the TV set behind the bar downstairs from eight o'clock until the place had closed. He had no way of telling just how much he'd drunk, except that near the end the barman had looked strangely at him, and the programs were a blur of ads and station breaks. And don't forget the stock reports. Oh, my, yes, not the stock reports. But out here stock was not the closing points of Xerox, Kodak, or the rest of them. No, stock was cattle, and the market prices came on first at eight and then at ten and then again at sign-off time. Hey, he could not have drunk too much if he could recollect all that in detail. No? Then why was he shaking? Why was he so sick that breakfast was a thought he couldn't tolerate? He had to have a drink before he dared go down the hall and shave, and then another when he came back, before fumbling with the buttons on his shirt. It scared him. This much he could recollect, a time when he had not required one drink in the morning just to function. Now, this morning, he had needed two, and if he weren't careful, he would soon need a third. But there's a difference, he was thinking. Needing one and taking one. Let's make sure you keep in mind the difference. Dunlap picked up his tape recorder and his camera where he'd set them by the television. Vowing to himself that he would clean his life up, feeling virtuous, determined, he didn't pick up his pint of bourbon when he walked out the door.

The hall went to the right, then left, then right again, then opened on three sides to show the lobby down there, a moose head on the wall—from thirty, forty years ago, no doubt; the thing looked shabby enough for that—gray tile floor, discolored wooden check-in counter, a bald wrinkled man in denim clothes behind the counter. Dunlap took a breath and instantly regretted it: the must was even worse up here. He asked himself again what he had ever done to deserve being sent to Potter's Field, then trudged down the stairs, crossing the lobby toward the street.

The sun was like a knife jabbed into his eyes. Eight o'clock, and how hot would the day be with the sun so fierce this early? He didn't want to think about it. Eight o'clock, but he'd been awake since well before dawn, and that was something else his drinking had affected. Now he hardly slept at all, and when he did, not deeply, waking often, drifting back and forth from grotesque dreams. He didn't want to think about that

either. Not the image that had constantly been coming to him. He walked toward the corner, concentrating on the coffee he was going to taste. Sure, you could buy a drink back at the hotel, but there wasn't any place to get some coffee. "Try the Grubsteak at the corner," he'd been told, and hell, they either didn't know the way to spell it, or they maybe were more clever than he thought. The one thing he at least was getting was a mess of local color. You don't talk like that, he told himself. You're here one day, and they're infecting you. You'd better keep your mind on what you're doing. Which was fine with him because he didn't want to think about a lot of things, but work was hardly one of them. He sensed that he was on to something.

Dunlap entered the diner. The counter was a horseshoe, the curved end in the middle of the room, and sure, what else did you expect? he thought. He looked at all the men in cowboy hats who in turn were looking at him, and he passed them to sit in a far corner booth where, quicker than he had expected, a waitress—her hair pinned up beneath a net—came over to him. Half a minute later, he was sipping coffee, but although he'd been eager for it, he had to drink it slowly lest he throw up. Yes, he was on to something. "Christ, he's dead, all right," the voice had blurted through the static on the two-way radio. "Lord, he doesn't have a—" The only thing that Dunlap had been able to discover was that two kids had been playing in a field where they had stumbled upon the body of a man named Clifford whose face had been so mutilated that policemen couldn't tell at first exactly who he was. The woman who had sat behind the radio had tried to avoid Dunlap's questions and had finally suggested that he leave—the chief would see him in the morning. Dunlap had lingered even so, but when policemen from the day shift had begun to come in for debriefing, they had made it clear that he should leave, and he'd had no choice but to go out on the street. He had hoped to talk to Rettig and a new recruit named Hammel whom Dunlap gathered were the men assigned to this investigation, but they hadn't come in yet, and he had quickly gotten the picture that unless he had the chief's permission, no one would be talking to him.

Nonetheless, the symmetry appealed to him. A murder twenty-three years ago, and now another as he arrived to do the retrospective. The contrast would be worth reporting, how the separate murders had been handled, if this second killing were indeed a murder. Well, a dead man with no face, that surely wasn't ordinary, and as far as Dunlap cared, the difference was the same. That first murder had been something he hadn't counted on. There hadn't been a mention of it in the files that he had looked through in New York. When Parsons mentioned it in passing—yesterday in Parsons' office—Dunlap had required all his discipline not to show his interest. He had just kept sitting there and nodding as if vaguely bored by all this ancient news, but really he had felt his heartbeat quicken, felt that tug inside him as he guessed that there was more here than he had anticipated. He had kept his guard up all the time he and Parsons made their bargain. He had still looked bored when he had gone down to the paper's morgue and asked the man in charge to bring the microfilm. But when he was alone, he'd squinted in suspense for it, and in an issue twenty-three years ago, the first week in October, he had found it.

It was pretty much the way that Parsons had described it. The town had evidently feared another rush of hippies coming through, especially if reporters showed up, publicizing what had happened. Once the town had adjusted to its shock, it must have worked to keep the news from going farther. And the tactic was successful. As much as Dunlap knew, the story had been strictly local, a headline the first day, a third-page feature the next day, then a few paragraphs buried near the sports section. A rancher had wakened to find that his eighteen-year-old son was missing. At first the rancher wasn't bothered, thinking that his son had gone out with some friends and simply stayed the night. He'd made some calls but couldn't find him, waiting through the afternoon until at suppertime the boy was still not home, and he got worried. On a chance he phoned the state police, fearing that there'd been an accident or maybe the boy had gotten in trouble and was too afraid to call. The police hadn't heard a thing about him, doing what the father had already done, however, checking with the young man's friends. The friends, though, didn't know a thing about him either, hadn't seen him in a couple of days. He'd been moody, staying to himself. He'd even broken up with his girlfriend. Someone thought of suicide, and then they really did get worried. This was sure—no vehicle was missing from the ranch. The son had either walked off or had gotten a ride. Had he run away? The father spoke of arguments that they'd been having, and as Dunlap had gone through the story, he had sensed that the arguments were severe. Small town rancher's son who wanted something more. Father who repressed him. Reading through the microfilm, Dunlap had been puzzled why it took them so long understanding. But it did. Indeed it took them several days. But then a friend remembered how the boy had hung out with those hippies when they'd caused that trouble in the town. The friend had even seen him smoking marijuana. The son had talked about the hippies often after they had left. The father and the state police considered this for a while, and then they finally had it figured out. The father wanted to go up and get him, but the state police insisted that they go alone. They evidently saw how furious the father was and concluded that they'd save some trouble if they went up on their own. Besides, there wasn't any guarantee that the boy was up there. This was just a chance. No point in making judgments until they knew.

The next few details Dunlap had to guess because, while there was plenty of space devoted to the missing son to start with, once the murder occurred the lid came over the story. Dunlap was impressed by someone's thoroughness. That was Parsons, he suspected, working to protect the town. There wasn't any way to know exactly what went on. The rationale was obvious. To guarantee that the trial was fair. To keep the jurors free from bias. After all, a small town, if the trial took place here, news about the murder had to be subdued and dignified. Oh, it was dignified all right. Hell, it was almost non-existent, and back in 1970, a small town in the boonies could get away with that. There hadn't been those recent major court decisions about freedom for reporters at a trial. Not that any local newsman would have worked against the blackout. No, the point was to keep outside newsmen ignorant of what had happened here. Conspiracy is what some people call it, Dunlap thought and sipped his coffee. Now you're thinking like a Woodward or a Bernstein. Let's not make too much of this. Well, make too much or not, he sure as hell was going to find out what went on up in that compound.

He walked toward the counter and paid fifty cents for his coffee. As he left, he glanced back toward the elderly waitress who was staring puzzled at him, then down at the two-dollar tip he'd put on the table. What now? Showing off? Well, why not? If he felt like being a big-time spender from the city, he was maybe condescending, but at least he didn't hurt somebody, and besides it made him feel good. He might be a boozer, but at least he wasn't stingy. He went outside, and once again the sun stabbed his eyes. It was even worse, though, hotter, more intense, and his elation as he left the diner suddenly was gone. He felt nervous and impatient. He had planned to go back to the newspaper's morgue, but he was doubtful that he'd learn much more. He'd tried to get in touch with the police chief several times last night, but Slaughter had been neither at his home nor at the station when he'd called, and Dunlap was determined now to speak with him. He hitched the straps of his tape recorder and his camera around his shoulder and marched through the glaring sunlight up the street.

The time was half-past eight. He noticed lots more traffic, mostly pickup trucks with people crowded in them, come to town on Saturday to shop or merely look around. He noticed that the stores were open, and he was thinking that he maybe ought to stop at one and buy a hat. Oh, that would look just great. A city suit and a cowboy hat. Well, keep your pride then, but before long, out here in the sun like this, your face'll be as parched and leathered as those people in the pickup trucks. He passed the newspaper's office, wishing he could hail a taxi, but he hadn't seen a taxi since he'd come here, and he trudged on, beginning to sweat. Well, this would be the last time he would let them send him to a jerk-off town like this. He sensed that there was some good story here, and when he put it all together, he would show them he was just as good as he had once been, and he wouldn't have to take this kind of job. But then an odd dilemma started working on him. Dunlap was anxious to get out of here, but if he meant to guarantee that he would never find himself this low again, he'd have to take more time than he could tolerate. He might be here a week from now. And that was too much for his mind to bear as he walked underneath the trees at last and up the front steps to the police station.

Of course, the chief had not come in yet. What was worse, the chief had phoned to say that he didn't plan to come in at all.

He'd had some kind of trouble. "And what am I supposed to do?" Dunlap asked the policeman on duty.

"Well, maybe if you told me why you had to see him."

Dunlap slumped in a chair. He'd gone through this the day before, but there had been a different person then, a woman, and Dunlap studied the policeman, sighed, then passing through frustration told him very calmly what it was he needed.

"That's no problem."

Dunlap blinked. He didn't think he'd heard correctly. "What?"

"If you had told me who you were to start with. When the chief called in this morning, he explained you might be stopping by. Just hold on while I call him back."

And fifteen minutes later, Dunlap stood across from a row of dingy houses, staring at a barren field with stockpens up at one end and a bar, the Railhead, down at the other. He had carefully avoided mentioning his interest in the recent killing, concentrating only on the compound twenty-three years ago. As a consequence, when he had found out where the chief was sending him, he'd been astonished by his luck. The Railhead. He had heard that name on the two-way radio yesterday. This was where the mutilated body had been found. Dunlap looked at the two policemen who were standing in the middle of the field. They turned to study him when the cruiser that had brought him here pulled away. The sun was stark. A wind hurled bits of sharp, hot sand at him. He licked his gritty lips and started through the field.

The two policemen met him halfway. "Yes, sir, may we help you?" one of them asked.

And Dunlap thought that things might just be getting better as he told them. But the one named Rettig didn't want to talk.

FIVE

Oh, that's wonderful. Just god-damned great. I'm out here in the middle of this stupid field, and this guy Rettig doesn't want to talk. Well, what else did you think would happen? Dunlap asked himself. Just because it got a little easier a while ago, you figured everything would be simple now? Hell, you're the one who's simple. Wake up, do your job. Dunlap knew that Rettig wasn't just the man in charge of this investigation: Rettig had been with the state police back then. Dunlap had learned that from the man on duty at the station. He had learned as well that Rettig was the one who'd spent the most time with Wheeler. Twenty-three years ago. "Look, way back then. I don't see what the problem is."

But Rettig didn't want to talk.

Wheeler was the rancher who had lost his son. "All right, then, you don't even need to talk about it. Let's try this. I'll tell you what I know." And guess, and less than that, just make up on the spot, Dunlap decided, but at least this was a way to draw out Rettig, to get him talking. "You just tell me if I'm right or not. I'm going to do this story anyway. You'll want to make sure that the parts about you are correct."

Dunlap studied him, and Rettig wasn't certain, staring back. So as another gust of wind came up, the dust obscuring them, their faces specked with grit, Dunlap started prompting him, anxious to fill the silence and keep Rettig from having a chance to say no. "You drove out toward the commune, looking for the boy. You headed up the loggers' road. The sentries wouldn't let you through the gate. They made you go back to the town to get a search warrant. But in the meantime Wheeler had decided not to follow your advice. He went up on his own, despite what you had warned him."

"No, that isn't true." Rettig hesitated, then continued. "Wheeler didn't go up in the meantime. We had made him wait back at the station—not the one in town, but the state police barracks out on the highway—and he heard us call in that we had to go to town to get a search warrant. That's when he drove out. The man on duty at the station went to take a leak, and Wheeler left while he was gone."

"And Wheeler was upset enough, the man on duty called you to go back up to the compound," Dunlap said.

"That's right."

"So you couldn't have been very far behind. Wheeler didn't have to go home for the gun. He was a rancher, and he likely had it in the trunk or car or Jeep, whatever he was driving."

"A pickup truck."

Dunlap had an image now of all those pickup trucks that he had seen this morning, families come to town: the guns in racks behind the driver's seat.

"A rifle or a shotgun," Dunlap said. The last word made Rettig's eyes flicker. "Yes, a shotgun," Dunlap said, and now he understood why there'd been no details about the murder. "Wheeler was cursing, angry at the boy for running off, angry at the compound for the trick that it had pulled. More than that, he didn't understand those hippies. He was afraid, going up to find the boy and rescue him. He roared his truck right up that loggers' road and crashed straight through the gate. He drove until the road came to an end, then jumped out with his shotgun, running through the woods, the sentries racing after him. He almost made it to the clearing when they tackled him. There was a fight. He jumped back, shotgun ready, and he blew one bearded hippy's head apart."

Dunlap had to pause, to check for some reaction. He was guessing, based on what he'd read, but it made sense, except he didn't know exactly how the shooting had occurred, especially what part of the body. But it had to be the head. Head or groin—otherwise the paper would have been more specific. But a shotgunned head or groin was something that you didn't mention if you wanted to be delicate, and since as far as Dunlap knew there was no sex involved in this, the head, its long hair and its shaggy beard, would have been what the rancher likely shot at. Hell, it was symbolic of the trouble. Dunlap kept waiting as the wind died.

In the silence, Rettig murmured, "His face looked like somebody had squashed a quart of strawberries on it. Just this mushy red stuff, no eyes, no mouth, nothing. Just this mushy red stuff." Rettig guided him toward the cruiser. "I've said more than I intended."

"Look, I understand. I'll make a deal. You call your chief, and he'll explain that it's all right. I told you at the start. I cleared this first with Parsons, then with him."

Rettig looked skeptical. "I have to go to his place. I'll be sure to ask him."

"Take me with you?"

Rettig frowned.

"I mean, I don't have any car. You can't just leave me."

"I can leave you. If you cleared this as you say, I don't want any trouble, though." Rettig thought about it. "You get in. We'll drive you. But you'd better not be lying."

Dunlap smiled and hurried into the back. The other cop got in the front beside where Rettig drove, and both were taking off their hats, and Dunlap wished that they had rolled their windows down when they had parked the cruiser. The heat had built up in here so that his clothes stuck to him and to the seat.

They drove up past the stockpens, Dunlap glancing at the cattle in there and then watching how the slums diminished as they turned left and headed toward a newer section of the town. They were going through an underpass, and quicker than he had expected, they were in the country. Dunlap had noticed in the phone book that the chief's address was R. R. something, but he hadn't really understood how far out that might be. They went past sun-baked grassland. No one spoke. On occasion, there were static-distorted voices on the two-way radio, but neither man picked up the microphone to answer.

Dunlap studied them. Rettig with his red, curly hair. The other man, much younger, blond, his hair cut short in imitation of the style back in the fifties, with the difference that out here the style was not an imitation, rather a continuation. They both looked like football players, big and tall and husky, and the man back at the station had been big and tall as well, and Dunlap was thinking that their size might be a part of what the chief had looked for when he hired them. If that were true, then Slaughter maybe had some big-time notions about how to handle trouble. He might not be just some hick, and Dunlap considered that, then tried to get Rettig talking again.

"You were close enough to hear the shot."

Rettig stared at his rearview mirror. "Look, I warned you—"

But you answered me regardless, Dunlap thought. Oh, you were close enough, all right. Hell, you were nearly there to see it happen. Once you heard the shot and saw that shattered gate, you sped up through it, stopping by the pickup truck and running farther up the trail to find the rancher with his shotgun aimed at several other hippies. Oh, yes, Dunlap could imagine what the scene had been like, the hippies looking down the barrel of the shotgun, terrified, not knowing what to do. If they ran, Wheeler would fire. If they stayed, he'd likely do the same, the rancher too far gone to maintain control, his eyes wide, his face stark, breathing hard and tensing his finger on the trigger. And the two of you, the last thing that you wanted was to shoot the guy. You didn't want him shooting someone else, though, either, even if that someone else was just another hippie, the first one spread out on the ground, his face like someone had squashed a quart of strawberries on it. And the others. Sure, there would have been other hippies from the compound who'd heard the shot and come running through the trees, and when they saw the body, they stumbled back or maybe just froze in shock, and soon the rancher became more nervous, seeing people all around him, hippies, his finger tight on the trigger as he squinted at the two cops who had their guns out, telling him to stop this, inching toward him.

"How'd you manage to take it from him?"

"What?"

"The shotgun. How did you take it?"

Dunlap hoped that the question would appeal to Rettig's pride, but the cop just stared down the highway.

"Some dumb hippie tried to grab him," Rettig said abruptly. "Wheeler turned, and I jumped close to get the shotgun. I had it pointed toward the ground when it went off. It blew up bits of dirt and pine needles. But I had him, and he couldn't work the pump to slide another shell in."

My, my, my, and sure, you didn't have much trouble telling me how well you did, Dunlap thought. He knew that soon he'd have it all, especially what happened to the rancher's son.

"Hey, tell me what you saw up there."

But Rettig didn't answer.

"I mean—"

"Look, I said we'll clear it with the chief first," Rettig told him, and their little game was finished. Dunlap didn't even try again. He sat back, his clothing sweaty against the seat, and watched the country they were passing, flatland mostly, clumps of brush out in the fields. They turned left through an open, listing, wooden gate. Then they were on a weedgrown wagon road, and he heard gunshots, many of them, louder as they sped along the dusty road. Dunlap leaned ahead.

"Trouble?"

But they didn't answer. They sped down a hill, dry red earth on either side, and there were buildings in a hollow: first a modest house, four rooms maybe, with a porch in front, painted white; and then a barn, about the same size as the house, and painted white as well; some kind of shed, and *it* was white. And all three were beside a fenced-in pasture where two horses shied from what disturbed them in the gully.

## SIX

Slaughter watched them shooting by the gully. Then he turned to face the medical examiner. "It was a cat, all right. I shot its fucking head off."

The medical examiner narrowed his eyes. "You're sure?"

"You think I never saw a cat before? The god-damned thing attacked me. Some big tom. I mean a *big* tom, fifteen pounds at least. And if I hadn't shot it, I'd have had my face scratched off."

The medical examiner scowled. It didn't make sense. Not only the attack, but Slaughter's fierce reaction. And then he understood. Sure, Slaughter must have been terrified. Lying in that hollow, thinking he would end up next like Clifford. He likely hadn't felt that kind of fear since he had worked back in Detroit. He wasn't used to it, and he was angry now because he'd lost control. The medical examiner had never thought of Slaughter's being capable of fear. The thought was oddly new and made the medical examiner feel sympathetic, liking him even more.

Over by the gully, the men continued shooting.

"What about that scratch? You'd better let me have a look at it," the medical examiner said.

But Slaughter only waved the offered hand away. "I fixed it up myself." The scratch was long and deep across his cheek, thickly scabbed and ugly. "Old Doc Markle made me keep a decent first-aid kit out here. Just in case. From when I tried to raise those horses. First I washed it. Then I disinfected it."

"I was thinking about stitches."

"No, it isn't bad enough for that. I should have gone to see you, but all I wanted was to get home."

Slaughter turned toward the sound of the cruiser angling down the red-clay road between the hillocks. Rettig and the new man were in the front. But as Slaughter watched them drawing closer, a dust cloud rising, he could see as well another person, this one in the back, a man in a gray, wrinkled suit, his face—it was obvious even through the dusty windshield—as gray and wrinkled as the suit.

But when the cruiser stopped and they got out, the man hitched up what seemed to be a tape recorder and a camera, and his body wasn't stooped or wasted, and if Slaughter's judgment was correct, his age was forty, forty-five. A face like that, though. Slaughter knew there wasn't any question. This guy was a boozer. Dry and brittle hair, gray like the rest of him.

Slaughter stepped from the porch. "There's some beer inside," he told the medical examiner. "See you later."

"Wait a minute. I have questions."

"Later." Slaughter walked toward the gray-faced man who had the tape recorder and the camera.

Rettig and the new man didn't even bother looking toward the sound of the shots in the gully, but the gray-faced man was staring in that direction.

"We did everything you told us," Rettig said as Slaughter reached them. "Nothing."

"I expected." Slaughter held his hand out. "Mr. Dunlap." And that earned the look that Slaughter had anticipated. Dunlap was impressed. Slaughter always made a point of keeping track of names. He'd learned that in the city, understanding that a name could mean the difference between trust and panic. "People tell me you've been looking for me."

Dunlap gripped his hand. "You're a hard man to find."

"Not so hard. You're here, after all." Slaughter smiled, and Dunlap turned once more toward the gunshots in the gully.

"Look, if you don't mind my asking."

"Anything. That's what you're here for," Slaughter said.

"That shooting."

"Target practice. It's a pattern we got into. Saturdays, I have the men I work with out to drink some beer and eat some chili. At the start, though, before they drink the beer, they go back behind the barn and do some target practice. Some towns don't require that, but I insist my men shoot two times a month at least. The shift on duty today will come out next week, and we alternate like that. You care to see?"

As they walked toward the barn, Rettig joined them. "He's been asking about Quiller and the compound."

"I know it," Slaughter said. "Parsons phoned about that. Quiller was before my time. That's why I sent our guest to you."

"He said that he had cleared it, but—"

"You did exactly what you should have. I tried calling on the radio, but evidently you weren't near the cruiser. There's no problem. In your place, I'd have been suspicious, too."

They passed the clean white barn, the gunshots louder, echoing, and then they came around the back, the dirt here hard and brittle, and five men were in jeans and rolled-up shirt sleeves, spread out by the gully, shooting revolvers at tin cans below a ridge across the ditch. The ditch was maybe twenty feet across, the cans another five feet farther on, and three men were reloading, glancing at where Slaughter came with Dunlap and then Rettig past the barn to reach them.

One man said, "That beer had better be as cold as you pretend it is."

"I lied," Slaughter said. "It's even colder."

They laughed.

"Looks like we could use some new targets." Slaughter pointed. All the cans across there had more holes than metal, barely held together by the seams that joined them.

"Well, we figure once we blast them till there's nothing left, we can say we earned the beer."

"A hundred rounds per man. No less than that." Slaughter gestured toward Dunlap. "This man's from New York. He's a reporter, and he's doing research on that commune in the hills. I want you to cooperate. I don't know all that happened back then, but I don't see much use hiding it."

They studied Dunlap and nodded.

"How come you're not out here shooting?" one man asked Slaughter.

"I put in my time before you came."

"Oh, sure you did." They looked amused.

Slaughter glanced at Dunlap, then at them, shrugged, and drew his revolver.

Dunlap stepped back automatically. He stared at the gun as Slaughter approached his men and concentrated on the cans on the other side of the gully. He braced himself, his body sideways, his feet apart, and aimed, then squeezed the trigger. A can flipped, the shot loud, the recoil spreading smoothly through Slaughter's body, and he cocked again and fired, cocked and fired, six times altogether, the shots echoing on top of one another as the can went through its clattering dance and, with the last hit, fell apart. Slaughter had worked his hand as quickly as the eye could follow. His men were laughing, clapping, as he shrugged, then pressed a button that allowed him to swing out the handgun's cylinder. He pocketed the used cartridges and reloaded.

"I see you've got some rounds to shoot yet," Slaughter pointed toward the half-full boxes by their feet. "That beer is getting colder." He winked, then walked toward the barn. "And pick up all your empty cartridges this time."

"Yeah, yeah," they told him, looked toward the riddled cans, and started firing again as Slaughter led Dunlap and Rettig back to the house.

"That's impressive shooting." Dunlap said.

"Nothing that a little practice doesn't help," Slaughter said. "I wasn't kidding. I did my stint before they got here. Sometimes I shoot with them. Mostly I just sit up on that porch and welcome people. There's a western gentlemen inside me trying to get out." He noticed that Dunlap smiled then. That was good. The message from the mayor had been emphatic. Give this man a good impression. "You must find this country different, coming from the East and all."

"A little," Dunlap said.

"Yeah, I felt that way myself at first."

Dunlap shook his head. "At first?"

"I came here from Detroit. Five years ago. A little while out here, and you can get to like the easy way of life."

Which Dunlap didn't buy, so Slaughter didn't try to sell it anymore. Slaughter had been just about as friendly as he'd planned, but he had other things to occupy him, and he didn't have the time to give this man a guided tour.

They passed the police car Rettig had brought, walking toward the porch, and Slaughter saw that the medical examiner was up there, drinking beer, talking to the new man. Slaughter was just about to ask if Dunlap wanted any beer when the medical examiner interrupted him.

"Your man here says it's still down in that hollow. Look, I want to know if that thing bit you."

"No, I thought about it, and I checked," Slaughter said. I even took my clothes off back here, and the only mark is where it scratched me." The scab was thick on Slaughter's cheek.

The medical examiner persisted. "Scratched, not bit you?"

"Does this mark look like it bit me? No, I'm certain."

"Well, I want to check that cat regardless. Cats don't go at people that way."

"Some cats do. When I was in Detroit, I had my share of bites and scratches. Cats gone wild and living in abandoned tenements. I know exactly what you mean, though. This is different. Cats might fight back, but they don't come looking to attack you."

And the five of them were silent. Dunlap had been listening with interest. Slaughter turned to him. He noticed that both Rettig and the new man had been looking at him, too.

"You're right," he told the medical examiner and then explained to Dunlap, "You see, we've got a situation here, but it's not the reason you're invited. I could ask you to go in the house and have a beer, but then you'd think that we were hiding something from you. So I'm going to let you stay. But understand this. Anything about the commune, that's your story. What we're saying now is strictly off the record." Slaughter waited.

"Sure. I guess you have your reasons."

"You'll know soon enough." Slaughter turned toward the medical examiner again. "My handgun's a .357. I loaded magnums before going in that field. I told you, when I shot that cat, I blew its fucking head apart. I'm no pathologist, but I'm aware of this much. If you want to check for rabies in an animal, you run some tests on portions of its brain."

"That's correct."

"Well, brain, hell I can give you all the brain you want. It's scattered, bits and pieces, all across that goddamn field. But they'll be so contaminated, you won't have a use for them." Slaughter pivoted toward Dunlap. "There. I've said it. Now you understand. If word about rabies ever gets through town, there'll be a panic."

Dunlap's face was ashen. "That's what happened to this fellow Clifford?"

Slaughter studied him. "You do your job. I'll give you that. No, we're not sure about him. We've been edging around this subject since last night." He asked the medical examiner, "You're sure it was a dog that killed him, not a cat?"

"I told you."

"Swell." Slaughter stared down at the porch. "I need a beer. He looked around.

"Sure," Dunlap told him. "I'll take one."

Rettig: "Me as well."

The new man and the medical examiner already had one.

"I'll just bring a cooler." Slaughter entered the house.

SEVEN

Christ, what's the matter with you? Slaughter thought, trembling once the door was closed. You're damn near cracking up. A cat attacks you, and it's like you never used a gun before. What's happening to you?

I'm out of practice.

Weak and soft is more the truth. That easy life you told that guy about—you really fell for it. Hell, life's so easy for you that you lose your nerve when some stray cat jumps at you.

No, that isn't true. I do my job. I'm good at it.

But you know you're lying. You can go through years and years of doing what you think must be your best. But then you get in some real trouble, and you understand that you were coasting, and you didn't even know it.

Hell, I don't know why I even bother trying.

Sure you do. That emptiness inside. That grocery store. Those two kids. What they did to you.

You want to prove yourself.

And that purely was the truth.

He stood inside his small, neat kitchen, staring at two coolers filled with ice and beer, and he was thinking that he'd open one can right away. But that would be a public show of weakness, drinking before he brought out the cooler for the others. Maybe not in their eyes weakness. But in his. So he lifted one of the coolers and returned to the porch.

They didn't even look at him, just concentrated on the cooler as he opened it, the glinting ice, the cans of Bud. They made a ritual, all snapping tabs at once and raising beers as if in toast, then sipping.

"All right, so what do you suggest?" Slaughter asked the medical examiner. He hoped the beer would relax him.

"Well, no matter what you say, I want to see that cat. Tell your men to keep watching for animals that act strangely. I'll check the hospital for anyone who comes in bitten. The truth is, though, there's not a lot we *can* do until we have another incident."

"That's *if.*" Rettig hadn't spoken in some time.

"Right. That's not until but if. Let's hope at least," Slaughter said.

"Don't wait for a dog or cat that's foaming at the mouth. A symptom like that shows up late," the medical examiner said. "What we're looking for is an attack without a reason. Totally irrational aggression."

Something clicked in Slaughter's mind. "That's funny."

"What?"

"You said the same about those dogs up in the hills."

And everyone became silent.

Too much so, Slaughter realized. It wasn't only them but everything around them. Sure. The men had stopped shooting. They were walking past the barn now, laughing, holstering their weapons as they joked among themselves and came near, rubbing their hands together as they stepped up for a beer.

"Who died?" one of them asked, noticing how somber everyone was.

"We've got a little problem. Did you pick up the empty cartridges?"

They nodded.

"Good. When you get a chance, reload them. We might need them."

And they paused where they were reaching for the beer.

"I have to check the horses," Slaughter said. "Let's take a walk. I'll tell you all about it."

He stepped from the porch. "There isn't much to tell," he heard behind him and saw where Rettig had moved back a little, talking now with Dunlap.

Rettig evidently noticed how Slaughter looked at him. "You're sure it's all right if I talk to him about what happened at the commune."

"Hell, I don't care." You're getting jumpy, Slaughter told himself and walked with the other men to reach the horses.

#### EIGHT

Rettig watched them go, then again faced Dunlap. "Really. There's not much more to tell." Despite permission to discuss this, he was nonetheless reluctant. He still remembered the secrecy with which the case had been conducted. There had been such trouble in the town, such bad publicity that summer, that the council had arranged for secret sessions to discuss this new development. Parsons had been mayor then, as he still was, and the general agreement had been to keep news about the murder quiet. Otherwise those hippies might come back, and those reporters, and the trouble might begin again. The trial had been delicate, the matter kept within the valley, with some understanding from the nearby towns beyond the mountains, and the valley had gone back to being normal. Even though the state police had jurisdiction in the case, and they were separate from the town, they had nonetheless cooperated with the town, realizing that the valley was related to the town, and Rettig in particular had been warned to keep his mouth shut. Oh, nobody ever said that quite so forcefully, but the implication had been clear, and he was very careful. It was twenty-three years now since he'd thought about the case, but he remembered the way things had been back then, and it was hard for him to break his habit. "Really. Not too much. You figured most of it already."

"But the son? What happened to the son?" Dunlap took his coat off, setting it across a chair on the porch.

"He was fine. I went up with another man and searched the compound. The rest of the men stayed back to get the hippies' version of what had happened. Wheeler had cracked up by then, and they were helping him into a cruiser. We went and—"

"Tell me what it looked like."

"Oh, not much. I'd heard too many rumors, and the place seemed ordinary by comparison. Just rows of barracks lined up to form streets. Like in the Army but more like migrant work-camps. Like in the Depression. Pathetic, really. There were gardens by each bunkhouse, dying flowers in them, but the flowers never really had a chance up there. All that shade, the thin air, and the lousy ground. The worst part was the fields they'd tried to plant with corn and beans, tomatoes, stuff like that. They'd put the seed in too late, and a farm crop never does well, even down here in the valley, so I can't imagine why they thought that corn would do well in the mountains. It was awful, all these little stumps of corn that never quite developed, little ears on them, all browned by the early frosts. They had a mess hall, I remember that, crude log tables in there, and they had a kind of officer's command post with a sort of square in front where people must have stood to get their orders, but it was obvious that things weren't going well up there, and I couldn't help wondering what they were going to do when winter hit. Oh, yeah, we found another building that was like a big garage."

"The Corvette."

"What?"

"The red Corvette. The classic 1959 that Quiller drove. You found it?"

"I remember hearing about that. No, we never found it. Oh, we found a van and then a pickup truck. But that was all. No red Corvette. Believe me, I'd remember it."

"Christ, what the hell is going on?"

Rettig stared at him.

"I've done some checking," Dunlap said, "and as far as I can tell, Quiller never sold it. But I know he took it up there. What in God's name did he do with it?"

"You've got me," Rettig said. "All I'm telling you is what I saw. If I'd been looking for that car, I might have found it. But I had my mind on searching for the boy."

"You found him?"

"In a while. It took us *quite* a while. We checked the buildings and the forest. If I hadn't stopped to take a leak, I maybe never would have found him even then. But I went over by an outhouse, and I found him in a trench. He sure was dirty. I remember that. And scared, although he never said what happened to him in the compound. Mostly he was scared about his father. Even when we brought the boy down to the cruisers, he refused to get in with his father. We were forced to drive them separately."

"And what did Quiller have to say?"

"Excuse me?"

"Quiller."

Rettig shrugged. "Nobody ever saw him."

"What? You searched the compound, and you never saw him?"

"No one did."

"Well, where could he have hidden? Why would he have hidden in the first place?"

"Don't ask me. He might have been out in the forest. I don't see the difference it makes."

"No, I don't either," Dunlap told him, frowning. "But there's something strange about all this, and I wish I understood it."

"Are you getting what you wanted?" a voice interrupted.

Dunlap turned to where Slaughter stood beside the porch, his deputies with him after they had come back from the horses.

"Mostly," Dunlap said. "There are still a few loose ends."

"Well, tie them up. We want you satisfied."

You bastard, Dunlap thought. Putting on this country show for me. You're ten times more sophisticated than you pretend. He glanced at Rettig. "So what about the trial? I never read the end of it."

"Oh, Wheeler was convicted," Rettig said.

Dunlap nodded. Sure, the coverup was just to keep the town safe from another bunch of hippies coming through. If Wheeler had been freed and word had gotten out, there really would have been some trouble then. The town had done the wisest thing.

"His lawyer tried to plead insanity, but people here don't understand that sort of thing," Rettig said. "The charge was manslaughter, extenuating circumstances, and the son was such a prick when he was on the stand, clearly out to get his father, that the jury sympathized with Wheeler, recommending that the judge go easy. Two years was the sentence, and the day the trial was over, Wheeler's son got out of here. The town police had kept a watch on him to make sure he didn't leave before then. Also to protect him. There were plenty of ugly feelings toward him, people angered by the painful choices he had caused, and he just packed his gear and left. Some people figured that he went back to the compound. But I always doubted that. Once his father was released, the father surely would go looking for him again. The kid was scared enough that he would want to run much farther than the compound. He would want to put a lot of miles between him and his father."

Slaughter stepped up on the porch. "All that happened here? I take it back about country life being easy." He stooped to pick up another beer, then restrained his impulse. "Look, I think we'd better break this up. If we've got the trouble I think we have, we should all be on duty. Grab that phone," he told the new man. It was ringing inside, and as the new man went in, Slaughter faced the rest of his men. "You know what to do." He told the medical examiner, "I'll go with you to get the cat I shot." Then he told Dunlap, "How else can I help you?"

"Well, I'd like to see the compound, talk to Wheeler—"

"I don't understand what you're looking for, but you can see the problems I've got. I'll make a deal. You let me have today, and I'll go out with you tomorrow."

"Can somebody drive me back to town?" Dunlap asked. "I'd like to examine the records in your office."

You're pushing, Slaughter thought. You know I don't have time to watch you. He was just about to answer when the new man appeared in the doorway.

"That's the state police," the new man said, and Slaughter felt his apprehension intensify. His mind seemed to tilt, and he knew that normalcy was on the other side now.

"Did you phone them yesterday about a rancher named Bodine?" the new man continued.

"That's right. Damn it, tell me what they want."

"Well, the ranch is still deserted. Not only that, but . . ."

When Slaughter heard the rest of it, he murmured, "Jesus," and rushed in toward the telephone.

## NINE

The helicopter circled high above the foothills. It was just a speck up there, and Slaughter barely heard it as he sped across the bumpy rangeland, squinting upward, then glancing straight ahead to make sure he didn't hit a rock or a clump of sagebrush or a gulch he wouldn't see until he was almost on it. He glanced to the left as well, worried by the wide, deep drywash over there, and hoped that he'd made the proper choice when he drove down along this side instead of heading across the bridge back near the ranch and moving down along the opposite side. He was aiming toward the helicopter, closer to it, closer to the drywash too and worried that he'd have to stop the cruiser soon, to cross the gully on foot and walk the rest of the way.

He didn't have to. One bend in the wash, and then it straightened, almost in a line up toward the helicopter high above the foothills. He was taking chances, speeding faster.

"Aren't you worried that you'll break an axle?" Dunlap asked beside him.

"Not in this car. It's designed to go through anything. I made sure we got the best."

Slaughter concentrated on the bumpy terrain. Bringing Dunlap with him was something he regretted. But he hadn't wanted Dunlap going through his files when he wasn't around, and certainly he hadn't wanted Dunlap asking people questions about what was happening in town—that would surely start the panic Slaughter wanted to avoid—and so he'd made a quick decision, taking Dunlap with him. Slaughter told himself that there was no place where Dunlap would be harmless. At least this way the man would be in sight. But Slaughter wasn't confident. Of all the weekends for a reporter to arrive, he thought, and he was speeding faster toward the helicopter high above the foothills.

"What about that cow the medical examiner mentioned?" Dunlap asked.

"The steer."

"I beg your pardon."

"Out here they call beef cattle 'steers'."

"I didn't know."

"It's all right. I called them 'cows' too many times myself. It takes a while to get adjusted."

Maybe I've changed the subject, Slaughter hoped. The night before, he'd told the medical examiner to check the steer that had been found next to old Doc Markle's corpse. But it turned out that someone at the veterinary clinic had mistakenly had the carcass incinerated. Slaughter had been furious. Wasn't anything about this trouble going to work out easily?

"But what about the steer?" Dunlap asked.

So the subject hadn't been changed, after all.

"A different problem," Slaughter told him. "Something got a steer two nights ago. We don't know what did it."

"The steer was Sam Bodine's?"

And how did you know that? Slaughter thought. "Yes, that's right. Bodine's."

"So then this problem isn't really different from the other."

The helicopter now was lower as the foothills loomed before them. Slaughter had to look away, the helicopter in a straight line with the blazing sun, and then he saw the state-police cars where the rangeland ended at the bottom of the thickly wooded slope. He drove as far as he was able, stopping by the other cars, his bumper up against some sagebrush, and he scrambled out, putting on his hat, holding it as dust was swirled up by the helicopter coming down. He looked around, puzzled, wondering where everybody from the cruisers had gone.

The helicopter's roar was deafening, so he didn't hear them coming through the trees. Abruptly, they emerged from the underbrush, Altick and three men he hadn't seen before. They all belonged to the state police, but Altick was the ranking officer, a captain, so Slaughter focused his attention on him. One thing about Altick, he was good at what he did, so good that no one ever made jokes about his unflattering mustache. He'd been forced to grow it after he had tried to stop a knife fight and had nearly lost his lip when two drunken cowboys turned on him. The scar was partly visible beneath the sandy bristles. He had his hat off, wiping at the sweat across his forehead. Then he put it back on, stepping down toward Slaughter, on a level with him now and just about as tall.

They tried to talk but couldn't hear and turned to watch

the helicopter set down, rotors slowing, engine dying.

"Nobody told me you'd be in on this," Slaughter said.

"Well, Bodine was a friend." Altick's voice was raspy. "That's why we got on this so fast. I knew the forestry department had its helicopter out this way. The land's so dry they're checking for fires. So I asked them to look for Bodine's truck."

"The phone call said they'd found it."

Altick pointed toward the trees he'd come through, motioning for Slaughter to follow. They hiked up through the underbrush and stopped where the ground eased onto a level before sloping sharply upward again. There were fir trees, boulders, and a small streambed that wound down the slope. The pickup truck was before them, its blue paint scratched from the trees it had squeezed past, one wheel in a sinkhole, both doors open, covered with dust.

The helicopter pilot joined them. "I almost didn't find it. I was looking for it out on the range."

"What made you even think to look here?" Slaughter turned to Altick.

"Just a guess," Altick said. "I thought that Sam had maybe taken his family on a trip. That appaloosa mare of his, though. It's won half a dozen trophies. No one came around to feed it. So I knew something had happened to him. I checked all the traffic accident reports. When nothing turned up there, I figured he was out on the range in some trouble and we'd better take a look. This pilot is something. He wasn't out here half the morning before finding this."

Slaughter walked toward the pickup truck. He circled it, then glanced at where the streambed angled toward the flatland. "Looks like Sam was in a hurry. He chose the only route that he could follow, rammed up the streambed until he couldn't go much farther, then jumped out, and ran."

"Not just him."

Slaughter squinted at Altick.

"Both doors are open, don't forget," Altick said. "We haven't touched a thing. Sam and someone else. It's my guess his wife and son were with him. Otherwise, where are they?"

Slaughter slumped against the truck. The shade in here was welcome, cooling him. He tried to think. "It could be nothing's wrong. Maybe he just drove up for the hell of it. The truck got stuck, but they were going camping, something like that, so he left it until he'd come back. Then he planned to get help to move the truck."

"Why would he leave the doors open?"

"I have no idea."

"There's something else." Altick pointed up past Slaughter.

When Slaughter turned, he saw a patch of brown and red among the fir trees. His apprehension increased as he straightened and breathed and walked up toward it. He heard someone, likely Altick, walking behind him. But he didn't look in that direction. He only stopped and kept on staring.

Sure, he thought. The freshly mangled carcass of a steer, its mutilated guts protruding, flies swarming over them. What else did you think it would be?

He felt dizzy.

"When we started searching, we also found this," Altick said. "The fifth one we've had news about today."

Slaughter leaned his head against a tree. "Better make that six."

"What?"

"Bodine found one like this Thursday, but we only learned about it Friday morning."

"Jesus."

"That's not all," Slaughter said. "We've had some animal attacks in town. A man's been killed. At first we figured it was wild dogs from the hills, but now we're worried about rabies."

Altick paled.

"That's right. Now you feel the way I do," Slaughter told him. "We've got trouble." He pointed toward the mountains. "What's up there?"

"Nothing. Wilderness. The forestry department lists this as a recreation area." Altick suddenly understood. "Rabies? Christ, what if people are camping up there?"

Slaughter's forehead throbbed. "Let's assume wild dogs are what did this. Bodine saw them on the range. He chased them into these foothills."

"I'd better get the helicopter looking for them." Altick turned, scrambling down the hillside, followed by the pilot.

"And for anybody else up there. Check the lakes, the likely

camping spots." Slaughter hurried after Altick. "Look, I know this is your jurisdiction, but we'd better work together on this. Leave a man to watch the carcass and the pickup truck. Get some other men out here with rifles. Have them search the hills as far as they can go today."

They reached the bottom, Altick turning toward him, and for just a moment Slaughter thought that Altick would be angry, that Altick would tell him not to interfere, to keep his opinions to himself. But Altick only nodded, saying, "I'll go you one better. Dogs. We'll get some bloodhounds out here. We'll pick up Bodine's trail."

TEN

"Warren!"

She heard him screaming and ran from the living room to the kitchen. Staring out the screen door, she saw him racing through the backyard toward her.

"Warren!"

He was clutching his hand. She saw the blood, the mangled flesh, and she was pushing at the screen door, rushing out to meet him.

He kept screaming.

"Warren! Tell me what it is that happened!"

She was holding him, the blood across her sleeve now. She could feel his frantic tears drop off his cheek to wet her blouse.

He just kept screaming.

"Warren! Please! You've got to—"

"It's the glass!"

"But—"

"Broken glass!"

"You've got to show me, Warren!"

She stared at him, at the blood. She wasn't certain what to do. She knew she had to stop the blood. But what had caused it? How bad was the cut?

She tried to lead him. "*Show* me, Warren."

He pointed toward the backyard. She squinted past the backyard toward the metal barrel in the old man's yard across the lane. She saw the blood across the rim, and she was running.

"Oh, my God."

The blood covered everything, the rusty cans, the broken glass, the ashes from the garbage fires that the old man used to set before the town denied him permission. Warren must have climbed up on this cinder block and reached in there for something, but he lost his balance, and he cut himself.

She swung around. Warren was clutching his hand, running toward the back door, and she called to him, but he was in the house already. She scrambled toward him, across the lane and past the bushes, the back door getting larger as she reached it, fumbling at the handle, charging in. She saw the blood across the floor, and she was racing down the hallway toward the bathroom, but he wasn't in there. Where? She doubled back. He sat in his bedroom, crying, blood across the sheets. She hurried to grab him, wrapping a sheet around his hand and guiding him into the bathroom.

"No!"

"I have to wash it. I have to see how bad it is."

"Don't touch it!"

Warren kept crying as she freed the bloody sheet and pushed his hand down into the sink. She turned the tap on.

He wailed again.

Too hot. She turned the other tap, and now the water felt lukewarm, and she was brushing at the bleeding flesh. She saw the wound, but blood kept oozing out, and she was brushing at it, freeing all the dirt and black clots, and Lord, the hand was mangled. Deep and wide and jagged. Oh, my baby, she was thinking as she felt his weight against him, and she knew before she looked that he had fainted.

ELEVEN

Warren smelled something strange, something like the powder that his mother put inside the washer when she did the clothes. His eyes fluttered. He winced from the light all around him, and he saw the strange man in the white coat leaning close. He started wailing.

"Warren, it's all right."

His mother's voice. His father close beside her. They looked angry.

"Mommy, I—"

"It's all right, Warren. Please don't be afraid. You're with a doctor."

Back now to the man, his white coat flecked with red spots down his arm. The man was holding something like a plastic pill that he had broken open, and the strange smell seemed to come from it. Warren kept on crying. This man was much younger, thinner, than the doctor he always went to, and the freckles on his face looked like the blood specks on the white coat, and Warren couldn't stop from crying.

"Ssshhh, it's all right, son. We're here now. You're just fine."

Then Warren slowly understood that they had him on a table, that his hand felt numb and awkward. He was raising it. The hand was like a white club, bandaged so he couldn't even see or move his fingers.

"He's still suffering from shock. He'll take a while to get adjusted," he heard the doctor saying.

Someone dried his eyes. His mother. She was smiling. So she wasn't angry, after all.

"Warren, can you tell us how it happened?"

He turned toward the doctor, trying to remember what the plan was.

"Yes, the glass," he told them slowly.

"In the barrel?"

"Yes, I cut myself."

His father clenched his fist. "I'm going to sue that old man."

"Harry. Please, not here," his mother said.

So I got away with it, Warren thought.

"Warren, let me tell you what I did for you," the doctor said. "You have to make sure you keep the bandage on. I sewed you up. I gave you stitches. Do you understand that?"

"Yes, like Mommy when she makes a dress."

They smiled a little.

"Something like that," the doctor said. "You were cut too deeply to let the wound heal on its own. I took some string like this, except it wasn't string. It's more like what we used to call a piece of catgut, and I sewed the cut together."

"Will the string stay in there?"

"No. A week or so from now, I'll take the stitches out, and you'll be like before, although you'll maybe have a scar," the doctor said. "But you've got a lot of growing to do, and most of the scar will disappear. What you've got to understand is that you can't put much weight on your hand. If you try to pick up heavy things or make a fist or anything like that, you'll risk the chance of pulling out the stitches too soon. Take things easy. Let your mother or your father do the lifting for you."

"Will they make my bed for me?"

"You bet we will," his father said. "And I'll still pay your full allowance."

Warren grinned then. Yes, he'd gotten away with it, and he was wiping at his tears, trying to sit up.

"Here, let me help you." His mother held him.

"He's going to be all right, I think," the doctor said. "Take him home. Here are pills for when the local anesthetic wears off. Call me if there's any trouble. But I think that all you'll have to do is bring him in a week from Monday."

"What about the bandage?"

"Change it every night. The first few times you ought to soak the bandage before it's removed. I don't want any dried blood tearing at those stitches."

"Dressing?"

"Anything you have around the house. First-aid cream is fine. I gave him an anti-tetanus injection. I don't see any problems coming up."

"Thank you."

"I'm just pleased that you got him here so quickly. He was bleeding quite a lot."

More talk, but Warren didn't listen. He looked around the room, at the cabinets and shiny metal objects, and abruptly he was dizzy. He almost toppled off the table.

"Here, young man. I think we'd better get you home."

Despite an itching, burning pain along his hand, Warren couldn't stop from feeling happy. He had gotten away with it. All night long, he'd tried to figure how to hide the bite. His hand had swollen so much that it scared him. At breakfast time, his mother had come in to wake him, but he'd snuggled in the sheets as if he wanted to keep sleeping. He had stayed there until he knew that she would surely come to wake him. So he'd listened until he heard her in the living room, and he had managed then to dress himself. The pain had been so bad that he shook. He had slipped and smeared some blood across his sleeve. But he had figured what to do by that time, and he'd snuck outside to reach the barrel over there. The worst part had been leaning in to let some blood drip onto the glass. When he had pulled the bloody rag off, he had seen the swollen throbbing ugly cut, caked with dirty blood. He'd shivered, reaching down to touch his hand against a broken bottle. That had been his plan at least. But he had lost his balance, and the cut had burst, not from the glass but from the pressure. He had never felt such shrieking pain. He couldn't stop his screaming.

### TWELVE

"Okay then, sure, why not?"

And Slaughter turned up onto the loggers' road. "I've heard so much about this place I guess it's time I had a look myself."

He hadn't planned to do this until tomorrow, but he didn't like the thought of Dunlap's staying any longer than was necessary. It was fine for Parsons to instruct him to be friendly. "Give him all the help he needs." Parsons had been clear on that. But Parsons didn't have to babysit this man. Parsons didn't know about the trouble that was going on.

There wasn't much that Slaughter had to do in town, regardless. He could sit and wait for calls to come in on the police station's two-way radio. Or he could drive out, troubleshooting on the streets. But hell, the compound wasn't even ten miles down the road from Bodine's place, halfway from the ranch to town, and he was out here, going past it. He might just as well drive up and get this nuisance finished. Slaughter saw the road and made his choice, and this would help take Dunlap's mind away from what was happening in town.

Slaughter knew the turnoff, although as he had said he'd never taken time to go up it. There had never been a need to, never been an interest. Back in the sixties, he'd seen freaks enough to last a lifetime. They could smoke dope up here until they couldn't tell their ass from grass for all he cared.

He angled up the loggers' road, if "road" was what it could still be called. No one had come up here for some time. There were bushes in the ruts, pine needles, fallen leaves, young trees growing in the mound between the ruts, and branches dipping down from all the large trees on each side. The place was shadowy, cool, yet strangely humid. Slaughter suddenly was worried that, if he got stuck, he wouldn't have the room to turn around, that backing down would be a problem, given all the ruts and bends, and several times he had to squeeze around some young trees that he couldn't just drive over, narrowly avoiding large trees at the side. He wished he hadn't been impulsive. Hell, I need a Jeep to get up in here. Why'd I do this? But he had no choice now, and he eased his foot off the gas pedal, slowing, bumping, working up this god-forsaken lane to nowhere. "What kind of place is this to build a commune anyhow?"

"I asked myself that several times," Dunlap said.

Slaughter glanced at him. "Not too happy where they sent you, huh?"

"I've had a little trouble. But I'm working on it. This is what you'd call my penance."

"I can see that from the way your hands are shaking."

"It's a bumpy ride."

"But wouldn't a beer go good now?"

Dunlap stared at him. "I said I'm working on it."

"Hey, I don't mean to rile you. I'm just making conversation."

Dunlap's stern gaze weakened. "All right, I apologize."

"It's *my* fault. I was mixing in your business."

"But the fact is, you're right. I shouldn't be so jumpy when somebody says the truth. You really like it here?"

"Love it."

"I find that baffling."

"It's simple. Back east in Detroit, things got out of hand. I got so I couldn't keep control. My wife divorced me. I was fed up with my work."

"You were a cop?"

"That's right, and finally I simply quit. I didn't know what else to do. I couldn't keep doing what I had, however. So I spread a map out on my kitchen table, and I asked myself where I'd rather be."

"And you chose *here?*" Dunlap looked incredulous.

"Sure. Because I'd never been here. I was having day-dreams. Mountains. Horses running free. I'd never really seen those things, never been around them. What they represented were the things I wanted, though. I knew that much. So I came here."

"Just like that."

"I left the next day, and I loved it. Oh, I had some hard times at the start. I tried my hand at raising horses, but I made a mess of it. The next thing I was in police work again. But I was talking earlier about control, and that's the point. My life here is exactly what I want to make of it. Things aren't so complicated that I have to give in to them. I have freedom."

Slaughter looked ahead and eased the cruiser past a clump of bushes. He didn't see the pothole just beyond them and felt the cruiser jolt down into it. "Now it's me I'm being personal about. I'd better watch it."

Dunlap rubbed his forehead. "I think I'll soon be divorced as well."

"Who wants it? Her or you?"

"Oh, she's the one who'll do it, I suppose."

"Is that why you drink so much?"

"It's that obvious, is it? No, I started drinking long before. It could be I caused the problem with her. But you know, a person has ambitions in his work. He wants to prove how really good he is, and I just never lived up to my expectations."

"Or you maybe liked the booze so much that it distracted you."

Dunlap shrugged. "The chicken or the egg. What difference does it make? I ended here. No matter how it happened, I know where it got me. Nowhere. Nothing personal."

"Well, why not just give in then? Maybe settle in a place like this?"

Dunlap started laughing.

"No, I mean it," Slaughter told him. "Things could be a whole lot worse. Sometimes we end up exactly where we should be."

"Or deserve to be."

Slaughter gave up trying to convince him.

"They were all idealists," Dunlap said.

"Who? What are you talking about?"

"Quiller and the others up here," Dunlap said. "They truly thought that, if they left the world and went up in here, they could live the kind of life they'd always wanted. They were fools."

"It's worked out fine for me."

"I wonder how it all worked out for them, however," Dunlap said. "This Quiller. Do you know about him?"

"Just from talk I pick up now and then."

"Well, he was evidently something. Six foot eight. Thin beyond grotesqueness, and that maybe helped him. Newsmen who were near him said he wasn't real. You know, as if they couldn't quite believe that he was there. It's like he radiated something holy. Charismatic like the best of that type, and those newsmen saw the best, believe me. If this way of life had any chance, Quiller was the man to do it."

"He was rich, I hear."

"An understatement, and that money would have helped as well."

They squeezed up past a fallen pine tree. Its needles were dead, dried and scattered across the road, the branches skeletal, and Slaughter looked up past them toward a wall of vines and bushes, slats of brown that showed through, and he knew that they were almost there. He slowed around a curve and, before he even stopped the cruiser, said to Dunlap, "See if you can budge that gate."

But Dunlap only stared ahead.

"I said—"

"I'm going." Dunlap stepped from the cruiser. First he viewed the wall of vines from several angles, took several photographs; then he left the camera in the cruiser, and he walked up to the weed-shrouded gate.

Slaughter watched him through the windshield. With the filtered sun, the frame around his windshield, Slaughter sensed that Dunlap was much farther than he really was. Sitting here, the motor idling, Slaughter was abruptly conscious that there weren't any other sounds around him in the forest. Sure, the noise we made has frightened everything away, he guessed.

He watched as Dunlap stopped and looked at all the vines and weeds that wound around the gate posts. Dunlap reached out. Then he brought his hand back.

"Poison ivy?" Dunlap called.

Slaughter laughed. "A city boy. No, I don't know exactly what they are, but they're not poison ivy."

Dunlap nodded. Then he turned back to the vines and almost touched them before looking at him again. "You're sure?"

"For Christ sake."

"Never mind. I'll do it."

Dunlap tugged some vines away. He did it cautiously at first, and then he used more strength against them. He was pushing at the gate.

"We'll maybe have to clear the whole bunch," Slaughter leaned out, saying.

"More than that. We'll have to break the lock here."

"What?"

"A rusted chain and lock."

"Tug at it. The chain might be so old you'll break it."

"That's what I've been doing."

"Hell, I thought that was more weeds."

"You'd better have a look."

Slaughter thought about all the time they were wasting, thought about the town, and shut the motor off. He stepped from the cruiser, walking toward the gate. "I should have known they'd have fixed the gate once Wheeler drove up through it," Dunlap said.

Slaughter didn't understand the reference.

"I'll tell you later. But they fixed it, all right. Christ, they really did. Just look at those thick timbers. They'd stop any pickup truck."

The two men stood in the shadowy, cool, yet humid forest that was close around them, grass and fallen pine tree needles underfoot, and they were silent for a moment.

"Here, let me try it," Slaughter said. He put his full weight against the gate and pushed, but nothing happened. Oh, a little creaking in the wood and some slight movement as the chain went taut, but nothing else, and Slaughter felt the awkward pressure in his shoulder, stepping back and rubbing at it. "What about the hinges?" he asked.

But although rusted, they were large and solid, and the screws were sturdy in the timber.

"Well, that does it," Slaughter said.

"You don't mean we're leaving."

"No. I came up this far, and I don't intend to waste time coming back. We're going to have to climb the fence and walk."

They looked at one another.

"Wait a second while I get my camera." Dunlap went down to the cruiser for it. When he came back, Slaughter waved for him to climb up first, and Dunlap put his shoe on one thick timber, grabbing at another timber, easing over. Slaughter climbed up just behind him, and they stepped down into the compound, on the edge of Quiller's fifty acres.

"Something wrong?" Slaughter asked.

"No, I'm just shaky," Dunlap answered. "You were right. I need a drink."

"Well, you'll be done with this before you know it."

They walked along the next part of the loggers' road, which was as overgrown as the first part. Slaughter heard a noise in the bushes and turned, but there was nothing he could see. He kept walking.

"Are there any people up here yet?" Slaughter wondered.

"I meant to ask you that myself. Parsons says there might be two or three."

"Oh, swell. Some commune."

"In its day, it was," Dunlap said. "I read that Quiller started with a couple thousand. Then he cut them down to just five hundred."

"Even so. If only two or three are up here."

"Yes, it isn't hard to measure Quiller's failure."

"What's the point then? I don't see your story?"

"*That's* the story. How it failed, and more important, why."

"Well, you must know your business."

They kept walking. Once again, Slaughter heard a noise behind them. He turned, but there was nothing.

"Now who's jumpy?" Dunlap asked him.

Slaughter had to laugh then. But the laughter echoed through the forest, and he quickly stopped.

The loggers' road disappeared a hundred feet ahead of them.

"Or could be that the forest just reclaimed it," Slaughter said.

They reached the dead end of the lane and glanced at the maze of trees around them.

"What now?" Slaughter asked.

"Well, the road was going straight up, and the clearing I suppose was somewhere near it. Let's just keep on through these trees."

"We could end up walking in a circle. We'll have to pay attention to our landmarks." That big boulder up ahead, Slaughter thought. And then that line of cliffs below the ridge.

They veered through the pine trees, the needles lancing at them. Dunlap stumbled, falling on his camera, and he groped up, clutching at his chest, staring at the camera that was dangling from his shoulder.

"Is it broken?" Slaughter asked.

Dunlap didn't know. He hurriedly checked the camera, but it seemed intact, and he'd made certain that he kept the lens cap on. "I don't see any damage."

"What about yourself?"

"Oh, just the wind knocked out of me."

"It could be worse. You want to try to walk?"

Dunlap nodded. Bent a little forward, limping slightly, he pushed farther through the trees. The forest now was thicker, darker, dead trees fallen among the live ones, intersecting, thick vines growing up around them. Dunlap stopped and took deep breaths. "There has to be a better way. They brought their cars and vans up here. But it's sure as hell they didn't bring them this way."

"Maybe we should go back to the loggers' road and angle right or left," Slaughter suggested.

"And maybe lose our way as you just said? I wish I knew."

"Well, let's keep going then. If this gets much worse, we'll have to change direction."

So they pushed up through the pine trees, and the clearing wasn't fifteen steps away, the trees so dense they didn't see it until they stepped free from the forest.

There were stumps that stretched off through young forest, all the growth here up to Slaughter's chest so that he looked out past the new tips of the pine trees toward the compound over there. Slaughter was reminded of a camping trip years ago. He'd gone with his father to a small lake in northern Michigan. They'd pitched their tent and eaten, so exhausted that they soon had gone to sleep. Rain pelting onto the canvas had wakened them, and they had talked and dozed and wakened again as the storm got worse, and in the morning when the storm was finished, they had crawled out from the tent to stare across the lake. A billowing mist hung over it, but they were camped up high enough that they were just above the mist, the pine trees visible along the other bank, and Slaughter now remembered how he'd thought about what he couldn't see below the mist—the fish that would be rising, and the ducks and frogs and other things. It wasn't real. That thought again. Like now. That sense of life around him but unseen. Except the compound was deserted.

They started through the new growth toward the compound. Dunlap took a photograph. "Hope the camera works." They continued walking.

"Sure," Dunlap said. "They used the timber here to build the barracks." He thought that Rettig had been accurate. With the difference that the walls were like log cabins, Dunlap was reminded of a deserted Army camp. Lanes and squares, a parade ground, everything was here. No, not exactly everything. He didn't see a flagpole. Hell, this kind of culture, they'd have called it a Maypole.

The compound loomed as they approached it, wide, the buildings all one story and with slanted roofs. At least the hippies knew enough to compensate for deep snow on the roofs in winter, Slaughter thought. And then he paused as Dunlap took another picture.

"Watch these branches on the ground here," Slaughter told him. "We don't want another accident."

Dunlap nodded, staring toward the compound as they walked around the branches, coming toward the nearest buildings. There were weeds and bushes, young trees growing in the lanes, and vines enmeshed around the shutters. There were broken windows, doors half off their hinges. And the slogans on the walls, the symbols, Day-Gloed green and red and blue, now faded, flowers, flags with rifles for the stripes and bullets for the stars, a skull and crossbones and a DOWN WITH NIXON, the

DOWN WITH slashed out, then TO HELL WITH scrawled above it, that too slashed, a simple FUCK above it. VIETNAM WILL CLAIM OUR CHILDREN. Skeletons across a pentagon.

"Sure. They took the time to do all that, but they didn't even think to treat the logs for insects," Slaughter said and pointed. There were tiny holes in all the logs, and down below the holes, thick piles of what seemed sawdust, dirty, flecked with dead leaves from the vines.

Dunlap took more photographs. As they reached the buildings, Slaughter had the odd sensation that he'd been here before. "Is anybody around?" And then he knew what he was thinking of. Sure. Bodine's ranch when yesterday he'd gone there and he'd heard the kettle.

"You look in this building. I'll check the others," Dunlap said, and Slaughter stopped him.

"No, we'd better stay together."

"What's the matter?" Dunlap asked.

"Let's just say I've got a bad feeling. Anybody here?" he called again.

He waited, but no answer.

"No one's been here for quite a while," Dunlap said.

They stepped inside one building. There were bunk beds, wooden slats instead of springs, no mattresses, but many spiders, cobwebs, leaves piled in one corner as a nest for something. The floor—decaying planks—looked unsafe.

"Let's try a little farther on," Slaughter said.

But almost every building was the same. Slaughter glanced around to notice how the compound had been situated in a canyon, cliffs beyond the trees on three sides, and the slope behind them descending toward the loggers' road. A wind came from below there, rustling trees and cooling him. He took his hat off. Then his back felt unprotected, and he looked behind him. "Well, they picked a good spot anyhow. Except they would have needed water, and I don't know where they got it."

"Higher up. Those cliffs might have some streams."

"Could be. But I don't have time to look."

That made his point, Slaughter hoped. He *didn't* have time. He hadn't thought it would take this long getting up here. While he felt more sympathetic toward Dunlap, all the same he had his job to do, and he was anxious to get out of here.

Because you're thinking of Bodine? he asked himself.
That feeling you had yesterday? You're scared. You might as
well admit it.

No. Because I have to get back if there's trouble. Sure.
And now he followed Dunlap past some bushes toward a larger
building. Its door had toppled. The steps were rotted. They
looked past the spider webs at what must once have been the
dining room. Rettig had been accurate again. Logs made into
trestles, tables that went down the whole length of the room. A
bird sat in a glassless window, staring at them. Slaughter
blinked, the bird flew away, and Slaughter felt that spot between
his shoulder blades again. He turned, but there was no one out
there.

"Are they hiding?"

"Little children laughing?" Dunlap asked.

"What the hell is that?"

"It's from a poem. T.S. Eliot."

"I *know* who he is. That's not what I meant." And Slaughter started running toward the small low building in front of the
parade ground. "I saw something moving."

He ran harder, glancing at the buildings on each side,
staring toward the trees beyond them, and he had his gun out,
lunging past the listing door, finding just a table, spider webs
and dirt, more pine needles.

But there wasn't any back door, and he didn't understand
what he'd seen moving. Then he did. The wind blew toward
him, and he saw the thick, rotted curtain moving. A blanket
really. Torn in half and hung up on a branch before a broken
window. He was nauseated by the smell that he'd been register-
ing all along: must and crumbling wood, the fetid, sick-sweet
smell of buildings left to ruin. Then he saw the hornet's nest in
the far right corner. Something moved inside its portal, and he
stepped out into the open.

*Dunlap.* Where was Dunlap?

"Over here!"

Now he reads my mind, Slaughter thought as he ran
toward the muffled voice inside another building. The emotion in Dunlap's voice worried him.

This building didn't have planks for a floor. Only dirt.
There weren't any windows. Two big doors hung open. Dunlap

stood in a shadowy corner, staring at dark stains on the ground.

"That's blood?" Slaughter asked.

Dunlap only shook his head.

"Well, what then? Christ, you scared me."

"Did I? Well, I didn't mean to. No." Dunlap picked up the dirt and sniffed it.

Slaughter suddenly was angry. "Tell me what that stuff is."

"Even after all these years, you can still smell the oil. This is where the Corvette would have been."

"Except it isn't."

"Where then?" Dunlap wondered.

"Look, there's no one up here. Quiller drove out years ago. He maybe let the others walk, but he kept the car in case he needed it to leave."

"I hate to say it, but I think you're right. And now my god-damned job is almost over."

"You can still track Quiller."

"No, it's finished. I'll be out of here by Monday. After I talk to Wheeler and see your records."

"And visit Parsons," Slaughter told him.

"Right. I haven't let that slip my mind."

"Twenty-three years? You really thought that they'd still be here?"

"Well, I had my hopes. I needed some big story to impress them."

"In New York?"

Dunlap's face was blank. "You're luckier than you imagine."

"Well, I made my own luck."

Dunlap took a breath and nodded. "Maybe," he said. "Maybe after this I'll have to spread out my own map." He looked all around. "The new republic." He snorted. "It's not all that failed." He started past the sagging doors, and Slaughter thought about the town as he went after him. The sun was descending. The wind had died. The compound felt lonelier than ever. Well, we'd better reach the car before the woods get too dark to see landmarks, Slaughter thought. "Let's get a drink," Dunlap said, and they walked along the lane between the ruined barracks.

# THE
## PART THREE
# MANSION

T SNIFFED AT THE SHOE.
MUD AND DAMPNESS. AND IT CHOKED. IT SCURRIED BACK AND SET-
tled on its haunches, puzzled by the odd sensation in its throat.
Then the choking spasm passed, and it was staring at the shoe.
It waited, almost sniffed the shoe again, then made its choice,
and scuttled toward the pile of clothing in one corner. Blue
and stiff, yet muddy, damp just like the shoe. And once again it
felt that sharp constriction in its throat—which made it angry—
and it cuffed at the clothing. Then it snarled.

Over to one side, another kind of shoe, this one dark and
scuffed, light spots showing through the surface, a faint odor,
partly sweat, and partly from the animal the hide had once
belonged to. It was sniffing closer. Then it bit the leather, and
it shook its head, the shoe flopping one way, then another. But
the clothes that hung down brushed against its head, and that

annoyed it, so it pawed up at the clothing, snagged a pocket, pulling, and some clothes dropped down upon it. Smothered, frightened, it fumbled to get out from under, snarling, pawing, and the clothes dropped free. Then it smelled soap and chemicals, and it was growling. As it bit hard into the cloth and held the garment, tearing, it heard noises coming down the hallway out there. It turned, staring, But the door was closed. The noises stopped. It went back to the garment, snarling, tearing.

Something rattled. It swung toward the door. The handle moved. It stiffened, garment hanging from its teeth. The handle kept moving. Then the door came open, and she stepped in. Dropping the garment from its mouth, it bared its teeth and snarled at her.

She breathed in sharply. "Warren?"

And it sprang at her. She stumbled back. Her elbow hit the door. The door swung shut behind her, and she fell against the doorjamb, fumbling with the handle, as it sprang at her again. She scrambled toward the dresser to avoid it.

"Warren!"

But it only snarled and kept coming.

"Warren!"

She kicked at it, throwing pictures off the dresser, dodging toward the bed, climbing, screaming. When it leaped the final time, it caught her not quite balanced on the bed so that they both went crashing off the other side, her back slamming hard on the floor as it came clawing at her throat. She screamed and hit at it. She struck it on the nose, the throat. It felt the blood pour over its lips, a salt taste in its mouth, and gagged. It pawed to clear the salt taste, angered by the gagging, slashed its teeth down toward her face, but in that moment's hesitation, she had gripped the table near the bed and scrambled from the floor to kick at it. The shoe came toward its face, but there was time to dodge, and now it sank its teeth hard into her leg. She wailed and kicked to free the leg, but it was growling, biting, and it felt the blood spurt into its mouth, that same salt taste. It gagged again as, shouting, she twisted her leg and jerked free. Something hard smashed against its shoulder, glass and a lampshade falling past. The pain surged through its shoulder. Whining, it was stunned. Then she wasn't before it any longer. She was stumbling past it toward the door, and it was turning, snarling, leaping as she reached the door and grabbed the handle, pulling, squeezing out to reach the hallway, slamming the door.

It banged against the door and clawed to move the handle. She was out there, screaming. But the handle wouldn't move. It heard her out there screaming, and it dimly understood that she was gripping at the handle, pulling at the door. It knew that there was no way to reach her. More than that, it understood the danger. Others would be coming. They would trap it. Have to get away. It swung to find an exit, saw the open window, the screen, then the porch and the open air, and it was charging forward, leaping, slamming at the screen. The mesh pressed, cutting at its face. The screen gave way, and it was falling through, the porch rising up to meet it. Darkness. Pain. It shook its head, the salt taste flooding its mouth. Then it could see again, and spitting, gagging, it vaulted across the railing toward the bushes.

"Warren!" it heard someone screaming.

### TWO

Slaughter heard as he came driving toward the outskirts. He reached for the microphone. "I've got it, Marge." He switched on the siren and the emergency flasher, staring now at Dunlap. "Well, that drink will have to wait." He pressed hard on the gas pedal, racing past the houses, swerving onto a sidestreet, people staring, as the siren wailed and he was concentrating on the street that stretched before him.

Five o'clock. The forest had become increasingly dark as they hiked down through it toward the cruiser. The sun had been low toward the mountains, and the dusk among the trees had lengthened. They'd almost lost their way, but then Slaughter had noticed the big boulder that he'd chosen as a landmark. It was farther to the left than he had figured, and they'd cut across, then found the loggers' road, and worked along it to the gate. He'd heard that skittering noise again but hadn't paid attention, just had wanted to get over to the cruiser, and he'd slowly backed the cruiser, Dunlap outside watching to make sure the rear wheels didn't jolt down into a sinkhole. Soon he'd swung the cruiser so the front was facing downward. Dunlap got in, and they'd bumped across the saplings and bushes down the road to reach the highway. Even so, the fading light made driving harder, and Slaughter's eyes were strained as he finally moved out from the trees to cross the rangeland. All he wanted was a drink and then some supper, thinking he would check in at the station first, but now he wouldn't have the chance, staring at Dunlap who was fumbling with his camera, both hands shaking, his tongue persistent at his lips.

"You ought to have a bottle with you for emergencies."

"I left a pint back in my room. I figured I'd be brave."

"Well, I can't take the time to drop you off."

"Hell, I wouldn't want you to."

Slaughter squealed around a corner, swerving just in time to miss a young boy in a wagon, thinking, Sure, if you're not careful, you'll hit one kid, rushing to find out about another. Slow down. There's no point in racing if you never get there.

But he couldn't force himself to slow. He strained to watch for people stepping from a corner or from cars parked on the side. He roared through an intersection, one car coming at him from the other way, then swung around another corner as he saw the people up there and the cars along the street and one tall woman standing, crying, other women grouped around her.

As everyone turned toward the cruiser, Slaughter reached down to flick off the siren and the flasher. Other people were crossing toward the house, and at last he was forced to slow. He stopped by a car before the house, double-parking, switching off the engine, reaching for his hat. A plumber's truck was coming toward him. It stopped as he slipped out from the cruiser, walking toward the lawn. He glanced toward the truck and saw a tall man jump out, running toward the group of women, and he guessed that this was the husband as they both came to the women at the same moment. Pushing through, Slaughter vaguely had the sense of Dunlap just behind him. He didn't want Dunlap learning too much, but he couldn't take the time to send him to the cruiser.

The woman clung to her husband.

"Peg, what happened?"

"He attacked me."

"Who?" And that was Slaughter, stepping closer.

She kept sobbing. "Warren did." She gasped for breath.

And Slaughter had a name at least.

"My God, what happened to your leg?" the husband blurted.

They stared at the blood that oozed down her leg and across her shoe.

"He bit me."

"*Bit?*" her husband said.

"I'm telling you. I couldn't keep away from him."

"Where is he?" Slaughter asked.

"The window. He was crawling like an animal."

Slaughter hurried toward the house. It was a single-story with a porch along the front and down the left side. He guessed that Warren was the boy he'd heard about when Marge had called, and he was thinking that he'd better look in through the windows rather than go into the house and risk the chance of something coming at him. He passed the aspen in the front yard and charged up the stairs. The porch rumbled under him as he looked first in at the living room and, seeing nothing, rushed along the side. Another window toward the living room, but he didn't look through it. He stopped, frowning at a broken screen that hung out from another window. Then he drew his gun—a gun against a little boy?—and swallowed, looking in at what had been a bedroom. But the place was wrecked in there, and he could see the blood, both on the floor inside and on the porch out here, turning toward where it was on the railing just above the broken bushes at the side. He stared off toward the gravel lane back there and sprinted toward the front again.

The woman had continued sobbing as her husband held her. People stood back from them, watching, murmuring to each other.

"Did he break out through the bedroom window?" Slaughter asked.

She nodded, gasping for more breath.

"He ran down toward that lane in back?"

"I didn't see. I only heard the noise, and when I looked in, he was gone. What in God's name made him do it?"

"I don't know yet. But believe me, I'll do everything I can to find out."

"I don't understand why he would bite me." She sobbed

uncontrollably as Slaughter ran toward the cruiser, picking up the microphone.

"Marge, we've got a situation here. That young boy had some kind of breakdown. He attacked his mother. Now he's running loose. I want everybody looking for him. Have you got that?"

"Affirmative."

"The same address you gave me. And one thing more. I want the medical examiner."

"Somebody's dead?" Marge asked in alarm.

"Just get him. There's no time to talk about it. I'll call back in fifteen minutes."

Slaughter hung up the microphone. He hadn't thought to ask the mother, but he knew the answer even so, although he had to check for certain, and he slipped out from the cruiser, staring at Dunlap who was near him, and then running toward the woman yet again.

She continued to cling to her husband.

"Mrs. Standish." He had seen the name on the mailbox. "Mrs. Standish, look, I know that this is hard for you, but please, I need to ask some questions."

She slowly turned to him.

This would bring the trouble into the open, Slaughter knew, but he had to ask the question. He glanced at the people near him, turning so his back was to them.

"Did your son complain about an animal that maybe got too rough with him? A dog that bit him, or a cat? Anything like that?"

They stared at him.

"But I don't understand," the woman said.

"No bites at all," the husband said. "We told him not to play with animals he didn't know."

"He cut himself," the woman said, and Slaughter looked at her.

"What is it?" she was asking.

"I don't know. Just tell me how he cut himself."

"Some broken glass," her husband said. "A barrel in the lane back there."

Slaughter felt puzzled. He'd been certain that the boy was bitten. "Several weeks ago. Think back. Did anything seem strange to you?"

"This morning."

"What?"

"He cut himself this morning. Why a dog bite? Why is that important?"

Slaughter couldn't bring himself to say it. "We've had trouble with those wild dogs in the hills. It's nothing. Look, I need a picture of your son. To help my men identify him."

He hoped that he'd changed the subject, and they looked at him and slowly nodded, walking toward the house, Slaughter just behind them. He really didn't understand now. If the boy had not been bitten, why had he behaved the way he did? Maybe what he'd said to Marge was true. The boy just had a breakdown. Maybe they mistreated him. Maybe he fought back and ran from home. The only way to know was to find the boy, and as the couple went inside the house, Slaughter turned to frown toward the sun. It was almost below the western mountains. Dusk would be here soon, then night, and how on earth they'd find the boy when it was dark, he didn't know.

He peered in at the living room. The place was absolutely clean and ordered. Surely anyone who kept a home so well was not the type to beat a child. But he'd been fooled that way back in Detroit, and he was wishing that his men were here so they could set out, looking for the boy.

The husband came back with a picture. Blond and bright-faced, blue eyes, in his Sunday suit. The boy was much like Slaughter's son had been at this age, and he had some trouble looking at the picture. God, the boy must be in terror out there. Slaughter couldn't show his feelings, though. He simply told the father, "Thank you. I'll return it."

"Listen, my wife's too upset to come back out and talk about this. Find him, will you?"

Slaughter heard the sirens, pivoting as two cruisers pulled up in the street. "We'll have him back. I promise." Then he paused. "I think your wife should see a doctor."

"She'll be all right once she rests a little."

"No, I mean her leg. A human bite. It's probably infected."

"I'll take care to clean it."

"Take her to a doctor," Slaughter told him. "I'll check

back to see about it. Look, I have to go."

He stepped from the porch, the photograph in his hand, the policemen coming toward him.

"This is who we're looking for," he said. "Warren is his name, and he's no doubt scared. But stay away from him. He's just a kid, but he attacked his mother, and I don't want any of you hurt."

They waited, looking at the picture.

"You two check the streets down this way. You two check the other way. I'll take the lane in back. Remember. Don't get careless just because he's little. I don't know what's happened here, but something isn't right."

Abruptly Slaughter faced the people on the lawn. "Everything's okay now. We'll take care of things. I want you all to go back to your homes."

But they just stood and looked at him.

"Come on. Let's move it."

Slaughter approached them, gesturing for them to leave, and slowly they dispersed.

"You'll know soon enough how this turns out. Just go back to your homes."

He turned toward his men. They were getting in their cars, and he was all alone, except for Dunlap.

"There's no chance to take you to your room," Slaughter said.

"I was hoping there wasn't."

"Hey, I know you need a story, but if word of this gets out, I told you there'll be a panic."

"I'll be careful."

"I assume I have your promise on that."

Dunlap nodded, looking puzzled. "But if the boy wasn't bitten."

"Yes, I know. It doesn't make much sense." They got in the car.

At the corner, Slaughter steered right, then right again, slowing as he started up the lane. He'd had to make a choice: here or where the lane continued to the left. But this direction took them toward the house the boy had fled from, and he figured that would be the place to start his search, so he was staring up the lane, then at the backyards and the houses on each side.

"I can't watch for everything. You check the yards on your side. I'll check over here."

"Hell, a kid, he could be anywhere."

"Just think of how the yards would look to someone small. A crawl space underneath a shed. A low spot in some bushes. Places an adult would never figure."

"Or he's maybe half a mile from here."

"Don't even think that," Slaughter told him. He was driving past the backyard of the house now, slowing even more, then stopping.

"What's the matter?"

"I just want to look at something."

Slaughter stepped from the cruiser, walking toward a metal barrel near the gravel lane. What made him stop was the blood along the rim and down the barrel. He studied the blood on the ground as well, noticing the large drops leading toward the house. He peered inside the barrel, saw the rusty cans, the broken glass, the blood across it, and the woman had been right. So why then had the kid behaved the way he did?

He glanced around for places where the boy could hide, stooped to check underneath some bushes by the shed, then straightened, walking to the cruiser. Dunlap asked him, "Anything?" But Slaughter only shook his head and worked the gearshift, driving slowly down the lane.

The radio crackled. "Chief, it's Marge. I haven't found the medical examiner."

Slaughter grabbed the microphone. "Well, keep trying. Stay there until you get him. I need lots of help on this. I've got plenty of questions."

They were at a side street now. Slaughter saw a German shepherd on a chain in one backyard. The dog was lunging, held back by the chain as it glared at them. Slaughter studied it a moment. Then he looked across the street toward where the lane continued. Far along it, at the end, he saw the large trees of the city park and all the places where a boy could hide, not to mention all the places in the backyards of the lane. He was looking both ways on the side street. A cruiser went by, and Slaughter nodded grimly to the driver. Then staying to the search plan, he moved across the side street and down the lane. The thing is, he was thinking, we don't have much time until it's dark, and what the hell is that kid doing now? He maybe just was angry at his mother. What, though, if he's crazy? How do we behave if someone traps him and the kid attacks again?

#### THREE

The medical examiner scowled. He had been a star in his profession once, back in Philadelphia, but that had been ten years ago. Born and raised in Potter's Field, he had left the town to go to school. A doctor's son, he'd wanted to be like his father. He had guessed that he would be a surgeon, but when he had finished pre-med, staying on at Boston for his training, he had found that diagnostics more than surgery attracted him. His father had approved. After all, those specialties were quite compatible. A lot of men could cut, but not as many could detect a cause, and a combination of both could earn considerable fees.

But the son had soon determined he would specialize much more than that. Searching out diseases not just in the living but the dead as well. Pathology, and in particular those duties strictly relegated to a medical examiner. The father had been livid, but for reasons that the son had not expected. Granted that a medical examiner had little chance to make the money that a surgeon could. "But autopsies!" the father had shouted. "You should want to cure the living, not dissect the dead!" The son had not been able to explain himself. The best that he could manage was the notion that determining the cause of death could help prevent another death just like it. But the argument was not convincing, even to himself. He sensed that there was another reason, although that reason wasn't clear to him, but he had made his choice, and despite his father's angry objections, he had continued with his studies.

Even when his father threatened not to pay his tuition, he'd persisted, working part-time, getting money any way he could. As well as with his father, he had trouble with some teachers. They felt that working with the dead was self-defeating for a doctor, and they had tried to change his mind, but he was adamant. Everyone agreed, though: he was good at what he did. He finished in the upper tenth of all his classes, and when he completed all his training, he had little trouble finding work. By then, he and his father no longer spoke to one another. He was certain he would not go back to Potter's Field. The place he chose was Philadelphia, and in five years, he rose from simply being on the staff to acting as assistant medical examiner. The hard jobs he was always given. More than that, he sought them out: the murders that were mystifying, and those deaths that no one understood, those suicides that maybe had been awkward accidents. He solved them all. It got so other members of the staff would come to watch him do his work. There were betting pools to see how long he might be stymied by a body's puzzle. Homicide detectives hoped that he would be assigned to their investigations. Reporters interviewed him. Magazines did stories on him. Once he even had an article devoted to him in *Time*.

And so his star had risen, with it self-understanding. He grew to comprehend that what attracted him were riddles from mute witnesses, the pleasures of the chase. Oh, sure, if he had stayed in diagnostics, he'd have had his share of puzzles, but the kind he worked with now were so much different, so more final and detached. He didn't have to bother with compassion, even fear, both in himself and in his patient. He could be objective, logical, and most important, uninvolved. A body there before him, he had this and this to learn about it; he would learn these things, and then this problem would be finished. Except for his excitement as he sensed that he was getting closer to the clue that he was looking for, he never felt emotion. No, that wasn't true. He often felt frustration, but excitement and frustration were related, one the polar feeling of the other, and the satisfaction of his work was in his scientific method, in his order, in the truths that he uncovered.

"After all, it doesn't matter. Nothing does," he often told himself. What profit if you diagnose a living person and that patient dies because there isn't a way to cure him? Granted, there were times when you could find out what was wrong with someone and stop the illness. But the end was still the same. If not on this occasion, maybe the next time, and finally the end was certain. Every person died. There wasn't any way to stop that. People just marked time. He couldn't bear the thought of caring for a patient and then failing.

"Self-defeat," his father had said when he first suggested that he'd like to be a medical examiner. His father had been wrong, though, for the self-defeat was not his study of the dead but how his father had prolonged the agony of someone's living. Tomorrow and tomorrow. Life is just a sequence of small losses. All those phrases now occurred to him, but back then he had not been wise enough to understand them, to call them up against his father. It was just a matter of one's viewpoint. Life was either good, or else it wasn't. In the long run, did it matter if you saved a man from this disease and spared him for another? The final truth was what he studied on the table.

Something else. A corollary. He would never have the strength to watch a patient die. He didn't have the courage. He was fearful of mistakes, and even if he made none, he was fearful of the look in someone's eyes should he be forced to pronounce a death sentence. He could never tolerate responsibilities of ultimate consequence. Certainly he had responsibilities in this profession, but if he failed, what difference did it make? A murderer would walk the streets. A suicide would never be detected. But he couldn't change what they had done; he couldn't replay time and alter things. The pain of what they did was past. He hadn't been connected with it.

The medical examiner was not so unaware that he didn't realize the causes for his attitude. His mother, for example, who had died when he was very young but not so young that he didn't remember how her body tortured her. Lung cancer. And he'd seen his father helpless to preserve her. Yes, his father the physician who was powerless when it most counted. Each day watching as she wasted. No, although he himself had long since learned to mute the power of that memory, he had not forgotten. She had been the only person close to him who'd ever died and filled him with grief. He didn't know why that should be, how his mother had made so strong a mark on him. Perhaps because he loved her, and that startled him. Because he knew a child's love had little substance. So he told himself. But if he'd really loved her, she had been the *only* one he ever loved. For sure, he didn't love his father. New thought: could it be that he had set out, insecure, to imitate his father, and then facing up to how he felt about the man, he had determined to annoy him? Self-defeat? His father maybe had been right. It could be that he himself had ruined his own chance to have a lucrative career just to get back at his father.

But he knew that wasn't true. He'd chosen this job because he liked it. The pleasure of practicing medicine without the obligations. His mind worked best without the setbacks of emotion. So his talents made him famous, but his life became a muddle. He could not commit himself to anyone. He had no use for friendship. People only let you down, he thought. Or die or get sick or leave. There were only different ways of losing. Better to be careful. So he concentrated exclusively on his work and lived alone and went out seldom. Personal distractions didn't matter either, he was thinking. Have a drink and just forget them.

One day he had been too busy for a shower. One day he had guessed he didn't need to shave. His pants went unpressed, his shoes unshined. He wasn't so slovenly that his manner and appearance were offensive, but the edge was off, the shimmer gone, and now in retrospect he knew that he had started acting like a loser. Self-defeat? Could it be that he had always been a loser, but that losing wasn't any good unless you first had been a winner? Had he courted his own losses? Or else could it be—he thought about this often—that when he had made his choice between the living and the dead he himself had started dying? Other people whom he worked with didn't have that problem, so the job was not at fault here. For a time he had a lover, but she couldn't tolerate his lifeless manner, and indeed he'd forced her to leave, certain that she'd one day leave him anyway. Besides, the dead were much more lovely. He would often go down to the morgue at night and, solitary, stare at certain corpses. Not the ones who were disfigured by a fire, say, or a traffic accident. But those who having died peacefully were much more radiant than they could ever have been when alive. The peace that passeth understanding. Quiet and at rest. A pewter sheen upon their faces and their bodies. Like some statues but much better. Or when working late at night, he'd pause before he cut a body open, meditating on perfection, and when he at last was forced to cut, he would do it lovingly, with care, so much so that, responsive to his care, the body gave up all its secrets. But the process took much longer each day. What before had taken two hours now would last a half a day. And sometimes all alone and working late, he'd occupy himself with just one body until the dawn.

So that was how they brought him down. Because when all his theorizing had been prolonged and exhausted, after he had put up all his layered explanations, he in time had come to understand his motives. He was fascinated by the dead, in love with them, and all he needed to discover that truth was one late hour's gentle touching of a young girl's lifeless body. He had looked up, and his supervisor had been standing in the doorway, watching him. There was no need for accusations or explanations. No word passed between them, but they both knew what had happened. One week later he resigned, effective when a person could be found to take his place, and without thinking, he went back to his birthplace, Potter's Field. His father had been dead by then, so it was easy to return. He sometimes thought that he had wanted to return since he'd first left the place, except his father would have been there. His credentials had been so impressive that he hadn't required a recommendation from his superior in Philadelphia. He'd asked; the local hospital had hired him.

And here he'd stayed, and here he had been happy. Understanding bred control. He settled in his father's house. He did his job, and he passed the time. He continued drinking but not as much as before. On occasion, he looked at Slaughter's sometimes puffy face and thought that Slaughter ought to cut back on the beer, but really it was he himself who liked the beer, and he at last had found a friend in Slaughter. Because Slaughter's life was his profession, as his own was, and a friendship based on work was something that the medical examiner could handle. People who were good at what they did, who related to you on that basis, seldom disappointed you. And besides, although this was a weakness, he had come to like the man, perhaps in part because he sensed that Slaughter felt that way toward him.

And so he frowned at it. The body of the cat down in the hollow. He stood along the rim and looked down at the mangled head, and it was blown apart, all right. Slaughter's magnum bullet had shattered the skull. There were bits of blood and brain and bone and fur that had been blasted back along the slope behind it. There were insects crawling on those pieces, on the carcass and the bloody skull, flies that clustered buzzing on the blood as well.

When he had parked his car and walked across the dusty field to reach the hollow, he had heard a noise down in there. He'd seen a dog run from the hollow, glancing furtively, its ears back, its tail low, as it had loped away. He had seen a bloody strand of sinew hanging from its mouth, and although he'd have to check the textbooks in his office, he was certain that he'd read somewhere that rabies could be passed on from the meat of tainted animals. He didn't have a gun. He wouldn't know how to use it even if he had one (that had been another block between his father and himself; his father was a hunter; he himself had not been interested). If Slaughter had been here now, the medical examiner would have been eager for Slaughter to shoot the dog. Either that or trap it. But that second way was risky, and the dog might be too clever for them. Better just to shoot it. Never mind who owned it. Never mind that he himself would want a living animal for observation and testing. That dog was a danger. It was running toward the cattle pens, and he was bothered by the damage that the dog could do if rabies were indeed the problem here. Oh, this soon the dog would not develop symptoms, but it certainly could leave the virus if it drank from where the cattle drank, and they would then contract it. He watched as the dog disappeared among the bushes by the cattle pens, as the cattle shifted slightly, brown shapes in a group across there, and he licked his lips and looked up at the summer sun.

It was noon, and he was thirsty, worn down by the heat. He'd left his suit coat in the car, had pulled down his tie and fumbled to open his top shirt button. Now he rolled his sleeves up, and he walked down into the hollow. Every sound he made was vivid to him, the dry sand crunching underneath his shoes—he never wore the cowboy boots so many of the townsfolk wore, his suits still those that he had owned back in the East—and he was positive that he would waste his time by doing tests on what was in a heap before him. There were only bits and hints of brain, and worse, they were contaminated, fly eggs on them now, corruption settling in. The cat had been a large one, black, a massive tom. He could understand why Slaughter had been startled when it suddenly came leaping at him, but he wished that Slaughter had shot it somewhere else besides the head. Well, that couldn't be changed, and for certain, he couldn't leave it here. In case it was contagious, he would have to seal it in a bag and then destroy it.

He waited, thinking, at last climbing back up the slope and crossing through the dust and bushes toward his car at the curb. He opened the trunk and reached in for the kit he always carried with him for emergencies. Lab coat, rubber gloves, a cap and face mask. Once he had them on, the face mask stifling in the mid-day heat, he chose a plastic bag, a pair of forceps, and he returned to the hollow. There, he used the forceps on the bits of bone and brain, dropping all those pieces in the open bag he held.

The process took a half an hour. He made sure that he found them all. Then he went up on the rim and searched among the bushes. When he was satisfied, he used a stick to push the carcass into the bag, put the stick in there as well, and noticed a piece of ragged flesh that had been hidden by the body. When he gripped it with the forceps, setting it inside the bag, he paused to guarantee that he'd been thorough. Sure, the blood that soaked the sand, dry now, rustlike, but he couldn't leave it, and he had to go back to the car again, to get the shovel in the trunk, the lye he always kept there, and fifteen minutes later he was finished, the sand scooped into the bag, the hollow pale with sprinkled lye. He walked back to his car, tied the plastic bag and put it in another bag and then inside the trunk. He put the sack of lye, the shovel, his lab coat and cap and face mask in yet another bag, careful with the gloves he took off, locked the trunk, and didn't know another way he could have done it. He would drive now to the office, go down to the furnace in the basement, and arrange for what he'd gathered to be incinerated.

Abruptly he was conscious of silence. No wind, no cars going by or people talking, no sound over at the cattle pens. Well, Saturday, he thought, there won't be much going on. But he had the odd sensation that he was not alone. Of course, he thought. My rubber gloves, my lab coat, cap, and face mask. I'd have looked like I was from another planet. Sure, the neighborhood is inside, staring past the drapes at me. But when he looked, he saw no movement at any windows, and he did his best to stop his premonition as he got in his car and drove away.

He headed toward the hospital, glancing in his rearview mirror where he saw two men come from the Railhead bar. He saw a woman emerge from a house and get in her car. He thought he saw, reflected dimly, workers from the stockpens walking down the street behind him. It seemed as if the world had once again resumed its motion the instant he left that place, and he was thinking he should get control of his imagination. Keep your mind in order.

Because really this was something that engaged him. If he didn't dare consider all the trouble that was maybe on the verge of breaking out, he found the problem in the abstract quite attractive. He was intrigued the way he once had been in Philadelphia. A riddle to be solved. A secret ready for him to discover. He was driving, glancing at a cat that perched in royal splendor on a porch rail. He was passing a young boy who walked a cocker spaniel. And because the day was hot, he leaned his elbow out the open window, his arm hairs shifting in the wind that the motion of the car made. He was almost startled by the excitement that he was feeling. Ten blocks later, he turned up the driveway toward the parking stalls behind the hospital. He waved to a man from the childrens' ward who drove out past him toward the street. He reached the back and pulled in at his parking space, getting out, his key in hand to open the trunk when something slowed him and then stopped him.

It was something that he'd grown so used to that he'd long ago stopped being aware of it. Except last night when he and Slaughter had been talking in the office, and he'd noticed it, but Slaughter had first turned to it, unconsciously reminding him, and anyway the thing had been so much in keeping with their conversation that of course he would have noticed then, but normally it simply blended with the background, and it wasn't worth consideration. Now when everything that he'd been mulling through distracted him, the sound had changed, had drawn attention to itself.

He stood motionless, his head turned, his hand still outstretched to unlock the trunk. Even when he shifted his body toward the trees back there, his hand remained outstretched and stiff until he noticed it and lowered it slowly to his side. He felt his muscles tighten. He almost couldn't make them work as he walked squinting toward the trees. In all the years he'd worked here, he had never gone back in them, never once been curious. There was a dry streambed, he knew, that in the spring was filled with rushing snowmelt from the mountains. But a flashflood was not a thing to walk near, and he'd always watched it from the distance of his parking space. The trees here all had leaves, their branches bare in the early spring, and there had been no trouble seeing. But in June now, everything was like a jungle back there, the trees thick, drooping, the bushes full and vine enshrouded, not to mention that there was a rusty fence.

He had a fear of snakes, of things that crawled and he couldn't see, but he was thinking only of the sound beyond the trees now as he reached the fence, and glancing at the thick high grass beyond it, he gripped the sagging post to balance for a foothold on the wire.

There was no need to climb the fence. The post continued sagging as he gripped it, and his weight kept pressing, and the post snapped softly, weakly, toppling toward the ground where it hung bobbing in the wires.

He looked down at ants, a hundred of them, next a thousand. They were scurrying to flee the ruptured nest inside the base of the post, rice-shaped eggs gripped by their pincers, rushing off in all directions. He lurched back, revolted. All those ugly crawling things. His skin began to itch. His mouth tasted sour. He was conscious of the irony that he could look at burned and mutilated corpses, maggots on them, and be concerned only about how much damage had occurred within the lungs, and yet he couldn't bear to see these insects and their crazy panicked scurrying below him. Well, he thought, in the morgue he had control, but here the situation governed him, and as the sound beyond the trees became even stranger, he made himself go near the fence. He stepped across the sagging fallen wires, avoiding where the ants were, staring at them even as he worked around them toward the trees.

He felt the bushes clutch his pants, and he was turning forward, stooping underneath a tree branch, soon encircled by the trees. The ground sloped: long grass, vines that clung hard to his pant cuffs. Everything was close and dark and humid. Then the trees gave out, and he was looking at the streambed. It was deep between the banks, dry, with sand, and here and there a rock or water-polished piece of driftwood. He saw tiny tracks of animals in the sand. He glanced along one track and saw movement ten feet to his right along the bank— a chipmunk up on its hind legs staring at him, in an instant darting into a hole beside a tree root. Then the chipmunk poked its head out, blinking at him.

He glanced toward the streambed once more, swallowed, and with one leg cautiously before him, he eased down the loose earth of the bank. The sand at the bottom was soft beneath him, and he didn't like that feeling, didn't like the lacerated tire he saw wedged among the silt and rocks. He was eager to get up on the other side, edging slowly up, then listing off balance, clutching at a tree root up there, but the clutching was instinctive, and abruptly he released his grip, scrambling upward, dropping to his knees and clawing.

At last, he reached the level, and he stood there, breathing, glancing all around. He brushed the dirt from his pantlegs, staring at his hands. The noise was even stranger, though, and slightly to his left, not straight ahead. He angled toward it, stooping past more trees, avoiding bushes, suddenly free of them, stark sunlight on him, open air before him, just the houses past the yards here, the white fence all along this back end of the houses.

He prepared to climb the wooden fence when he thought better. Down there to his left, the sound was even closer, stronger. From that backyard two lawns down. He walked along the fence, and then he saw it, tangled in its chain, the doghouse scratched and bitten, splinters and blood spots on the lawn, an Irish setter, and the sound it made was chilling. Not a growl exactly, not a bark. Much lower, almost speaking, deep within its throat, long and drawn out, suddenly a sequence of quick choking, then that drawl-like laryngitic moaning. He stared at the bloody lips, the froth that dripped in great gobs from their corners, and as it stopped biting at the chain and went back to the bone-revealing sore that it was chewing on its left hind leg, he gripped the fence, peered down at the unmowed yard, and gasped, desperate to control the churning in his stomach. He'd seen what he could only term the face of evil. Later he would recollect how those peculiar words occurred to him. He'd judge and weigh them, hoping to condemn their wild emotion, but he knew that they were fitting. He had never seen such open, brutal, insane evil, and his instinct was to flee, to repel the image from his sight.

Instead, he rushed along the fence until he faced another backyard, climbing over, straining to see every portion of this yard in case there was a dog in here as well, but there was nothing, just a tiny plastic wading pool, and he ran past it, hurrying along the side until he reached the sidewalk in the front, and then he swung across the next yard toward the front door of the house in back of which the dog was baying even more grotesquely.

If he'd been the man he claimed to be, he would have known what next would happen, would have paid attention to the weed-choked lawn, the untrimmed bushes, would have understood the owner here. But he was taken up with urgency. He gripped the wobbly railing, charging up the stairs. On the porch, he pressed the doorbell, but the sound of a television blared out from the open windows so he couldn't hear the doorbell. He couldn't even hear the dog now, and he pressed the button once again, staring through the screen door past the open main door in there, toward the shadowy living room. He realized that the doorbell wasn't working. As a crowd cheered on the television, he banged at the screen door. He shouted, "Hey, is anybody home?", hammering so fiercely that the wood trembled and a shadow moved in there, pale against the murky sofa, a man coming to the door.

The man was husky, naked to the waist, a can of beer in one hand. He was surly, unshaven. "Yeah, what is it?"

"Look, your dog—"

"I know. The bastard won't stop barking.'

"It needs treatment."

"What?"

"You've got to get it to a vet," the medical examiner blurted.

"Up your ass. I told the neighbors I was working on it. Hell, I even got a special collar."

"I don't—"

"One with batteries. The kind that every time the dog

barks sends a shock to stop it barking."

The medical examiner was speechless.

"Who the hell are you? I've never seen you anywhere," the man said.

"I'm . . ." The medical examiner explained who he was.

"You live around here?"

"No, I—"

"Then up your ass, I said. If this isn't where you live, why don't you mind your own damned business?"

There was no way that the medical examiner was going to make him understand. He gripped the door to pull it open, heading in.

"Hey, now wait a minute. What the hell do you think you're doing?" the man demanded, blocking him.

"I've got to use your phone."

"The beer store has one on the corner."

"There's no time."

The crowd cheered on the television. As the medical examiner squirmed to get past the man, he saw beyond the sofa where the television showed two boxers slugging at each other.

"Hey, buddy, I'm through being patient." The man shoved him hard.

"Rabies."

"Don't be nuts. The dog just had her shots."

"Christ, go back and look at her."

"The collar makes her act that way."

"I can't afford to take the chance."

The two men struggled toward the middle of the room.

"I have to phone a vet."

"If you're not out of here, you're going to have to phone an ambulance."

The medical examiner slipped past the man, dodging toward the phone that he had seen beside the sofa.

"Get out," the man ordered.

But the medical examiner was dialing.

"Okay, buddy, don't forget I warned you."

As a woman's voice came on the phone to tell him "Animal Associates," the medical examiner turned just in time to see the hand that held the beer can lunging toward him. He was vaguely conscious of the other hand that set him up and held him steady. But the blow that split his lips and shocked him backward he was never conscious of at all. He had a sense of someone moaning, and he wondered through the spinning darkness what that murky cheering was about.

## FOUR

They ran with the bloodhounds up the steep slope through the trees. The dogs were silent, sniffing as they forged up higher, and the men who held their leashes were exhausted.

"This is crazy," one man said and pulled back on the leash to slow the dog. "If we keep on like this, we'll be useless in an hour."

He was gasping, taking in long breaths, exhaling like a bellows.

"Never mind an hour. Fifteen minutes is more like it," another man said and swallowed, breathing, reaching for a tree to get his balance. "I say take it slower."

They were five miles up from where they'd left the pickup truck. They hadn't organized the search until almost three o'clock. It took that long to get their knapsacks and their dogs. Then there had been instructions, and the dogs had needed time to find the scent. The search had really started at three-thirty. Running with the weight of knapsacks, rifles, walkie-talkies, and ammunition, they had labored through the forest, climbing bluffs and crossing ridges, stumbling down and up through gorges, and a tangle of dead timber had been just about enough to finish them. They had to carry each dog through the tangle, but the dogs had not refound the scent across there, and the men had struggled with the squirming dogs to carry them back to the first edge of the tangle. Bodine must have tried to cross, then given up. But they themselves had managed to get through here. Why not Bodine? "Never mind," one of the state policemen said. "Let's just keep moving."

So they had worked higher, and although they'd only gone five miles, they'd needed several hours.

"Christ, six-thirty."

"Hey, it must be time to eat."

"Another mile yet. If this guy's in trouble, one more mile could be enough to help him."

Which was understandable, so looking at the shadows stretching darker through the forest, they moved farther, higher, through the mountains. Slower, though. They couldn't run up ridges as if they were sprinting around the local baseball field. They knew their breathing should be constant, their heartbeats steady. Keep things smooth and even. They had hurried at the start, but that had been because they were impatient. Now that this had become routine, now that it was boring, they were moving much less frantically. Something broke a branch up to their right, and they were staring, but the deer that showed itself and ran away only made them laugh.

"I don't see why that guy went up here anyhow. If it was me, if I was chasing some wild dogs, I wouldn't try it on my own."

They heard the helicopter roaring closer. It had been a muffled droning far off to their right, but now it skimmed across the trees above them, and they saw the insignia of the U.S. Lands and Forest bureau.

"Air search to police," a man's voice crackled from the walkie-talkie.

They halted on an open bluff and squinted toward a line of trees that obscured the helicopter. They had little trouble hearing it, however.

Once again the static from the walkie-talkie. "Air search to police."

The man in charge, a sergeant, gave his dog's leash to a trooper beside him. He fumbled with the straps that looped his walkie-talkie across his shoulder. Then he pressed a button and put the walkie-talkie to his ear as he leaned back against a boulder. "Roger, air search. We can hear you. What's the problem? Over."

"Is that you on the bluff I just passed?"

"Roger. Affirmative. Ten-four. Over," the sergeant answered.

The man beside him winced. He was well aware that there were special words you had to use with walkie-talkies. "Affirmative" was better than "yes," which sounded like a hiss. But he'd seen some men pick up a walkie-talkie, and they suddenly were like some god-damned hotshot actor in a police movie. "Roger. Ten-four." A smug look in their eyes like they were getting screwed while they were talking. Jesus.

A crackle from the walkie-talkie. "I just wanted to be certain. I'm done for today. The ground's too dark to see much."

Except us, the second man thought. Sure, you saw the bunch of us, all right. You're just eager to get back to town and celebrate Saturday night in a bar.

"Roger," the sergeant responded.

Christ, the second man thought.

The sergeant continued, "Anything that looked suspicious? Over."

"I checked all along the slope to the north of you. I checked the lakes up that way. Nothing. Some nice elk at Windshift Basin."

"Well, we'll keep moving with the dogs then. There's a lake another mile above us, and we'll camp there. Over."

"Just make sure you cuddle close, boys. It gets awful lonely on your own in the woods."

"We've got the dogs to keep us company. Over."

"Yeah, but you should see what I'll have. Nighty-night, boys."

"Roger. Ten-four. Out." The sergeant brought the walkie-talkie down.

"Aw, go screw yourself," the second man grumbled. He wasn't certain if he meant the man up in the helicopter or the sergeant, but the sergeant grinned at him, and so the second man decided, raising up his hand to make an obscene gesture toward the far-off roaring of the helicopter. Soon the noise dimmed, becoming fainter, at last inaudible, and the men now looked at one another. Throughout the afternoon, they'd heard the chopper roaring near them in the mountains. They had gradually become accustomed to it, at last so familiar with it that they hadn't been aware that they were hearing it. They heard it now, though, or rather heard its absence, and they missed it, somehow incomplete without its reassuring presence. "Let's get moving," the sergeant said. He reached for the leash he'd handed over, and they let the dogs go on, straining to keep up with them.

"What a way to spend a weekend," someone said.

"Saturday, and hell, we won't be back at least till Sunday evening."

"Well, if you boys worked as good as you complained," the sergeant told them, "we'd have found this Bodine long ago."

The dogs began to slacken and then cower.

## FIVE

It was crouched behind the deer cage, watching as the black and white police car reached the end of the lane, stopped a moment, and then drove toward the swimming pool. The thought of water made it gag again, and when it crawled out from its cover to be certain that the car continued moving, it saw people diving from the high board, splashing into the water, and it had to turn away to keep from retching. There were people over by the swings and slides, children and a mother. They were laughing. A man and a woman strolled toward the deer cage. In the cage, the deer had long since shifted toward the side away from it. They stared at it, their withers rippling nervously, and it was bothered by them just as much as by the people coming near. It only wanted to be on its own, to hole up somewhere safe, to stop the spasms racking through it. Finally the man and woman reached the deer cage, and it scurried through the bushes up the slope. It dimly recollected that a walkway angled across the slope above there, and it reached the walkway, wooden steps that cut up high across the slope, and it was running up them. In the sunlight, it pawed at its eyes and squinted. Once it stumbled, falling, and it scrambled up on all fours, rasping, whining. Then it reached the top, and it could see the mansion over there. Once its mother had taken it here to visit the place, a big, tall, old-time house with many rooms and stairways, and it still retained the image of those dark corners, all those sheltered crannies it could hide in. Squinting far around, glancing toward the park down there, the people, it shivered and turned toward the mansion again. It saw the trees around the place, the bushes, and the gravel driveway that led up to the front steps, and it saw the car parked in the front, and it was ducking toward the bushes, moving closer. All those shadowy rooms. The front door suddenly came open, and it paused among the bushes. Now a man came out, and he was talking to a woman. They had boxes in their hands.

"The afternoon's been slow. I don't think anyone will come up now."

"Well, I've got guests. I can't stay any longer."

They closed the door. The man reached to put a key inside the lock.

"No, I didn't tell you," the woman said. "Eva phoned to tell me she couldn't find her key."

"Well, she can get mine from me in the morning."

"No, she wants to do her work before tonight. She has to go away tomorrow."

"I can't leave the place unlocked," the man said.

"Only for ten minutes. I expected her before this."

"If vandals get here sooner, you know how the owners will react."

"From what I hear, they still have plans to sell the place. It doesn't make a difference."

"Just remember. It was your idea."

"Such a gentleman."

They started down the stairs.

It crouched behind the bushes, watching as they put the boxes in the car.

"I'll drive you home," the woman said.

"No, that's all right. I need the walk. So when's your next shift?"

"Not for two weeks. Sunday afternoon."

"They've got me chairing meetings."

"Well, I'll see you later."

Nodding, the man walked down the gravel driveway, and the woman got in her car, driving past the man. She blared her horn. The man waved, and soon both the man and car were out of sight.

It waited just a while. Then it crept out from the bushes, running toward the porch. It huddled by the steps and looked around, then scampered up the steps and turned the knob, and it was in there.

Very quiet. Everything smelled musty. It remembered the large big hallway, bigger than the living room at home, and there were tables, stacks of papers to one side, and a box where people put their money in.

Its mother had, at any rate, She had explained about historical societies and how an old house like this had to be preserved for people to appreciate the way things used to be. It hadn't understood the words exactly, but it sort of had the sense that this old place was special, and it hadn't liked the musty smell back then, but now it did.

The hall was shadowy, rooms on both sides, old-time furniture in there, guns up on the wall and maps and faded oval photographs. It listened, but there wasn't any movement in the house, and it crept forward. Now it faced a big room with the longest table it had ever seen, big-backed chairs along it, plates and glasses set out, knives and forks and more spoons than it understood, as if a party soon would be here, people eating. There were ghosts here, it was sure, but oddly, that was comforting. The staircase wound up toward the second floor, a caged-in elevator to the side. Its mother had explained about the elevator, how the platform rose without an engine. You simply had to pull down on the rope that dangled in there, and a pulley then would turn to raise you. But the cage had boards across the front, and anyway it never would have stepped inside there. All those bars. The place was too much like a trap.

It walked a little farther, pausing as the floor creaked. No, it had made that noise itself. There wasn't anybody in here, and it wondered where to go. Up the stairs or to the cellar. No, the cellar would be a trap as well, and boards creaking, it was inching up the stairs.

But it stopped as the front door opened. It turned, the daylight out there strong, painful, staring at the man who stood within the open doorway. This man had just left. He'd walked until he'd disappeared along the gravel driveway. That was why there hadn't been a warning, why there hadn't been a car sound to alarm it, and it hissed now as the man came forward.

"Yeah, that's just what I expected. Leave the door unlocked, she says. God damn it, kid, get out of here."

It hissed again.

"What's your name? I'm mad enough to call the cops."

It growled then, and the man hesitated, frowning.

"None of that damned stuff. You get your ass on down here."

One more step. The man was at the bottom of the stairs. He reached, and it was leaping, body arcing down the stairs to jolt the man and send him sprawling.

"Hey, God damn it." But the man apparently expected that it next would try to scramble past him toward the open door. The man lunged to the side to block it, his neck uncovered, and it dove in straight below the chin.

"Jesus."

They struggled. It could feel the blood spurt into its mouth. It gagged again. The taste was not unpleasant, even in a way compelling, although the choking was an agony. It chewed and swallowed, gagging.

Abruptly it couldn't breathe.

The man was squeezing at its throat. It felt the pressure in its chest. It squirmed. It twisted.

"God-damned kid."

Then teeth free, it was snarling at the hands around its throat. It tried to bite the hands but only nipped the acrid, cigarette-vile, suit-coat sleeves, and suddenly one leg was underneath it, pushing, as it flew high to one side, its body slamming on the wooden floor and rolling hard against a table.

Even so, its instinct was automatic. Turning, it scrambled on all fours and braced to spring again. The man rolled, coming to his feet. They stared at one another.

Then the man looked at the blood across his clothes. He touched his neck. "My God!" He understood now, his hands up, stumbling backward.

It leaped, but not strongly enough to drop the man, just knock him farther backward. "Oh, my God!" the man kept saying. And the open door was suddenly behind the man. The man was out there, kicking as it leapt again. Its shoulder took the kick. The jolt spread through its body. Falling, it landed on that shoulder. It crawled back and snarled.

Snarled not just toward the man but toward the carsound coming up the lane now. It could see beyond the man toward where the car was coming into view. A different car. A different woman driving. It was staring, crawling farther toward the stairs. Its shoulder wasn't working. It snarled and stumbled up the stairs. Then as it heard the car door out there squeak open, as the man glanced quickly out there, it mustered the little strength it retained and scuttled farther up the stairs. The stairs kept winding. It reached the second floor, and out of sight from down there, it huddled, tensing.

"Mr. Cody!" It heard the woman's voice outside, the rushing footsteps on the porch. "Good Lord! Your throat! The . . . Mr. Cody!"

It heard the heavy body slump to the floor.

"Never mind me. Get in there and use the phone," the man rasped. "Call the cops, an ambulance. Watch for some kid, something, on the stairs."

Panicked, much less certain now of what it should be doing, it swung to face the hallway up here, looking for a place to hide. It scurried. But at least the place was dark up here. At least its eyes no longer hurt.

SIX

"You've got to help me."

The medical examiner blinked at the shirtless man. The television news was droning.

"I don't—"

"Hey, you didn't give me any choice. I didn't mean to hit you that hard."

The afternoon came back to him. His head hurt when he moved it, and his lips and nose felt like they belonged to someone else. When he touched them, they were senseless, swollen, but he felt the blood, and he was groaning.

"Look. My dog. You've got to help me," the man said.

"What's the matter?"

"She's not moving. She just lies there, staring at me."

"Jesus, stay away from her."

"I am. My Christ, if only I had listened. Can I get it if she licked me?"

The medical examiner struggled to sit up. "When?"

"This morning. She was acting fine then."

"Wash your hands! I hope you didn't touch your mouth. You don't have any cuts she might have licked?"

"I can't remember."

"What?"

"I don't have any cuts. I can't remember if I touched my mouth."

"I told you, wash your hands." The effort of the conversation made him dizzy. He slumped back. "Use disinfectant. Mouthwash. Gargle. Change your clothes." He gripped the sofa to brace himself and stand. He fell back. Then he took a breath and made it to his feet. The blood was all across his tie and shirt. He started feeling angry, and that helped him. "Hurry up. Wash your hands." Then suddenly he thought about the hand that had split his lip and smashed his nose. He bolted down the hallway, shoving past the man who was going into the bathroom. "Get away. I've got to wash my face."

The medical examiner soaped his hands and scrubbed his face, scrubbed it until it hurt, and still he continued scrubbing. He peered at the blood that mingled with the soap upon his hands and dripped down toward the swirling water in the sink. He continued scrubbing. Then he grabbed a towel and scoured his face until the porous cloth was bloody.

"Rubbing alcohol!" he ordered, fumbling in the cabinet behind the mirror, but he couldn't find it. "Alcohol!" he shouted, and the man jerked open the door below the sink. They saw the bottle at the same time, and the medical examiner grabbed it, twisting off the cap, and splashing his nose, his lips. But he needed more. He leaned his face down sideways toward the sink. He poured. The hot sweet alcohol was flooding, burning. He snorted. Then the effort took its toll, and he sank onto his knees.

"My God, you're just as crazy as that dog out there," the man said.

"You don't know the half of it. Just wash your hands and face and gargle like I told you."

He slowly came to his feet. The man was at the sink, swabbing soap around his hands. The medical examiner cringed. Lord, I might need shots. Then he stumbled from the bathroom, down the hallway toward the kitchen. Out there, through the window, he saw the dog stretched out, the blood and foam around her mouth, slack-jawed, staring off at nothing.

That was all he needed. He groped from the kitchen toward the phone.

He had to concentrate to dial. The phone kept ringing on

the other end. At last, an answering machine told him to leave a message. What's the matter with them? Saturday. He peered down at his watch. Of course. They're only open in the morning. They won't be there this late. He was flipping through the phone book. Vets. Vets. And then he had it, dialing.

This time someone answered. A woman.

"Dr. Owens," he blurted.

"Who's calling, please?"

"The medical examiner."

"I'm sorry. He's not in right now. Give me your number. He'll call you back."

The medical examiner felt his heartbeat stop.

"No, wait a second," she said. "He's just coming in the door."

Muffled voices. Bumps and echoes as the phone was being transferred.

"Dr. Owens here."

The medical examiner identified himself. "There's a dog I think has rabies."

The vet didn't speak for a moment. "Rabies? You're certain."

"No. I told you I just think that's what it is. The dog has got some kind of collar that sends shocks to stop her from barking. Hell, this could be heat exhaustion or distemper. I don't know. You'd better get over here."

"Don't touch her."

"Hey, don't worry."

"Slaughter called and said this might turn up. I hope it hasn't."

"Well, we'll know damn sure in a little while." The medical examiner saw the man come down the hallway. He asked for the address. Then he quickly told Owens, and he hung up, and the two men tried to keep their eyes away from one another. "Turn that television off."

"*—Fifteen other steers have been discovered, disemboweled the same way. Local ranchers still are baffled,*" the announcer finished saying.

"No. I changed my mind. I want to hear this."

"*Weatherwise, the weekend has been—*"

"Turn it off."

The man went over, pressed a button, and the screen became blank, mercifully silent. The man shifted his weight from one foot to the other. "I don't know how to make this up to you. You want a beer?"

"I'd like a couple, but I can't right now." The medical examiner stared at his trembling hands.

"I didn't mean to hit you that hard. Hey, I'm really sorry."

"Just forget it."

They waited.

Thirteen minutes later, the van pulled up in front. It was white and dusty. ANIMAL ASSOCIATES, the red words said along the side. A young man got out, tall and trim. As the medical examiner hurried from the house toward the sunset-tinted street, the man yanked at the back doors of the van and leaned in to get something.

"You're the medical examiner?" the man asked, puzzled by the blood on his shirt.

"That's right."

"I'm sorry I took so long. I had to go down to the clinic for this van. I don't like taking chances."

He pulled out padded overalls, stepping into the legs, then tugging on the arms and drawing up the zipper. "Has it bitten anyone?"

"It licked its owner."

"I don't like that. What about your face?"

"The owner hit me."

"Broke your lip there?"

The medical examiner nodded.

"I don't like that either. Help me with this gear."

The vet brought out a padded helmet, its leather edges coming down around his shoulders. In the front, a wire grill kept the face protected, and the medical examiner helped the vet put on padded gloves.

"Your name's Owens?"

"That's right. Help me with these shoe protectors. Where's the dog?"

"In the back."

"Well, let's get to it."

Owens grabbed his satchel, almost like a doctor's. As they turned, the medical examiner looked up to see the shirtless man on the porch.

"That's the owner?" Owens kept walking.

"If you want to call him that."

The man stepped off the porch. "Look, I had no way of understanding."

"Never mind that. Show me where the dog is." They reached a gate along the side, and Owens told them, "On second thought, you'd better not go in there." He shut the gate behind him, walking down along the side of the house.

"It's on a chain," the medical examiner said.

Owens peered around the corner. Then he straightened, walking slowly out of sight.

The medical examiner and the dog's owner frowned at one another. Without speaking, they crossed to the next yard and walked along the fence.

The medical examiner kept staring toward the corner of the house. He saw the backyard getting bigger as his line of sight improved, and then he saw a shadow. Then he stopped as he saw Owens standing by the dog. But he couldn't see the dog too well, and so he walked a few more feet, and he was gazing at the slack-jawed, bloody, froth-edged mouth, the blinking eyes, the heaving withers. "Jesus."

"What are you guys doing?"

The gruff voice came from behind them, and the medical examiner turned to see a man in tennis clothes come out the back door, staring at them.

"Get your face back in the house," the owner of the dog said. "You're the cause of this."

"I beg your pardon?"

"This man's dog is sick," the medical examiner explained.

"Yes, I know it is. The damned thing won't stop barking."

The owner of the dog started toward his neighbor.

The medical examiner hurried to stop him. "Don't be foolish. You've got trouble as it is."

Behind them, he heard Owens saying, "What a mess," and they turned. "Whose idea was this collar anyhow?"

"The neighbors kept complaining."

"Hell, I ought to see you jailed for this." Owens set his bag down, reaching in to get a hypodermic, leaning close, preparing to slip the needle into the dog.

The dog bit his padded wrist, and Owens squirmed. "Take it easy, girl. What's the dog's name?"

"Irish."

"Take it easy, Irish."

But the dog kept its teeth clamped onto the padded wrist, and Owens had to slip the needle in with one hand while he squirmed to free the other.

Still, the dog would not release the wrist. Owens had to crouch there, waiting. In a minute, though, he tugged his wrist free, standing, watching as the dog's head settled onto the ground, its eyes closed, motionless.

"Christ, you killed her."

"Just as well as far as I'm concerned," the neighbor said on the steps behind them.

The owner of the dog again started toward him.

"I *didn't* kill her," Owens said, "although I'll likely have to."

The owner didn't know which man to turn to. "Is it rabies?"

"Rabies? What the hell?" the neighbor said on the steps behind them.

"I don't know yet," Owens said. "I'll need to get the dog to the clinic and run some tests." He pointed toward the bowls of food and water by the back door. "This dog's chain is too short. She couldn't reach her water. She could just be vicious from the heat. What the hell is wrong with you?"

No one spoke then, only stared at where the owner looked around, then glanced down at the grass. "I thought the bowls were close enough. I guess I wasn't thinking. I've had problems."

"Sure, his wife moved out last week," the neighbor said. "She couldn't stand him."

The owner suddenly began to sob. When the medical examiner avoided looking at him, he saw Owens fumbling with his thick gloves to release the chain hooked to the collar. Owens tugged to free the chain from where the dog was tangled in it. Twisting, pushing at the dog, he had the chain at last unhooked. Then he peered down at the mangled back leg, shook his head, and stooped to pick the dog up.

Still the medical examiner could hear the owner sobbing. "Let's get you inside. You've had a lot of things go wrong today."

He tried to ease the owner along the fence. The owner shoved his hand away and stared as Owens straightened with the dog.

The dog was large and heavy. Owens stumbled with the weight. The owner hurried along the fence and opened the gate to let him through.

The medical examiner frowned at the neighbor.

"Well, I didn't mean to make him cry," the neighbor said. "How was I to know?"

The medical examiner gestured with contempt, walking away.

"At least, the dog quit barking," the neighbor said.

Furious, the medical examiner kept walking. He joined Owens and the dog's owner at the van, where the owner obeyed instructions and stepped inside to spread a plastic sheet on the floor of a cage. Then he got out, and Owens set the dog in, making sure to lock the cage.

The owner wiped at his tears.

"I'll handle it from here. You'd better go back in the house," Owens said.

"I'm coming with you."

"No, I've got a lot of tests to run. I'll phone you," Owens said. "You'd be in the way."

"I promise."

"Sorry." Owens glanced at the medical examiner, then started walking toward the backyard. "I left my bag behind the house."

As Owens disappeared, the medical examiner told the owner, "Well, you heard him."

"This is *my* dog. I'm responsible."

"You should have thought of that before." And then, "I'm sorry. I didn't have to say that. Even so, he's right. There's nothing you can do. Just go back in the house. We'll call you."

"Hell, it's Saturday."

The medical examiner was puzzled.

"I'm all alone."

There was nothing the medical examiner could think to say. He turned as Owens came across the lawn, carrying his bag.

Owens peered in the van toward the dog and shook his head. "Even with that plastic sheet, I'm going to have to disinfect the van. I'm going to have to burn these clothes and get a new bag. What a mess."

"Well, maybe you won't have to. It could be this is something else."

"You wouldn't care to bet on that."

The medical examiner just shook his head.

"I thought not. Let's get moving. Do you need a ride?"

"My car is through those trees in back."

"I'll see you at the office then." Owens shut the rear doors.

Walking with him, looking in the front, the medical examiner was not surprised to see the plastic sheet that Owens had spread out where he was sitting.

"Hey, I think we ought to bring this man along." The medical examiner gestured toward the owner who was staring at the back doors of the van.

"Oh, that's just fine. That's really fine." Owens tried to keep his voice low. "Look, I did my best to play it down. I have to kill the dog to do the final tests. You want this man along to see that?"

There wasn't any need to answer.

"Fine then. I'll be at the clinic." Owens turned the key and got the engine going. Then he sighed and shook his head in disgust before he put the van in gear and drove away.

## SEVEN

Dunlap stared down at his trembling hands. Everything considered, he was doing very well, he guessed. Oh, sure, he'd started shaking, and his stomach felt like he was going to throw up, but he *hadn't* thrown up, and although he was sweating, that was maybe from the heat as much as anything. Who's kidding who? The sun is almost down. The air is cooling off. You're sweating for a drink, and buddy, do you need one. There were times when he suspected he would scream. That's just dramatics, he told himself. You were looking for a story. Now you've got it. He was not yet certain what was going on here. Rabies, maybe. Could be something more. Whatever, it was getting out of hand, and if he screwed this story up the way he'd screwed up many others, simply out of weakness, there was no one he could blame except himself. You'll get your drink. Just keep control.

This thing tonight is almost finished.

Is it? Maybe it's just getting started. And he shook his head and gripped the dashboard as the cruiser swerved sharply around the corner, skidding past the swimming pool and up the tree-lined gravel driveway.

He watched as Slaughter grabbed the microphone. "It's Slaughter, Marge. I'm almost there. Make sure you send those other units. What about the ambulance?"

"It's on its way."

"I hope so."

Dunlap focused his gaze down past the trees and toward the park spread out below him—the lake, a stream that twisted toward it, swings and slides, and cages that looked like a zoo, and people down there staring toward the siren. When he glanced ahead, the road curved, and abruptly he could see beyond the trees up to the hilltop, a wide three-story mansion up there, the last rays of the sunset glinting off the windows. The place was old, expensive, of a size that nobody could afford to build these days, the driveway curving past the front porch, columns with a roof above the driveway, like a Southern mansion, showing signs of age though, dark and rough and grainy, somehow very western all the same. He saw the cruiser that had hurried here before them, and another car, civilian, and two officers who stood at the front door, talking to somebody in there.

Slaughter skidded to a stop. Dust cloud settling, Dunlap got quickly out, Slaughter putting on his hat and hurrying before him through the dusk. They reached the front steps. These were stone, and both men rushed up, their footsteps scratching on the stone. The two policemen had already turned to them.

"He's up there on the second level," one of them said.

"Or the third. You're sure he's even up there?" Slaughter asked.

"Talk to these people."

A man was slumped inside the doorway, his shirt and suit a mass of blood, his throat ripped open, his hands clutched at his wound.

"The ambulance," a woman blurted.

"On its way. You're sure he's up there?" Slaughter asked.

"Mr. Cody—this is Mr. Cody—said the boy ran up the stairs as I stopped in the driveway."

"That's your car?"

She nodded.

"Better move it. There'll be a lot of traffic coming up here."

Even as he said that, they turned toward a cruiser speeding up the driveway. Just behind it, siren wailing, came the ambulance.

"Can you walk?"

The man nodded, struggling weakly to get off the floor.

"Here, let me help you. I don't want you in the way if something happens." Slaughter turned to face the two policemen. "Watch those stairs. Make sure the boy doesn't get away." Slaughter held the man and worked with him across the stone porch, then down the steps. Two attendants ran from the ambulance, policemen from the other cruiser running with them.

"Is there any place to get down from the second story?" Slaughter asked the woman who was helping him to move the man out of danger.

"A roof above the servants' quarters in the back. I don't know how he'd jump down and not hurt himself."

"The trees around the house. Are there any he could lean to and climb down?"

"I never thought . . . I just don't know."

"The back," Slaughter told the two policemen coming toward him. "Make sure no one leaves the building. It's the kid we're looking for."

"The kid?"

Slaughter realized that these two men had not been with him at the boy's house. "Never mind. Just make sure no one leaves. Be careful of the roof above the servants' quarters."

Slaughter gave the injured man to the two men from the ambulance. They stared, and Slaughter looked down at the blood across his own hands and his shirt. "A young boy bit him. That's right, isn't it?" he asked the woman.

She was nodding.

"Bit me," Dunlap heard the injured man repeating, his voice distorted, rasping. Added to what he'd been feeling, Dunlap was fearful that the jagged throat would do the job and make him sick. He had to glance away.

More sirens, two police cars skidding up the gravel driveway, a dust cloud rising behind them. Slaughter hurried toward them.

Dunlap frowned in the middle of it all. The two men from the ambulance had opened out the back and set the injured man inside. The woman was inside her car and moving it. Slaughter stood between the cruisers, talking to the officers who'd just arrived.

Dunlap turned to face the mansion, squinting through the dusk toward the two policemen at the front door. This was all too much. He was shaking even worse as he walked toward the woman who was getting from her car where she had moved it to the side.

"What *is* this place?"

"The Baynard mansion."

"Who?"

And Dunlap learned then about Baynard who had been the richest man around here. Back in 1890. "He had cattle all across the valley, and he built this place up here to suit a Southern woman he had married."

There was something automatic in the way she said it, Dunlap thought. As if she'd said it many times before. He listened with wonder as in bits and pieces she explained how Baynard had brought from the South the wood, the furniture, the bushes, everything to make his wife feel more at home. And then his wife had gone back South one summer where she died. Either that, or else she left him, and he lied about her dying.

"No one knows for sure," the woman said. "We've tried to find the record of her death. We never managed. She had reasons if she left him. He was hardly ever home, tending business, working as a senator. Plus, there were rumors about certain kinds of parties on the third floor. But he said she died, and everyone agreed to that, and he came back and never left the house again."

Dunlap was amazed that she seemed more concerned with what she said than with the preparations going on around them. He learned how people said that Baynard wandered through the house for days on end. The cause of death was claimed to be a heart attack, but everyone suspected he just drank himself to death. And one thing more—the rumors that he killed her, that she told him she was leaving, and an overbearing man like him, he flew into such a rage that she was dead before he even knew he'd struck her. Then he hid the body, and he wasted in his grief. At last he killed himself, and people in the family hushed it up.

"But those are rumors, as I said." The woman shrugged. "Nobody ever proved it, though in recent years they looked for her. They never were successful."

"But back in eighteen-ninety . . . how come you know all about this?"

"I'm a member of the Potter's Field Historical Society."

"I still don't understand."

So she explained. "No one lives here. Baynard had two children. They grew up to manage the estate. Then *they* had children, and this new set gave the mansion to the county to avoid the taxes. They're not very wealthy now. They live in houses down the hill beside the swimming pool. We've fixed this place up just the way it used to be. The plumbing's from the eighteen-nineties. We even shut the power off. To get around at night, you have to use a flashlight, either that or candles or a lantern if you want to be authentic."

Dunlap faced the mansion. Oh, that's swell, he thought. So now we've got a haunted house. The only thing that's missing is a thunderstorm.

Well, there wouldn't be a storm, but sundown would do just as fine. He saw the orange distorted disc where it was almost behind the western mountains. In a while, the grounds would be completely dark, except for flashlights, headlights, maybe even candles, lanterns as this woman had suggested, and the search up through the mansion for the little boy. He felt his scalp tighten as the woman said beside him, "Whose child is it?"

"I don't know."

Exhausted, Dunlap walked toward Slaughter, who spoke to four policemen.

"We need nets," Dunlap heard as he came closer.

"Nets?"

And Dunlap saw that it was Rettig, standing with the young policeman Dunlap had gone to Slaughter's with this morning. That seemed several days ago.

"You heard me. Nets. You think that we should club him, do you?" Slaughter asked. "Or shoot him?"

"But nets, I don't know where you'd find them."

"Try a sporting-goods store, or that zoo down in the park. Rettig, you're in charge of that. The rest of you, I want you watching both sides of the mansion. Let's get moving."

They stared at Slaughter. Then they hurried toward the mansion.

"Hold it," Slaughter told them.

They spun to face him.

"Give your keys to this man. I want your headlights on the building."

They glanced at Dunlap who had not expected this. Instinctively, he held his hand out. Then he had a set of car keys. Mindless, he expected more, but then he realized that Rettig would take one car. These keys fit another. Slaughter's was the third car, and the fourth had been driven by the two policemen who were in the mansion. They separated to watch the sides as Slaughter shoved a ring of keys at him.

"You understand?"

"I think so," Dunlap said. "I'll spread the cars out so they're pointed toward the windows."

"Run the engines. I don't want the batteries to die. And use the searchlights by the sideview mirrors."

"What about the woman's car?"

"You've got the right idea."

Dunlap nodded, running toward the cruisers. Slaughter's car he recognized, and Rettig now was driving down the gravel driveway, siren wailing. Dunlap went toward the car beside where Rettig had been parked, and got in, fumbling for a key to fit, and started the engine. In a while he understood that someone else could just as easily have done this, but the tactic was a way for Slaughter to distract him.

It helped. There wasn't any doubt about that. Breathing quickly, taken up with interest, Dunlap adjusted to the burning in his stomach. He was glad to be in motion, driving the cruiser toward the mansion, aiming straight ahead and stopping where he judged that the headlights would be most effective. He groped down to turn them on. He found the switch upon the searchlight, and he flicked it, and this right side of the mansion, almost to the second story, was bright against the dusk.

He got out, running now toward Slaughter's car and did the same, this time aiming toward the left side of the mansion, and the place was lit up there as well. The woman had been watching, and she didn't need to have somebody tell her. She was getting in her car to move it once again, aiming toward the front door, and the sun was down below the mountains, the park a murky gray below him, but the windows reflected all the headlights, and people wouldn't have to stumble in the darkness.

Dunlap heard another car. He thought it was a cruiser, but the siren wasn't wailing, and he didn't see the silhouette of domelights on the roof. As it stopped where he was watching, he could see the mother and the father. Oh, dear God, no.

They scrambled out. "Where's Slaughter?"

"I'm not certain."

Even as he said that, Slaughter came out from the mansion, standing on the porch, the glare of headlights on him, staring at them. He and the parents approached each other, the parents hurrying.

"You shouldn't be here," Slaughter told them. Dunlap saw that he was angry. "How'd you know?"

"We have a neighbor with a police radio. Have you found him?"

Slaughter pointed toward the upper stories. "He's in there. That's as much as I've been told. I'm asking you to go back home and wait to hear from me."

Dunlap thought that Slaughter, standing in the headlights' glare, seemed to age a dozen years, his cheeks sagging, dark lines underneath his eyes.

"But why should he be hiding? Let me go inside and talk to him," the woman said.

"No, I don't think so." Slaughter looked down at the ground and scraped a bootsole in the dust. "I think that you should let me handle this." He looked at them.

"You heard my wife. She's going up to talk to him," the husband said.

"I'm sorry. I can't let you."

"That's what you think."

The husband and wife moved forward. Slaughter stepped ahead to cut them off.

"Those headlights, those police cars. Hell, you've scared him half to death," the husband said.

"I didn't want to tell you, but you evidently haven't heard the rest of it. Your son attacked again. A man this time. The man was bitten in the throat."

The wife froze, her mouth open. "Oh, my God."

The husband gasped.

"The man is over in that ambulance. Go take a look, and then you'll know why I can't let you in there."

They turned toward where Slaughter pointed as the two white-coated men stepped from the back of the ambulance and shut the doors.

"We've done all we can here," one of them shouted.

Slaughter nodded, and the two men rushed to get inside the front. The siren started as the engine roared, the lights went on, and they were swerving in a circle, speeding down the gravel driveway.

Dunlap watched until he couldn't see it anymore. He turned and saw the woman crying.

"Please. I think that you should leave here," Slaughter said.

"I want to stay," the woman sobbed.

Slaughter raised both arms and let them flop down loose against his sides. "At least stay in the car. The best thing you can do is aim your car lights toward the house. And please, don't get in the way. We've got too much to do. I promise, we'll watch out for his safety."

She wept as her husband held her, both of them nodding.

"Thank you," Slaughter said.

They moved weakly toward their car.

And then they heard it. Everybody did. They all turned, mother, father, Slaughter, Dunlap, the policemen by the house, staring toward the upper levels.

Deep inside, above there, from which floor wasn't certain, something, someone started howling. It was like a coyote or a dog, a wolf up in the mountains, worse though, mournful, hoarse and hollow, rising, baying, howling, then diminishing, then rising once again.

It went on two more times like that, chilling, echoing from somewhere deep above there. Dunlap felt his backbone shiver. Then it ended, and the night, except for idling engine motors, finally was quiet.

"What the hell was that?" a man blurted from the right side of the mansion.

"I'm not sure I want to know," another shouted back.

And Slaughter started racing toward the front door of the mansion.


EIGHT


The state policemen huddled frightened by the fire. They had planned to reach the lake by sunset, but the dogs kept holding back and whimpering, and the men had traveled slower than they'd wanted. Soon dusk was thick around them, and they never could have seen Bodine even if he'd been ten feet away from them. They had struggled through the underbrush, their arms and legs scratched by bushes, and the dogs had held back so fiercely that the men were forced to grab the dogs and carry them.

"These dogs of yours are really prizes," one man told the sergeant.

"I don't understand it. They don't act this way without a reason."

"Sure, they figure they've gone far enough today. They figure it's about time we carried them."

"A cougar maybe."

"Down this low?"

"A bear then."

"Come on, Charlie. These dogs just gave out on us. Admit it."

But the sergeant didn't want to. He was speechless for a moment, a dog held in his arms as he worked through the underbrush. "All right, what about those wild dogs we've been looking for? Maybe *they're* what my dogs are smelling."

And everybody else apparently had thought of that already because no one spoke then, and their lack of banter was self-conscious as they struggled through the bushes.

One man tumbled, breaking branches, groaning as the dog yelped in his arms beneath him.

"Watch my dog."

"Your dog? For Christ sake, what about me?"

"Well, I know plenty of guys like you, but I'll never get another dog like that one."

"Thanks a lot."

"No, what he says is true," another said. "He'd never get another dog so lazy."

And that seemed to bring their spirits back. They laughed a little, waiting as the fallen man got up and struggled to lift the dog.

"Well, the dog isn't stupid anyhow," someone said. "He figures why walk if someone'll carry him."

And that helped even better. They were laughing freely as another trooper ordered, "Quiet."

"What's the matter?"

"Listen to those noises. Off there to the right."

They wrestled with the dogs to keep them silent, staring toward the darkness, and they heard it. Branches breaking, fir-tree needles brushing. Not a lot of noise and not too loud, not even close, but there was something nonetheless that they heard moving through the murky forest to the right.

And then it stopped.

The dogs struggled harder in their arms.

"It could be nothing."

"Well, I don't intend to wait here until I know. That lake can't be too far ahead."

The sergeant chuckled. "Some tough bunch I brought with me. A little noise, and you boys start to panic."

"You're the one who mentioned those wild dogs."

"But think about it. Five of us. Our own dogs. Nothing's going to bother us."

"So you agree then that those wild dogs could be out there watching us?"

"No. I agree to nothing. Except that it's late and I'm tired. Let's get moving."

"That's exactly what I said. Let's get the hell out of here."

Someone snickered then, and they continued through the underbrush. They glanced from side to side, and when another noise came louder from the right, they increased speed.

"Heavy pine cones."

"No, the sky is falling. Don't you know that?"

"Just shut up."

At last they were in the open, staring at the murky ripples on the lake. They had a distance yet to go, about a hundred yards, but there were hardly any bushes, just a few trees by the lake, and even in the darkness, they were more at ease now, walking with less tension toward the lake.

They heard a branch snap behind them, and they turned but kept on walking. As they reached the lake, they sensed the glow before they saw the moon begin to show above the mountains.

Their inclination was to build a fire, but they had to stake the dogs first, to take care that their leashes were secure. Then they had to feed the dogs, but only one man was required for that, so they let the sergeant do that while they looked around for firewood.

There wasn't much. People often camped up here, and there weren't many trees by the lake, the dead wood long since gathered, so the men, despite their apprehension, had to go back to the forest. They used flashlights, scanning the trees and bushes first before they stepped in, gathering dead branches, pine cones, fallen leaves, going back, their arms full, toward the sergeant and the dogs beside the lake.

"Well, what's the matter?" one man asked the sergeant.

"They're not eating."

"No wonder. Look at what you gave them."

"Kibble. That's what they eat every night."

"They must want something else."

"They understand they have to eat what they're served."

"I wish my kids would understand that."

Another man walked over. "You don't mean to tell me I packed that dog food up here just so your damned pooches could turn their noses up."

"They look a little sick to me," the first man said.

"No, they're not sick. They're scared," the sergeant said, and since until now he hadn't acknowledged that there might be trouble, they were struck by his remark. They stood there facing him, then glancing at the dogs.

"Well, never mind. Let's get that fire started." But the second trooper said that very faintly, and he turned to where the last two men were working on the fire.

They fumbled with matches, trying to ignite the leaves. One hand shook a little, and a match went out. The other match kept burning, though, and soon the flames spread through the leaves and pine needles, crackling toward the branches, and the branches now were burning, their large flames spreading toward the logs above them.

The men grouped around the fire, holding their palms out, rubbing them together, then rubbing their arms and shoulders. They glanced at the shimmer on the lake, at the ripple of the fire's light across the trees. They looked at the dogs, then at the darkness around them. It was several seconds before one man said what everybody else was thinking.

"We don't have a lot of wood."

"For now it's plenty."

"But in an hour . . ."

"Damn it, then, let's get some more. I'm hungry."

Even with the crackling of the fire, they heard a noise back in the forest.

"You go do it. I'll stay here and fix the supper," one man said.

"Thanks a lot for volunteering."

The sergeant patted one of his dogs and told it, "That's all right. I'm with you." Then he moved toward his men at the fire. "So you want to do the cooking? That's just fine. You stay and help him. You and you come with me."

They surprised him when there wasn't any argument. The two men he had chosen were reluctant, that was true, but nonetheless they turned and followed where he led them toward a section of the forest where the noises hadn't been. They aimed their flashlights through the trees before they went in for more wood, and this time they came out with big chunks, stout and heavy branches that would last them. Just to guarantee that the job was done, they made three other trips, always to a different section of the forest, and they came back, dropping wood where they had put the rest, and they could smell the coffee boiling.

"Not too hot. I don't like coffee that's been burned."

"Well, you can do the cooking then."

"I wanted to, but you were too afraid to get the wood. I did it for you."

"That's the last I want to hear about that. Everybody did his job," the sergeant said. He gingerly drew the coffee pot a little farther from the fire. "Ow," he said and reached his fingers to his mouth.

"Here, use these gloves."

They heard three noises then, in three separate sections of the forest.

But the sergeant, although he stiffened, didn't look. "So what's for supper?"

They frowned toward the forest.

"I asked you what's for supper," the sergeant said.

"Oh. . . . Spaghetti. Freeze-dried sauce."

"That sounds real fine."

The dogs were whimpering again, though, and the sergeant tried but couldn't hide his worry now. The moon was higher. He went over to the dogs and patted them again. "I let them drink some water from the lake. I wonder if they're still a little thirsty."

From the three separate places in the forest, they heard noises. Then, a distance to their left, they heard a fourth sound.

"This is stupid. This is just our imagination," one man said.

"Those noises? Hell, they're not my imagination."

"No, I mean what's causing them."

"Deer or maybe elk?"

"It's possible," the sergeant said. "They come down here at night to drink. They see us here and don't know what to do. Your water's boiling, by the way."

They looked down at the pot beside the fire.

"Right. I wasn't thinking." And the man in charge of cooking paused a moment before fumbling in his pack, then pouring noodles into the boiling water.

"Hey, you said spaghetti."

"What's the problem? Noodles are the same."

"Well, maybe they're the same to you. But—"

"Quiet."

And they listened to the noises from the forest.

"That's not deer, if you ask me."

"I *didn't* ask you."

"You're all crazy," someone said. "I've camped here a dozen times. I even brought my wife and kid once. You hear noises like that from the forest all the time."

"So how come you picked up your rifle?"

"I'm just checking that I didn't get some dirt in it."

"Good idea. I think I'll check mine as well."

"Now I've had just about enough," the sergeant said.

They turned to him.

"First of all, those noodles need some stirring. Second, if you wave those guns around, you're going to end up shooting somebody. Take it easy. What Jack says is true. You hear those noises in the forest all the time."

They stared at him.

"I'll help you with the sauce," the sergeant said. "Here, someone fill that plastic sack with water. Put more wood on the fire."

It was obvious what he was doing, trying to distract them, but they did what they were told, and everything was better for a moment, although the man who went down to the water's edge made sure he didn't stay too long. They heard him splashing by the lakeshore, and he came up toward them, water dripping from the plastic sack.

"Let's figure on the worst," the sergeant said. "Suppose it is wild dogs. They're not about to come at us. Hell, higher in the mountains, I've seen wolves so close their eyes were lit up by the fire. But they never came in toward us. They're just curious. The main job is to find Bodine. If you boys still are nervous when you bed down, we'll arrange to have a guard in shifts. That's fair enough?"

They thought about it, slowly nodding.

"Stir those noodles like I told you."

"I once knew an Indian," a man said.

"Good for you."

They laughed.

"No, just listen. He did odd jobs for my father when my father was alive and had the ranch. The Indian was David Sky-hawk, and I felt about him as if he was my brother. Oh, that

Indian was something. Six-foot-three and built like some thick tree trunk. He's the man who taught me how to shoot and hunt and fish. My father never had much time for that. Well, anyway, he used to take me camping. In the summers we'd go up here, sometimes for a week or more. We'd often go up so high that I'd swear to God nobody else had ever been there. And he told me lots of things about these mountains. Once we camped so far we needed horses. We rode up, leading pack mules till we reached this crazy draw. It wasn't much, just steep slopes like a V, a stream that wound along the bottom, boulders on the ridges. Hell, there wasn't any undergrowth. There wasn't much of anything. The only reason we chose it was a kind of gametrail that would take us to the high end, and we started up the gametrail when the horses went crazy. I was only twelve then, so if only *my* horse had gone crazy, that wouldn't have proved much. Skyhawk's horse began to act up too, though, and no matter what we tried, we couldn't get those horses up the gametrail. They were whinnying and shying back. Then the pack mules started acting up. They tried to turn, and there was hardly any room to do that. We were scared they'd lose their footing and tumble down the slope, so we dismounted, and we kept our hands across the horses' muzzles while we squirmed around to go back down the gametrail. Even as it was, we almost lost one pack mule. I asked Skyhawk what was wrong, and he just said that we should try another passage."

"That's some story."

No one laughed, though.

"I'm not finished. So we went back to the entrance to the draw and found another way, and all day I saw Skyhawk glancing past his shoulder toward where we had come from, and I asked him again what was wrong, but he just wouldn't answer. Everything went fine from then on. We came to a spring, and it was nearly dark then, so we camped and made a fire just like now, and we were eating, and I asked him once again. He almost didn't tell me, but he shrugged at last and said it was a superstition. There were places in these mountains where we shouldn't ever go, he told me. Places like that draw back there. You didn't know until you got up in them, and you never saw a bird or animal, but even then you might not notice if you didn't have a horse or dog or something like that with you. They could sense the trouble right away. There wasn't any way to keep from sensing it. They simply wouldn't go up in those places. If you tried to force them, they'd start acting crazy like our horses had back in that draw. 'What causes it?' I asked him, and he said he had no idea. His people knew that there were certain places that you never went to, and they didn't question that tradition. Spirits maybe. Some terrible thing that once had happened there. The point was that they marked those places and they didn't go there. Some bad medicine, he said, and Skyhawk was no dummy. He'd been to school. He knew the difference between fact and superstition, but he said the only difference was that people hadn't learned the facts behind the superstition. They just understood the consequences. He said that he had seen a whole pack train go crazy in a mountain meadow once. He'd seen a herd of elk go crazy like that once as well. The year before, he said, he'd gone out camping by himself. He'd pitched his tent and gone to sleep, and for no reason, he suddenly woke while it was dark and found that he was shaking, sweating. He crawled from his tent and packed his gear. He went as fast as he was able through the darkness to a different section of the mountains."

Now the man stopped, looking at them.

"That's the story?" someone asked. "Christ, what the hell was that about?"

"The point is, he'd been to that spot many times. It was a special place for him. But he said that those spooky feelings sometimes show up where they shouldn't be. They move, he told me, and he never went back to that site again."

"For Christ sake, that big Indian was fooling you. He was telling ghost stories by the campfire."

"No, I'm positive he wasn't fooling. He was serious."

"Hell, you were only twelve."

"That Indian was close to me. He never played that kind of joke. And anyhow, I saw the way those horses acted."

"So they smelled a cougar or a snake."

"Or something else."

"Hey, I know. Bigfoot."

They laughed.

"Yeah, that's right. That Indian was frightened by a Sasquatch."

They laughed even harder.

"You know, Freddie, sometimes that big mouth of yours makes me want to smash it in."

Now none of them was laughing.

"Take it easy," the sergeant said.

"No, the boy here wants to teach me."

"That'll do, I said," the sergeant told them. "We've got problems without starting in on one another."

And they did what they were told, because the noises were much louder now, and everyone was turning.

"Now you've really got us jumpy. You and those damned stories about spooks."

The rest of them were picking up their rifles.

"Supper's ready."

"Save it."

"I don't know," the sergeant said. The dogs were whimpering. The moon was higher. "Maybe that's Bodine. If he's been hurt up here, he might have seen our fire and tried crawling toward it. That would explain the noises we've been hearing."

"He'd have shouted."

"Could be he's not able."

"But the noises are from different sections."

"There's his wife and son, remember. Could be all three of them are hurt. Maybe separated."

"That's a lot of 'could be's."

"But at least an explanation."

The noises became louder.

"Hell, I'm going out there. I want to find out what that is," the sergeant said.

"I don't think that's a good idea."

"It's the only one we've had. And anyway, suppose it is Bodine. We've got to help him." The sergeant looked at them. "I can't order you, I guess. Is anybody coming with me?"

They glanced toward the ground, toward the dogs, anywhere except toward the sergeant.

"Yeah, okay. If no one else will, I'll volunteer." It was the man who'd just told the story. "This is getting on my nerves just waiting here."

The sergeant smiled. "That's fine. I'm glad to have you."

So they clutched their rifles, and they started from the campfire toward the darkness. Out there, they could hear the noises.

"Hey, be careful," one man said.

"Don't worry."

The sergeant and his companion now had disappeared beyond the firelight. Those who stayed beside the fire heard the footsteps brushing through the mountain grass. The distance was sufficient that in a moment the weak sound didn't carry, and the three men stood there staring at the darkness, and they waited.

"They should reach the forest soon."

"Just give them time."

"The sauce is burning."

One man stooped and grabbed a glove to pull the pan out from the fire's edge.

"They should turn on their flashlights."

"Just give them time, I said. They'll want to save the batteries. They'll need them for a lot of hours yet."

But there were no lights near the forest.

"Okay, I'm convinced. They're taking too long. They've had too much time to reach the forest."

At once they heard barking.

"What's that?"

"They're in trouble. Let's go help them."

"Wait. We're still not sure yet."

"What the hell's the matter with you? They're in trouble."

The man who had stooped to move the sauce was clutching his rifle. "I'm not going to wait here while they need me." He moved toward the forest. Then he turned and looked at them. "You're coming?"

They hesitated.

"To hell with you."

He continued moving forward.

"Use your flashlight."

He was just beyond the firelight as the last two men heard the howling. Not just barking as before, but howling.

"No!" somebody shouted from the darkness out there. "No, stay back!"

The howling intensified. Then they heard the rifle shot.

"No! Stay back! My God, no! Run!"

They started backing toward the fire, staring toward the darkness. There were sounds of movement in the darkness to their right and left. They lurched farther back, staring, aiming. As the snarling figures hurtled toward them, one man fired, but he was overpowered, and the other man kept stumbling back. He felt cold water in his boots and realized that he'd stepped into the lake. He was shooting, tugging at his rifle's bolt and shooting yet again, his eyes unsteady from his panic, peering at the swirling howling figures on the lakeshore, but the water held them back as he kept shooting. He dropped one and then another, and he worked the bolt and pulled the trigger, and the pin snapped down on empty. All his other bullets were inside his knapsack by the fire. The figures twisted, snarling, on the shore. He couldn't see them clearly, only made out silhouettes against the fire behind them, heard his partners screaming off there in the darkness as he drew his handgun, eager now to save his bullets for their final rush at him. The water. Sure. They don't like coming in the water. Otherwise they would have charged me. In a rush, he waded farther out, and suddenly, attentive only to what faced him on the lakeshore, he ignored what might be rising behind him, lost his balance as the muck beneath him sloped much deeper, and he fell back, completely swallowed by the water.

NINE

Everything was speeding up. The medical examiner didn't have the time to think things through, to make sure that he did things properly. When Owens left to take the dog down to the clinic, for example, he himself had stayed behind to calm the owner. All the while he stood there talking with the man, at last walking with him toward the house, the medical examiner wanted to rush through the streets to get to Owens and to watch him do the tests. At the same time, he was thinking that he ought to get in touch with Slaughter, to tell him what was going on. But *what* was going on? He didn't know yet. There was nothing positive. For all he could predict, the tests would indicate some other problem, and he didn't want to trouble Slaughter, didn't want to bother him without a reason. So he'd gone inside the house and stayed there briefly until he'd reassured the owner. Then he hurried from the house ("Don't go out in the backyard. You could be infected by the doghouse or the chain.") and frantically realized that he'd left his car at the hospital. He ran through the backyard of the house next door. The man in tennis clothes came out to tell him, "Hey, if I'd wanted people cutting through here, I'd have put in a sidewalk." But the medical examiner didn't answer. He simply clambered up the fence and jumped down on the other side, racing through the long grass toward the trees and then the dry creek. He no longer cared about the snakes or other things that might be hiding there. He thought only about his car, about the tests that Owens soon would be performing.

He scrambled from the dry creek, through the trees and bushes toward the fence that he had toppled, jumping across the ants' nest, running to reach his car. But as he stood there, breathing hard, fumbling in his pocket for his keys, he suddenly remembered the objects in the trunk of his car: the plastic bags, the dead cat, and the blood-soaked dirt. How much danger did they pose? He couldn't take the chance. They might be so contaminated that they'd spread the disease. Until he had time to examine them, he needed to make sure that they were safely stored in medical-waste containers.

The process took twenty minutes. Only then was he able to hurry to his car and speed away. He swerved up the driveway toward the back of the veterinary clinic. The sun had set now. In the darkness, except that the rear doors were closed and Owens' van was parked before them, this was much like when he'd come here Friday morning, seeing old Doc Markle dead and staring at the mangled steer, when everything had started for him. He skidded to a stop beside the van and jumped out. He gripped the door beside the two big double-doors, and Owens hadn't locked it. As he rushed inside, he squinted from the blazing lights and was mindful once again of Friday morning. Had it started only yesterday? He saw the dog up on the table, a protective plastic sheet beneath it, Owens there beside it in his lab coat and his face mask.

Owens turned to him, his voice muffled by the face mask. "The dog was dead before I got here."

"Is that common?"

"Sometimes the paralysis can set in very quickly."

The medical examiner understood what Owens was referring to. An animal with rabies would go through several stages. First it acted normally until the virus worked along the nerves. Then the brain became infected, and the victim was excited, furious. At last the virus spread back through the total nervous system, and the animal was lethally paralyzed.

"But I saw it in the active stage. Several hours later, and it's dead? Paralysis shouldn't be that quick."

"Maybe. I agree with you. This could be something else," Owens said. "You'll find a coat and face mask in that locker over there."

The medical examiner went across to get them, also finding a pair of rubber gloves. He put them on, and he was conscious of the buzzing lights up in the ceiling as he walked back to the table.

"First, let's get this collar off." Owens fumbled to unsnap it, staring at the battery attachment. "What I'd like to do to that guy." He set it aside. "You ought to meet some people who come in here, wanting us to make their dog mute, cut its voice box out, its vocal cords. Hell, I'd like to cut on them. At least they wouldn't talk so much then. And they wonder why a dog without a voice will bite somebody when it's got no other way to warn him off." Owens' face was red above his mask. He shook his head. "Well, let's get to it."

"How can I help?"

"I need that scalpel."

Four quick strokes, and Owens peeled the scalp off. They stared at the blood-smeared skull.

Then the drill. Owens flicked the switch. The bit was whirring, grinding through the bone. Four holes, widely spaced to form the corners of a square. And then the saw. Owens used it neatly, its motor buzzing as he cut from one hole to another, swiftly, gently, not too deeply. Then the job was done, and he was prying at the skull bone.

"Well, the brain is swollen and discolored. You can see that slight pink color. Indications. On the other hand, distemper sometimes looks like that. I need to take the brain out and dissect it."

The medical examiner again handed him the scalpel, then forceps, and Owens placed the brain in a glass dish on the table.

"Ammon's horn," the medical examiner said.

"That's right." Owens cut past the hippocampal region. Then he had it. "You can do the slides."

"Which way do you want them? Pressed or done in sections?"

"The sections take too long. Just do impressions. What we're looking for will show up just as well."

So the medical examiner, instead of placing tissue from that portion of the brain into fixing fluid and embedding it within paraffin, a process that took several hours, simply pressed a bit of tissue on the slide and smeared it evenly, then looked around to find a microscope.

"Over by that cabinet."

The microscope had a jar of Seller's stain beside it. The medical examiner put stain across the specimen to make sure that what he was looking for would stand out in contrast. He arranged the slide and peered down through the lenses.

"Can you see them?" Owens asked.

The medical examiner kept peering.

"What's the matter? You should see them."

But the medical examiner just turned to him and shook his head. "I think you'd better look."

"You mean you didn't see them, and we have to do the other tests?"

"I mean that you should have a look."

Now Owens frowned as he peered down through the lenses.

What the medical examiner had looked for was some evidence of Negri bodies. Negri was a scientist in Italy who first identified them in the early 1900s. They were tiny, round, and sometimes oval bodies in the protoplasm of the nerve cells in that portion of the brain called Ammon's horn. No one knew exactly what they were. In current theories, they were either rabies virus particles, or else degenerative matter from the cells affected by the virus. Maybe both. But seeing them was certain proof that rabies was at work here. And the medical examiner had seen them. On the other hand, he maybe hadn't.

"I don't get it," Owens said. "Something's wrong here. These things shouldn't look like that."

The medical examiner understood. He watched as Owens peered down through the microscope again. Because the things he'd seen were neither round nor oval. They were oblong with an indentation on one side.

"They look like god-damned peanuts," Owens said. "What's going on here?"

"This could be some related virus."

"What? You tell me what."

"I just don't know."

"You bet you don't, and I don't either. Rabies is something I'd recognize, and you can bet there's nothing in the books about these things we're looking at."

"We'll have to do the antibody test."

"It takes a couple of hours, and the mouse test takes at least a week. I want to know what this thing is."

"We have to guess for now it's rabies. Or a virus that has all its symptoms."

"Which is fine if no one were exposed to it," Owens said. "But what about that owner? And yourself? If this is rabies, you'll have to take the serum shots, but we don't know if they'd do any good."

They studied one another, and the medical examiner reached up to touch his mask, the swollen lip beneath it. He'd forgotten. Or more truthfully, he'd tried to keep from thinking of those shots. "I'll take them anyway."

"But what if they don't work well with the virus? What if there's a bad reaction?"

"Hell, if I've already got it, I'll be dead soon anyway. What difference does it make?"

The medical examiner suddenly remembered something that the owner had first told him, that he'd let slip by in the excitement, something that the rabies serum shots reminded him about.

"He said his dog had been inoculated."

"What?"

"The owner. He mentioned that the dog had received its shots."

"What's his name?"

The medical examiner told him.

"Okay, there isn't any other animal clinic, so his file will have to be here. Try some other slides. Make sure we didn't do them wrong. I'll come back in a minute." Owens hurried toward the door that led down to the offices in front.

The medical examiner obeyed the instructions he'd been given. His legs were shaking as he stumbled toward the microscope. He peered at all the slides, and each one was the same, and he was really scared now.

Owens pushed the door open so forcefully that the medical examiner flinched.

"He was right." Owens had a file in one hand, raising it. "That dog is five years old. It had its puppy shots, its boosters every year."

"Well, could the boosters be the cause of this? Contamination in the vaccine?"

"I don't know, but sure as hell I'm going to learn."

"Even if the vaccine were prepared correctly, could it have been so strong that it caused the virus?"

"In the case of rabies, maybe. With a weak dog. One chance in a hundred thousand. But I don't know how the vaccine would produce the thing we're looking at."

"One chance might be all this thing might need."

They frowned at each other.

"Look, I've got to make a call." The medical examiner grabbed the phone and dialed. Marge was answering. "I've got to talk to Slaughter."

"He's been looking everywhere for you," she said. "He's at the Baynard mansion."

"What?"

Then she told him the rest, and he felt sicker.

"I'm on my way."

He hung up, turning to Owens. "Run the antibody test, the fluoroscope. I'll get back as soon as I can manage."

"But what's wrong?"

There wasn't time to explain. The medical examiner tugged off his gloves and face mask. Urgent, he yanked at the door to meet the darkness.

TEN

It kept howling.

"Jesus. Lord, I wish that thing would stop."

The policemen stood in the glare of the headlights, a net spread out before them. Rettig had come back a little while ago. He'd looked everywhere to find a net, the sporting-goods stores, the zoo down in the park as Slaughter had suggested, but he hadn't seen one. He'd been frantic since the stores had all been closed, and he'd been forced to call the owners, but they hadn't been home. Then as he had given up and started back to Slaughter, he had slammed his brakes on, staring at the restaurant across the street. It hadn't done well, and the business had been sold. A seafood place in cattle country. Why had anyone put money in it? But the decorations still were in there, and he saw the heavy sea nets hanging in the window. He had run across. The doors were locked. He didn't know the owners. He finally pulled out his gun and smashed the back-door window.

Slaughter hadn't liked that, but he didn't want to say so. After all, the man had tried. At least they had the net now, and that really was what mattered. He told his men how they would have to do this as the howling kept on from the upper stories, and they clearly didn't want to go in. For that matter, Slaughter didn't want to go himself. "The main thing is, don't hurt the boy." He glanced to see if Dunlap heard that. If this thing turned sour, he wanted to avoid accusations about police brutality. He wanted all his men to know without a doubt that they were only to restrain the boy.

"But what if he attacks us?"

"Just don't hurt him. Keep the net between you and the boy. We'll get him tangled in it. After that, we shouldn't have much problem."

Slaughter looked at Dunlap again, hoping that Dunlap understood how clear and cautious every order had been. He squinted from the headlights aimed toward the porch. He saw the mother and the father, and they still weren't in their car. He saw the woman from the Potter's Field Historical Society, the other cruisers that had gotten here not long ago, the headlights of another cruiser speeding up the gravel driveway.

"Well, we've got enough men. Let's do it."

But the headlights weren't another cruiser. Slaughter recognized the car. It was the medical examiner's, and Slaughter told them, "Wait a second," as he stepped from the porch.

The medical examiner got out of his car and rushed forward.

"Where have *you* been? I've been looking—" Slaughter stopped talking when he saw the blood across the man's shirt, the mangled lips. "What happened to your face?"

"There isn't time to explain. I know this thing's a virus, but I'm not sure if it's rabies."

"Is it just as bad?"

"It's maybe worse. It seems to work much faster. There's a dog that passed through one stage of the virus sooner than it should have. We're still doing tests."

"Well, what about this boy up there?"

The medical examiner winced as he heard the howling from the upper stories. "That's a *boy* who's doing that?" His face was twisted with the shock of disbelief.

"I have to think it is. There could be some stray dog up there, but we don't have a reason to believe that."

"God, I once heard someone sound like that."

"A case of rabies?"

"Back in med school. But the other symptoms weren't the same as this. A victim of rabies might get vicious, even bark and snap at someone."

"Bark?"

"The muscles in the neck constrict. The person tries to talk, but all the words come out like barking."

"This is *howling.*"

"That's exactly what I mean. The symptoms aren't the same. It sounds more like an animal. Besides, I never heard of anyone with rabies who had actually attacked someone. Oh, I read cases in the medical books but never met a doctor who'd actually seen it happen."

"Then we don't know any more than when we started."

"That's not true. We know there's something, and we're fairly certain it's contagious."

"But the parents claim the boy was never bitten."

"Sure, and I just saw a dog that had its shots, and now it's dead back at the vet's."

The howling started again.

"Damn. I should have thought. The moon," the medical examiner said.

"Now you've lost me."

"Look at it." He pointed toward the almost full moon that was shining toward the mansion. "That symptom is at least consistent. Victims of rabies are enraged by light. Their eyes are sensitive. They seek out darkness. When the moon rises, they start reacting to it."

"Howling?"

"Rapid dogs will, and in this case one small boy."

"They say he cut his hand on glass this morning."

"That's too soon. It takes about a week before the rabies virus starts to show symptoms. But if this thing is quicker than the normal virus, if the glass had been licked by an infected animal, that would be enough to transmit it. When you catch the boy, the first thing I want to do is see that cut."

The howls were rising.

"It's like something, someone, crazy," Slaughter told him.

"Lunacy, they used to call it. Madness from the moon."

Slaughter didn't want to talk about this anymore. "I've got to go in after him."

"I'll bring my bag."

"We'll need it." Slaughter hurried up the stone steps to his men. "Is everybody ready?"

They nodded tensely.

"Keep your gloves on. Rettig, hold the net at that end. You three hold it at the other end and in the middle. Just remember. No one hurt him."

Slaughter looked at Dunlap again to make sure he'd heard, and they started in.

Dunlap followed.

"No, you stay out here," Slaughter told him.

"But I want to see the end of this."

"I don't have time to keep you safe from trouble. I've got plenty as it is to think about."

"I'll stay back out of danger."

"You're damned right you will. You'll stay there on the porch."

"You're hiding something, Slaughter."

For the first time, Slaughter felt enraged by him. "I beg your pardon?"

"You heard what I said. You're not sure you can keep your men controlled. You don't want someone like me up there to see trouble."

"I've had just about enough from—"

"Parsons told you to cooperate."

"About the commune but not this. He doesn't even know about this."

"But he'll be damned mad if you screw up his p.r. tactics. Look, you need as many witnesses as you can get. I've handled this about as well as anybody. I've been helping."

Slaughter couldn't stand here arguing. He squinted at the headlights, at the medical examiner approaching, and abruptly made his choice. "All right, I'm going to take a chance on you. The first time you get in the way, you'll find your ass out on the porch."

"That's what I figured."

"Then we understand each other." Slaughter turned to the medical examiner. "You'll need these gloves."

"Hey, I will too," Dunlap said.

"You won't be close enough to need them."

They crossed the long, wide hallway toward the curving staircase. Men were spread out at the bottom, the net before them.

"Ready with your flashlights?" Slaughter asked.

They nodded, turning on the flashlights, beams arcing up the stairs. He heard their breathing and smelled their sweat.

"Okay, let's do it."

Footsteps shuffling, scraping, they started, the net spread out before them, up the staircase.

<u>ELEVEN</u>

It was waiting for them. It had scurried to the final landing. Now it heard their footsteps and their whispers, saw their sweeping flashlight beams. They still were quite a distance down there, but in time they would be up here, and it hissed as it swung in search of cover.

But there weren't any rooms behind it, just this one big open space that stretched from end to end. It didn't understand, although it did retain a far off memory of someone who'd explained this. There were slight projections from each corner, spaces behind, but these would be too obvious. It needed something else. And then it saw what it was looking for. A perfect hiding place and one it could attack from if it had to.

It was scurrying to reach the place, and all the while, it kept glancing at the glow that swept in through the window and spread cold and pale across the floor. It started howling again. It couldn't stop itself, was powerless to fight the urge, just crouched there, head up, howling long and high, its throat constricted painfully, and then the urge had been relieved, and it was scurrying.

The darkness in this hiding place was wonderful, the blackness soothing and secure. It closed its eyes to rest them after all the strain of squinting at that cold pale glow that spilled in through the windows. It was breathing quickly, nervous even though the hiding place was comforting. It licked its lips and tasted yet again the scabs of blood that clung in specks against its mouth. That salt taste that it now had grown accustomed to and even had begun to crave. But the salt taste had been liquid, and that recollection made it gag again. Nonetheless it wanted that warm sweetly salted liquid. It was caught in oppositions, both attracted and repelled, and without conscious effort, it was howling even more fiercely.

<u>TWELVE</u>

They stopped down on the second landing.

"It's up on the third floor."

"Maybe," Slaughter told them.

"But you heard it howling."

"We don't know if there's a dog in here as well. I say we do this as we planned it. Dunlap, you're so anxious to be helpful. Shine that flashlight up the stairs. Don't wait to yell if you see movement."

"Oh, don't worry. If there's anything on those stairs, I'll

yell my god-damned head off."

"Are you sorry that you came now?"

"I wouldn't miss it for the world."

"You must want that story bad."

"You have no idea."

But then Slaughter saw the way the flashlight beam was shaking, and he took the light away from him. "I don't know if it's booze or nerves, but I don't want my life depending on you. Here, you'd better take this." And he gave the flashlight to the medical examiner. "You do it just the way I told him." He turned to his men. "Okay, we work along this big hall up here, checking all the rooms. I don't expect to find him on this level, but I can't depend on expectation."

With the net spread before them, they moved through the darkness. When they reached the first doors on each side, they stopped and looked at Slaughter.

"Try the left side. I'll stay here and watch the other."

Breathing hoarsely, they went slowly in. But there was nothing. They shone flashlights in the corners and the closets, just an old-time bedroom with a canopy above the bed, a net that came down to keep out mosquitoes. They looked underneath the bed, and they came out, checking all the other rooms along the hallway. Other beds, a playroom, and a study, all rigged out as if a hundred years ago, maps and photographs and guns up on the walls, a chair that looked as if old Baynard had risen from it only a moment ago, but nobody was in there, and they came out, staring down the hall toward where the medical examiner was aiming the flashlight up the stairs.

"I guess we know he's up there," Slaughter said.

They faced the stairs and started up. Their flashlight beams were making crazy angles on the walls and ceiling. The men shuffled as if at any moment they expected some small figure to come hurtling toward them, but instead they reached the final landing, and they swung their beams across the big top-story room.

"Well, I don't get it," Slaughter said. "What *is* this place?" His voice echoed.

"You've never been here?" Rettig asked.

"Always meant to. Never took the time."

"The ballroom," Rettig told him. "Baynard's wife was

Southern, and she didn't like the people out here. She was used to parties, dances, fancy dinners. Baynard built this place to suit her, and the ballroom was his special effort. Once a month at least he had a celebration. Ranchers, those with money, used to come from miles around, better people from the town, congressmen and senators. He paid their way. They'd come up from the railroad in carriages he sent for them. He even brought an orchestra from Denver. They would dance and eat and—"

"What's the matter?" Slaughter asked him.

In the dark, the flashlight beams angling across the ballroom, Slaughter felt his stomach burning.

"Well, I used to hear about it from my father's father, but I never knew if it was true or not. He said the parties sometimes got a little out of hand."

"I don't know what you mean."

Rettig continued, "You can see the way the balcony juts out from that end. Well, the orchestra played up there. With that solid wooden railing, the musicians couldn't see too much of what went on below them. In the corners and the sides there, you can see the slight partitions that come out."

"They're triangles."

"That's right. You see those padded benches on the sides."

"Well, what about them?"

"Rumors, I suppose. My father's father said that wives were swapped up here, that people went with different partners in around the back of those things. He said there were secret doors that you could go in for privacy."

"He knew that for a fact?"

"He never was invited. No one ever found a secret door."

"Then that's just a rumor, like you said. I mean, a thing like that, somebody would have told."

"And maybe not have been invited anymore."

"But Baynard's wife. Why would she have gone along with this? You said that she was from society."

"I didn't mention that she also had a reputation. Baynard was the one who had to go along with it. To keep her with him. Then the parties got a little out of hand. She found a man she liked much better than the rest. Some people say she left with him. Others say that Baynard killed her. But they never found the body."

"Oh, that's swell. So now you've got us searching through some kind of haunted house. Just keep your mind on what you're doing. Dunlap, you stay here. We'll check this right end. Then we'll move down toward the other. Shout if anything slips past us. Everybody ready?"

They nodded, then slowly worked across to search the corner to their right, moving around the triangle. They knocked the wood in case they might find a secret door. They crossed to search the other corner. Then they moved along the big wall, going around the triangle on that side.

"Nothing so far," Slaughter said. "We still have two partitions and the balcony. We've almost got him. Let's be careful."

They moved up toward the far end.

"Like I said, be careful."

There was nothing in the far left corner, nothing in the right.

"Okay, he's up there in the balcony. He's got to be."

They started up the narrow stairs but bumped against each other; there wasn't room for the four of them.

"This isn't working," Slaughter told them.

They were grateful for the chance to wait.

"Rettig, you stay back. You other three go up," Slaughter told them. "Rettig will be just behind you."

Rettig breathed out with relief. The other three looked tense, aiming their flashlights up the narrow stairway.

"What about on top of those partitions?" one man asked.

"No. How could he climb up on them?"

And in that brief distraction, their faces turned out toward the ballroom, everything began to happen. First, the snarling, then the hurtling body. It came off the balcony, a half-seen diving figure that swooped past them, slamming hard at Rettig, men now scrambling, shouting, bodies rolling on the floor. Slaughter heard the snarling, Rettig's screaming, as he tried to get in past the scrambling bodies. He saw Rettig struggling upward, something hanging on him. He saw Rettig falling backward then, the extra weight upon him as they crashed against the near partition, the old boards cracking, and the men were rushing forward with the net.

"Where is he?"

"Here, I've got him!"

Rettig kept screaming. Then the net swung through the flashlight beams toward where he struggled with the figure on the padded bench beside the triangle.

"Oh, Jesus, get him off me!" Rettig shouted, and he kicked, the figure thumping, snarling on the floor.

The net fell. They had him. Arms and legs were lashing out, entangled worse with every effort. Slaughter pushed between his men and saw them roll the boy and get the net around his back and chest, and there was no way that the boy could get out. He was powerless, except for where he slashed his teeth against the net and snarled at them.

The medical examiner hurried next to Slaughter, set down his bag, and reached inside to grab a hypodermic. "Keep him steady."

"You don't think we'll let him go."

The medical examiner pulled out a vial, slipped a needle into it, and eased out the plunger to get liquid into the chamber. Standing by a flashlight, he pushed slightly on the plunger until liquid spurted from the needle. Then he looked at Slaughter. "Pull his shirtsleeve up."

"You're kidding. In that net. I couldn't move it."

"Rip a patch out then. I don't care. Let me see some skin."

Through the webbing, Slaughter tugged and ripped the shirtsleeve. He was quick, afraid the boy might get at him. The medical examiner swabbed alcohol across the skin and leaned close to press the needle.

One loud yelp. The medical examiner kept pushing gently on the plunger. Then he straightened, and he looked at Slaughter. "In a minute."

"Why are these bricks here?" someone said, and Slaughter turned. Too much was going on.

"I don't—"

Then he saw where Rettig's fall had broken the partition. In there, as he shone his flashlight, he saw a wall of bricks. He glanced at Rettig who was slumped across the padded bench, his hands up to his throat.

"Are you all right? He didn't bite you, did he?" Slaughter asked.

Rettig felt all over his body. He breathed, gasped, and swallowed, breathing once again. He nodded, wiping his mouth. "I think I only lost my wind." He tried to stand but gave out, slumping once more on the bench. "I'll be okay in just a second. What bricks?"

"There behind you."

Rettig turned, still trying hard to breathe. "I don't know anything about them. I don't think they should be here."

Slaughter didn't even need to ask him. Rettig was already going on. "I guessed that this one sounded different from the others. Much more solid, heavier."

"What's that supposed to mean?" a policeman asked.

"Baynard's wife. I think we know what happened to her." The group became silent.

Slaughter felt Dunlap beside him.

They peered down at the small boy who was tangled, now unconscious, in the net.

"A little kid and all this trouble. Hell, I didn't really understand how little he would be," Slaughter said.

They stood around the boy and stared at him.

"We'd better get him to the hospital," the medical examiner said. "You too, Slaughter. Rettig, you as well. I want to check both of you."

"He never touched me," Slaughter said.

"The cat did. If this virus is like rabies, you're long due to start your shots. Rettig, I don't know. If you don't have a bite, there won't be any problem."

"But I wasn't bitten," Slaughter told him. "Only scratched."

"You want to take the risk?"

Slaughter shook his head to tell him no.

"That's what I thought. Don't worry. You've got company. I need the shots as well."

"But you weren't bitten either."

"No. But with this bloody lip, I can't take any chances. The boy is harmless now. You men can lift him. Stay clear of his head."

They looked at Slaughter, who nodded. One man held the boy's legs while another gripped his shoulders.

"Hell, he doesn't weigh a thing."

"That's what I said. A little kid and all this trouble," Slaughter answered. "It's enough to make you—"

Hollow and disgusted, he watched as the men worked with the boy to reach the stairs. "Here, someone grab that corner of the net before we have an accident," he ordered, and they moved clumsily down the stairs.

Slaughter kept his flashlight aimed before them. On the second landing, they turned, heading toward the bottom, and he heard the idling cruisers now. He saw the headlights glaring through the open door, the mother and the father out there, and the woman from the organization that ran this place, an officer beside them.

"Take it careful," one man said and paused to get a better grip around the boy's shoulders. "Okay. Now I've got him." They reached the bottom, moving across the hall toward the entrance.

"Rettig, tell that woman what we found up there. Those bricks could mean a dozen things, and none of them important."

"You don't think so."

"I have no opinion. But she should know about the damage."

They went onto the porch. The mother and the father now were running.

"Is he—?"

"Just sedated. Everything considered, he's been lucky. Stay away from him," the medical examiner said. "I don't want you contaminated. You can see him at the hospital."

They didn't look convinced.

"It's simply a precaution," Slaughter said, stepping close. "We still don't know what we're dealing with. Let's put him in the back seat of my car," he told his men.

"You'd better set him on a blanket. We can burn it at the hospital," the medical examiner said.

"Do we have to be that careful?"

The medical examiner only stared at him.

"I'll get a blanket from my trunk," the father said and hurried.

"Good. That's very good. We need your help."

They moved toward the cruiser. Slaughter opened the back door, and the father spread the blanket.

"Thank you," Slaughter told him. "I know how hard—"

He looked at where the mother stood beside the cruiser, weeping. "—how hard this must be for you."

They set the boy inside, and the medical examiner leaned in to check him. He stayed in there quite a while. When he came out, even in the darkness, Slaughter saw how pale his face had suddenly become.

"I have to talk."

"What is it?"

"Over there."

The medical examiner walked toward the trees. Slaughter followed.

"What's the matter?"

"I just killed him."

"What?"

"I should have thought." The medical examiner rubbed his forehead.

"Come on, for Christ sake. Make some sense."

"The sedative. I should have thought. The dog I found. I called a vet who came and took one look and gave the dog a sedative."

"But what's—?"

"The dog had reached the stage of paralysis by then. The sedative was just enough to kill it. That boy in your back seat isn't breathing."

"Oh, my God."

"You understand now. I'm not sure exactly how this virus works, but it's damned fast. I know that much. He was maybe on the verge of becoming paralyzed. The sedative precipitated everything. It slowed his body's metabolism until it killed him."

"You can't blame yourself."

"You're damned right I can. I should have paid attention! *I just killed him.*" The medical examiner closed his eyes, shaking.

Slaughter turned to see the father leaning toward the back seat.

"I don't . . . Something's wrong!" the father blurted.

Slaughter watched the mother crying as the father scrambled in. He saw his men, the cruisers, their headlights glaring at the mansion, saw the woman Rettig talked to start to run up toward the mansion. He sensed the moon above him and the medical examiner beside him shaking as he felt his world begin to tumble and a creature in the park below him started howling at the moon. Dunlap stood to one side, taking pictures. Slaughter didn't even have the strength for anger anymore. He let the man continue taking pictures, flasher blinking.

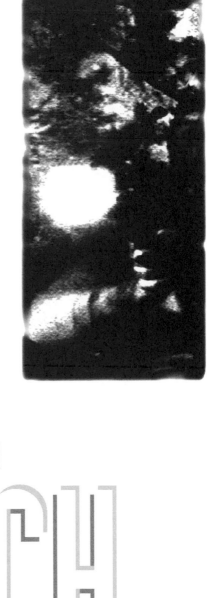

# THE
## RANCH

*Part* ART *Four* OUR

SLAUGHTER WAS DRUNK. HE HADN'T COME BACK HOME UNTIL NEARLY ONE O'CLOCK, AND HE HAD stayed outside just long enough to check his horses. Then he'd walked back to his house and with the porchlight on had stared down at the cooler filled with tepid water and the beer cans from this morning. There were empties on the porch as well. There hadn't been a chance to clean up. Too much had begun to happen. But he didn't clean up this time either, simply glanced out at the darkness and then turned to go inside where first he flicked the lights on to study another cooler in the kitchen before heading toward the cupboard where he kept the bourbon. That was something that he almost never drank, but this night had been special, oh, my God, yes, and he almost didn't even bother with a glass. He knew that would be too much weakness, though, and since he was determined to be weak to start with, he at least would set some limits. Reaching for the bottle and a glass, he fumbled in the freezer for some ice and poured the glass up to the top and in three swallows drank a third of it.

The shock was almost paralyzing. He put both hands on the sink and leaned across it, choking, waiting for the scalding flood to settle in his stomach. He could feel it draining down his throat. He felt his stomach tensing, and he knew that because he hadn't eaten since this morning, he might easily throw up. But then the spasms ebbed, and he was breathing, trembling. He leaned across the sink a moment longer. Then he poured some water with the bourbon, and he started toward the shadowy living room. Once, years ago, when he had learned that his wife was leaving him, he had felt emotions like this, ruin, fright, discouragement that bordered on despair. He had sensed those feelings building in him until the instant of the divorce, and going to his rented room, his legs so shaky that he didn't think he'd get there, he had stopped at a liquor store where he had bought the cheapest wine that he could find. A quart of Ruby Banquet, some god-awful label like that. And he'd somehow made it to his room where without pausing he had drunk the bottle in thirty seconds. Setting down the bottle, he had scrambled toward the bathroom, and the heave of liquid from him had evacuated more than just the wine. The sickness had been cleansing, purging all the ugliness, the hate and fear and anger. He had slumped beside the toilet bowl, and how long he had stayed there he was never certain, but when he got up and slumped across the bed, he found that it was night and that the slowly flashing neon sign outside his window was the pattern of his heartbeat, measured, weary. There was nothing in him anymore. He had passed the crisis, and he had a sense then of a new beginning. He was neutral.

Now he'd graduated from the cheap wine to the bourbon, and he would have forced himself to throw up, but he understood that this trouble wasn't over. No, his apprehension from the night before remained with him, and he was definitely certain that this wasn't over. First, there'd be the lawsuit. That much he could bet on. Against the medical examiner, and then like ripples in a pond, eventually against himself and against the town council that employed him. Then investigations to determine if the medical examiner and he should lose their jobs.

Hell, the medical examiner might even lose his license. That boy might have died because he was allergic to the sedative. There hadn't been the proper questions, proper cautions. They had let the trouble so distract them that they hadn't thought beyond it. They might very well *deserve* to lose their jobs.

He didn't want to think about that. He wanted only to shut off his mind and stare down at the bourbon in his hand. Avoiding the light in the kitchen, he sat in a dark corner of the living room and frowned at the darkness past the window. For a moment as he raised the glass, he didn't realize that it was empty. Better have another. So he went back to the kitchen, pouring more but putting ample water with it this time. He would have to talk to lots of people in the morning, and he wanted to be sober. He could recollect as if he still were there the father crying with the mother, cursing, saying that he'd warned them about so much force to catch a little boy. The hardest part had been his struggle with the father. "No, you can't go in to touch him."

"He's my son."

"I don't care. He still might contaminate you. As it is, your wife might be infected from that bite."

It took two men at last to keep the father from the back seat of the cruiser. Dunlap had continued taking pictures. Oh, my Jesus, what a mess. And when he'd finally mustered the energy to talk to Dunlap, there had been no sign of him. The man had sense enough to get away while he was able, likely fearing that his pictures would be confiscated. Slaughter didn't know if he would actually have grabbed the camera, but by then he had been mad enough to grab at something. It was just as well that Dunlap had not been around to serve that function. There wasn't much happening by the time he looked for Dunlap anyhow. The man might simply have walked into town to get some rest. The mother and the father had been driven home. The medical examiner was going with the body to the morgue. The officers were locking the mansion until they'd come back in the morning to investigate. He himself had stood in the darkness by his cruiser, staring at the mansion, and he'd heard that howling from below him in the park again, but he had been too weary and disgusted to go down there. He had seen enough for one night, and he had the sense that he would see a lot more very soon. All he wanted was to get home and anesthetize himself.

But not too much, he kept remembering as he walked toward the living room and sat again in the corner, staring at the night out there. He'd have to do a lot of talking in the morning. Dunlap, Parsons, and the medical examiner. He didn't know who else, but there'd be many, and he wondered how he'd manage to get through this. All his years of working, and he'd never had this kind of trouble. No, that wasn't true. There was the grocery store. And on one occasion, he'd shot a man. Three, to be precise, but only one had died, and the inquest had absolved him. He'd been bothered by the killing, but he'd never felt like this, and he was grateful that the bourbon finally was numbing him. Even slumped in a chair, he was slightly off balance, and his lips felt strange. Too long without sleep, without a meal, but he was too disturbed to want either.

He was thinking of the medical examiner, the green walls of the autopsy room, the scalpel cutting. That was something else Slaughter hadn't done right. Because the father would no doubt press charges, Slaughter never should have let the medical examiner go with the body. Even if the medical examiner were able to determine that the boy was not allergic to the sedative, the father would maintain that the evidence had been distorted. What was more, the sedative had almost surely not reacted well with the virus. It had helped to produce the fatal symptoms of paralysis, so any way the problem was approached, the medical examiner had been at fault. He couldn't be objective when he examined the body. There'd be accusations from the council. Slaughter wished that he'd forbidden him to do the autopsy.

"But don't you see I have to know?" the medical examiner had begged him. Slaughter knew how he himself would feel and in the end had let him. After all, what difference did it make? The boy was dead. There wasn't time to bring in someone else to do the job. They had to know right now how this thing worked. He sipped his drink and wondered if the medical examiner would find out that the boy had died from other causes. That would be the best thing anyone could hope for. If the medical examiner did discover that, however, was it likely that the town council would believe him? Or yourself, he thought. Would *you* believe him? Do you trust him that much?

Yes, he thought, and when the phone rang and he reached for it, he guessed that this might be the medical examiner calling to report. But it wasn't, just a dead sound on the telephone.

"Who is it?" Slaughter repeated, but there wasn't any answer. He wondered if this might be the father. "Is there anybody—?"

But abruptly the dial tone was buzzing, and he stared down at the phone and set it onto its holder. Which he would have done regardless, because from the field down by the barn he heard the horses. They were whinnying and snorting. Through the open window and the screen, he heard their hoofbeats skitter one way, then another. In a rush, he set down his glass and rose from the chair. The bourbon made him dizzy, and he waited until his brain was steady before walking toward the door. He'd turned the porchlight off when he came in, but now he turned it on again and stepped out, pausing as he glanced around, then swung left off the porch to face the barn. There was something different, and he had to think before he noticed that he didn't hear any insects. They were always rasping in the bushes and the grass. They had been when he drove in, parking, going down to check the horses at the start.

But now the night was silent, heavy, except for the skittish whinny of the horses, and he wished that he had thought to bring a rifle from the house. He had his handgun, though, and in the dark its range was good enough for any target he might see. This likely would be nothing anyhow. The horses sometimes acted like this if they sensed a snake or a coyote down that drywash on the rear side of the barn. Often all he had to do was calm them or else shine a light out into the bushes, and the thing would go away. But with the bourbon working on him, he'd left his flashlight in the house, and he was wondering if he was in control enough for this. Considering the trouble that was going on, this might be something, after all.

So, careful to approach the open barn door from an angle, he quickly reached inside to switch on the floodlights. There were two sets, one in front and back, that blazed out toward the drywash and the field beside the barn and toward the house. His eyes hurt briefly as he stared at where the horses galloped toward the right and whinnied and then swung fast toward the left. Their pattern was a kind of circle as if both felt threatened on each side, and although they were a distance from the fence before him, he could see their wild eyes and their twitching nostrils.

"What the hell?"

The words were out before he knew he'd said them, and their sound, mixed with the horses' panic, startled him. He'd never seen them act like this. When there was something here that bothered them, they always made some slight disturbance and then shifted toward a better section of the field. But both were in a frenzy, snorting, twitching, galloping, and he was just about to climb the fence and go out there to calm then when he realized that they might be infected. Sure, a sudden change in manner. That would be a symptom. He could not afford to go to them.

But what else could he do? Assume that something in the darkness frightened them. He hoped that was the case. He loved these horses, and he'd hate to lose them. Well, get moving then. He realized that his reluctance was an indication of how much he'd been bothered, and he took a breath, pulled out his gun, then forced himself to walk along the fence to reach the drywash.

The floodlights brightened everything for fifty yards behind the barn. He saw the red clay of the gully, saw the bushes on the slope across there and the trees along the far rim. He glanced behind him, fearful that there might be something crouched behind the barn, and then his back protected, he walked slowly toward the gully.

There was nothing at the bottom, just the red clay and the boulders and the branches he had thrown in to stop erosion. All the same, he *felt* that there was something. In the field, the horses continued skittering and snorting, and he didn't know exactly how to do this. Under usual circumstances, he would have no second thoughts before he went down into the gully and then up the other side to check the bushes. After all, what normally would be out there that could harm him? But this trouble made him reconsider everything. He had to distrust every living thing and even dead ones. But he couldn't bear the horses' panic, couldn't tolerate their agony. He had to stop what they were doing. So he started down the gully when he heard the branches snapping.

Over to his left, across the gully in the bushes, where the glare from the floodlights blended with the darkness. Stepping back toward the rim, he walked along it, frowning toward the darkness. His handgun cocked and ready, he couldn't be certain if the branches snapped from something that came close or backed off. Then he heard another group of branches snapping, farther to the left, and he relaxed a little as he judged that it was something moving off. The branches snapped close to the first place he had heard them now, however—farther to the left again as well—and there was more than one thing out here, that was certain. He was rigid, fighting the urge to flee in panic like the horses.

Keep control. It's just coyotes. Sure, then why the hell have you quit breathing? When he heard the snapping once again and couldn't pretend anymore that it wasn't coming closer, he reacted without thinking. His instinct now in charge, he fired in the air and saw the lean four-footed object, furry, scrambling backward through the bushes. Then he saw the other, and another, and he might have shouted as he saw yet another coming nearer. He would never know for sure. He heard a noise down in the gully to his right, another on the far side of the barn, and he was running up along the fence beside the barn to reach the house. The horses galloped in a line with him, and then they bolted toward the middle of the field. He kept running, hearing noises close behind him, not once looking, only gasping, racing, and he reached the house and burst inside, slamming the door, locking it behind him. He dodged through the living room to reach the kitchen and the back door which he locked as well. He closed the windows everywhere. He locked them, pulling down the shades, and he was reaching for the phone, gasping, frantically dialing.

"Hello," a sleepy voice said. "Who, uh—"

"Rettig, this is Slaughter. Get Hammel and get out here."

"Chief? Is that you? I uh—"

"Rettig, don't ask questions. Just get out here."

"To the station? What time is it?"

"My place. Fast. I need you."

Slaughter repeated his instructions and set down the

phone, hearing how the horses whinnied beyond tolerance. He started toward the windows on that side, reaching for a blind to pull it up and see why they were sounding like that. But the phone rang, and he stood immobile, one hand on the blind while he stared toward the phone. That god-damned Rettig. What's the matter with him? When Slaughter crossed the room and grabbed the phone, there wasn't anyone, however, just that same dead silence. "Tell me what you want!" he shouted to the mouthpiece, but the silence continued. Then he heard the dial tone again and scratching on the porch and only one horse out there now was whinnying. He faced the front door, his handgun ready, glancing at the window on the side that faced the horses. But he couldn't hear even one horse now, and as he scrambled toward the front blind, the scratching stopped. The night became terribly soundless.

## TWO

Dunlap set down the phone. He was in his room, the camera and the tape recorder on the desk where he was sitting, his notes spread out before him. He was almost out of cigarettes. He frowned at the pint of whisky that he'd left here in the morning. Even though his body was in agony, he held firm to his promise to himself not to take a drink. The promise was a recent one, although there'd been others like it many times before, but this time he was absolute in his determination not to break it. He had walked back to his hotel from the park. He'd seen the mother and the father leave, had seen the medical examiner go with the body, and he'd known that Slaughter shortly would be turning on him. After all, he'd seen too much. He'd even taken pictures—of the grieving parents, of the body, of the medical examiner who looked so guilty that an image of him would be damning. Dunlap didn't know if Slaughter was as good a man as he appeared to be, but he'd seen even good men try a coverup if they were threatened, and the way those parents had reacted, Slaughter would feel threatened all right. Dunlap wasn't going to take a chance on him. He hadn't come across a story this strong in too many years, six of them at least, about the time that his drinking had gotten out of hand and the magazine had shifted him to minor stories. Now, though, he'd been lucky. What had seemed little more than a routine story had developed into something that would surely get his reputation back. Indeed if this situation got much worse—and he was positive it would—it might turn out to be among the ten best stories of the year, and he was not about to jeopardize his comeback. Actually he hadn't walked back to the hotel; he had run. He'd slowed on occasion, fighting for his breath, but mostly he had run the ten blocks to his hotel, knowing from the vantage point that the hill provided which way he had to go to reach the downtown section, and he'd often looked behind him just in case a cruiser might be coming, but there hadn't been one, and when he at last had reached the hotel and his room, the desk clerk downstairs frowning at him as he hurried up, he'd fumbled to unload his camera, looking for a place to hide the film. His room would be too obvious. He went out in the corridor and braced the cartridge behind a picture on the wall. He hid the tape from his recorder behind another picture. He had all their voices from the moment they had reached the ballroom to the instant when the grieving parents had accused the medical examiner of negligence. Oh, it was all there, every blessed detail, and he meant to keep it. Slaughter might come after it, but Slaughter wasn't going to get it.

Back inside his room, Dunlap had locked the door, and that was when his glance had settled on the pint of bourbon. He was moving toward it, even twisting at the cap, before he stopped himself. No, that was how he'd ended in this dump. He'd ruined every piece of luck he'd ever had by drinking, had nearly lost his wife and almost screwed up his career. If he got drunk now, he'd do something stupid, maybe talk too much when Slaughter came or even draw attention to those pictures in the corridor. For sure, he'd need his senses to keep up with what was happening. The time lost from a drunken stupor would fit the pattern, though. Like gamblers who kept losing, maybe that was what he wanted. To keep losing. Maybe something in him was determined to seek failure. Well, not this time. This time he was going to be a winner. He had lasted since the morning without booze, the first day he had managed that in years, and if he'd suffered this long, he could suffer just a little longer. Make it through the night. The melody to those words occurred to him, and he was laughing. Face this one hour, then the next. That was how the A. A. people were successful, wasn't it? Sure, take this one hour at a time.

But although Dunlap had laughed, his hands were shaking. He suspected he would throw up, and he set the bottle by the television, went into the bathroom, and drank some water. Hell, you're hungry, that's all. A little sick from all that running. But no matter the reason, he was close to throwing up. He stripped and showered, and that helped, the hot sting of the water flooding all the sweat and dust and tension from him, but he nonetheless was sick and wishing for a drink. The drink might make him even sicker, but he wanted it. Attraction and repulsion. So he put on fresh clothes. Why, he didn't know. He ought to go to bed, but he was thinking maybe he would take a walk. Instead he sat down at the desk and tried a first draft of some notes, just to flesh out what was on the tape and film. He smoked and scribbled his impressions, in no special order, just to get the words down, staring at the way his hand was shaking, and the sentences were scrawled so poorly that he almost couldn't read them. Why not just one drink? To brace you, get you through this. No, and glancing from the pint of bourbon, he kept smoking, writing.

Then he knew he had to get some sleep. He flicked the lights off, stretched out on the bed, and concentrated to relax his stiff, tense body. Hard, it trembled, and he eased the muscles in his feet, his legs, his torso, slowly moving toward his head. It might have been that he was even more fatigued than he suspected, or that slowly moving up his body was like counting numbers backward or repeating nonsense phrases, but his consciousness gave in before he ever reached his head. He woke in what he later learned was half an hour, almost screamed in the darkness but stopped himself. He found that he was sitting in the bed, that he was sweating, and he wavered to his feet, switching on the light. He saw numerous insects clinging to his window. He leaned against the wall and rubbed his forehead. He had seen that image once again, that strange, half-human, antlered figure. But he always had associated it with nights of too much drinking. DTs, bourbon, nightmares. This time, though, he'd dreamed it even though he'd been sober. When the dream had first happened to him, almost three years ago, he hadn't thought much about it. Just another crazy nightmare. But the dream had come back in a month, and then another month, and he'd been slightly bothered by it. After all, his dreams before were always varied, and although he reacted to them as he dreamed, they never lingered after he wakened. This dream, though, was like an imprint, always vaguely with him, haunting. It was never different, an upright antlered figure standing with its back to him, and then the figure turning slowly, its body twisted, its head aimed past its shoulder, staring at him. That was all. But once a month became twice and then three times, and lately he had dreamed it almost every night. He had thought of going to a doctor, but he knew that the doctor would advise him to stop drinking, and he wasn't ready for that. Hell, if all the drinking did was cause a few bad dreams, so what? He willed himself to keep from dreaming it, and for a month, the tactic worked, but soon the dream was back again, and maybe its persistence, not its nature, was what bothered him. A repetition like that wasn't normal, but the image on its own was hardly normal either, part man, part deer, part cat, God knows what all, and that grotesque beard and that upright body turning sideways, its paws up, its round eyes staring at him. It was horrifying, monstrous. More than that, it was hypnotic, powerful, like magic, as if it were waiting for him, drawing him, and one day he would see it. He was frightened by it, by the riddle that it represented. What was happening to him? If he kept seeing this thing, he would end up in an institution. Never mind an institution. He'd be in the crazy house. He couldn't stand this anymore.

He had to talk to someone, but he didn't know anyone he could call. He crossed the room and grabbed the phone, surprised to find that he dialed his home number. That was something he never did when he was on a trip. The trouble with his wife was so great that they barely managed talking face-to-face, let alone long-distance. But he had to talk to her, to tell her that he'd managed to stop drinking, that everything was going to be all right. Maybe he was too optimistic, but he knew that he could stop at least as long as he was working on this story. After that, he couldn't say. "One day at a time," he reminded himself. Just take it one day at a time. He didn't even care that he would waken her, that in New York it was two hours later. He just had to talk to her and waited while the phone rang and kept waiting, but there wasn't any answer. Still he waited, and at last he had to admit that she was out. But where would she be at this hour? The doubts and the suspicions. He hung up and glanced at the bourbon before he picked up a cigarette. He had to talk to Slaughter and get their differences resolved so he could continue working with the man and have this story. When he found the number in the phone book and dialed it, he was suddenly uncertain, though. He didn't know how he would do this, how he would cancel the ill will he had created. As the phone rang, he was tempted to hang up, but Slaughter answered, and he found that he was speechless. "Yes, who is it?" Slaughter asked and then repeated. Dunlap waited, paralyzed. "Is there anybody—?" Slaughter asked, and Dunlap set the phone back on its cradle.

That was stupid. What's the matter with you? Dunlap thought. But he knew what the matter was, all right, although he had trouble admitting it. He was ashamed of what he'd done tonight, regretful and embarrassed. He'd grown to like the man. Granted, there wasn't any valid reason to pretend that they were friends. Dunlap nonetheless had thought of Slaughter that way. When they had gone out searching for the boy, Dunlap had felt that he was part of things, that he belonged and was involved. That feeling conflicted with his job, his instincts, and his training. No reporter ought to get involved with what he wrote about. His job was to watch objectively and then to write the story. But then maybe that had been his trouble all along, concentrating too much on himself and not on other people. For just a little while this evening, however, he *had* felt involved, and for that brief time, he hadn't felt hollow. Then they'd searched the mansion, and the boy had died, and he had remembered why he came here. He had realized how strong this story was becoming, had been mindful of the good that it would do him, and he'd switched the tape recorder on before he'd even considered what he was doing, and the next thing he had started taking photographs. Now he thought about the grieving mother and the father, how he'd used them, how he'd planned to benefit from what would happen to the medical examiner. He felt sorry for the boy and for the parents, sorry for what had happened up there, but he'd kept taking photographs. His career. That's where his sympathies had finally been strongest, and he couldn't stop his shame now and embarrassment. So what do you intend to do? Do you plan to give up those pictures and that tape? Do you want to back off from the story? No, of course not. You're damned right, you don't. Because that shame you're feeling is just one more way to be a loser. It's not your fault that the boy died. You're just here to write about that. You can go on feeling all the shame you want, but just make sure you get that story, just make sure that your emotions don't intrude on how you make your living.

He knew that he was right, but all the same he continued staring at the phone. Regardless of the friendship he imagined he had violated, he still had to talk to Slaughter, to smooth things, to fix them so he wasn't cut off from the story. Even so, he debated for ten minutes before picking up the phone again. He dialed Slaughter's number once more and waited while the phone kept ringing. This time Slaughter's voice was angry. "Yes, God damn it, Rettig, what's the matter? Get on out here." Dunlap didn't answer. "Tell me what you want!" the angry voice demanded. Dunlap set the phone back on its cradle. There was no way he could make a man who sounded like that sympathetic. He would wait until the morning. So he smoked his final cigarette and looked down at his notes, and then he did a thing that he had never done before, had never even dared because he was so bothered by it. Unsettled by his dream, the image fixed in his mind, turning, glaring at him, he was forced (he didn't will it, but was passive, worked on, compelled) to sketch it. He was staring at it, swallowed by its eyes. He kept on staring, couldn't shift his head away. He felt a darkness in his mind begin to open, and he didn't weaken all at once. It took him several minutes, and he fought it, he would later give himself that credit, fought as hard as he could manage, but resolve diminished into pointlessness, and he was reaching for the bourbon.

### THREE

The medical examiner gave himself the first shot in the lip, frowning at the mirror while he spread the injured portions and then slipped the needle in. It stung, and he was too quick on the plunger so that he felt the liquid spurting through his tissue. All he could be grateful for was that he held his breath and didn't spill the liquid up across his lip and hence he couldn't taste it. Human antirabies serum manufactured from the blood of persons who'd been vaccinated against rabies virus. That would help his system to produce the necessary anti-bodies and in tandem with a second kind of treatment, it was his best chance to survive contagion. He winced as he drew the needle out. Next he set it down, undid his pants and dropped them, pulling down his underwear and reaching for a second needle that he inserted into one buttock. This injection too was antirabies serum, and he wouldn't need another needle until just about this time tomorrow. Even so, that didn't give him comfort because, if he winced to draw this needle out, tomorrow's shot would be the start of worse things. It would not be antirabies serum; it would be the second kind of treatment: rabies vaccine. Anyone who'd been injected with it cringed when they remembered it. First developed by an Englishman named Semple who had done his research in India in 1911, it was rabies virus taken from the brains of rabbits, mice, or rats, and then killed by incubation in carbolic acid. The dead cells helped the body's immune system. Although harmless in them-selves, they encouraged the body to reject the not-yet-rampant live cells that were like them. But the trouble was that not just one injection of the vaccine was sufficient. Fourteen were the minimum, and twenty-one were even better. Each injection was given daily to the muscles of the abdomen. A clockwise pattern was required because the shots were so excruciating that the muscles became extremely sensitive. And maybe you could bear the first five or the second, but the last few were an agony, and this was not a thing the medical examiner was looking forward to.

He didn't have a choice, though. He had indirectly been exposed, and if indeed he had it, the disease would surely kill him without treatment. There were only two examples in which persons had lived through the virus, and there was doubt that they had really had it since their symptoms had been like encephalitis. With the treatment, he still took the chance that he would die from the disease, that it would be too strong for his precautions, but the likelihood was small, and anyway, as he kept thinking, he didn't have a choice. Even rare reactions to the vaccine, like a fever or paralysis, were nothing when compared with certain death. But all the same, the start of treatment didn't calm his fears. The dog had gone through pre-exposure vaccination. It had died, regardless.

The start of treatment didn't calm his sorrow either. He was thinking of the boy lying on the table in the autopsy room, of how he should have had the foresight not to give him the sedative. Those parents. How could he absolve himself? He could still hear the mother shrieking. Well, he meant to find out everything he could about this thing. When he was finished, he would know this virus more than any other he had ever worked on. He had once been famous as an expert in pathology. So now he would discover just how much an expert he could be. That's right. You think you know so much. Get moving. Now's the time to prove it.

So he pulled his pants up, buckled them, and thinking of the tests he would perform, he turned and started from his office. Owens would be here soon with the dog's brain to compare what he had found with what the medical examiner would find inside the boy downstairs. Meanwhile, he himself would use the simple test for Negri bodies. He would also use a more elaborate test in which a brain smear was treated with fluorescent antirabies serum and examined underneath an ultraviolet microscope. To watch the symptoms of the virus, he'd inject a half dozen newborn mice with portions of the boy's brain. He would also want a picture of the virus using the electron microscope. Whatever this thing was, he meant to have a look at it, and when he opened that body, he would understand why the paralysis occurred so quickly, why it worsened with sedation.

As he walked along the corridor, he saw the nurses staring at him. Word had gotten around, all right, and fast as only people in a hospital could spread it. They were looking at a man whose error had been fatal to a patient. Then he told himself to get control. They maybe were just frightened by a thing they didn't understand. Or maybe they were startled by the grim way he was walking. Well, he didn't plan to ask them, and if they knew what was good for them, they'd stay away from him.

He reached the door down to the basement. He thought of Slaughter who would need injections, and the mother and the man who had been bitten, and the man who owned the dog. There were too many details he had not attended to. What was more, he needed sleep. And food, he hadn't eaten since this morning. Well, he would do this and take care of everything. With Owens here to help him, he could find the time to call those people, get them down here for their shots. But he knew what he really wanted—to learn what had killed this boy.

The medical examiner reached the bottom of the steps and went through to the corridor. He came to the far end of the hallway and entered the morgue. In the anteroom, he washed his hands and put on a lab coat, a cap, a mask, and rubber gloves. Just to be exact and avoid contaminating his samples, he even stepped inside protective coverings for his shoes, and then with nothing further to detain him, he pushed through the door and he was in the autopsy room.

Green tile on the walls reflected the glare of fluorescent lights in the ceiling. A counter with steel sinks and trays of instruments was flanked by three tables, each with gutters and a drain for blood. The tables were arranged sideways as he faced them, one behind the other, and the third was where his eyes were focused, on that tiny lump beneath the sheet. He walked with slow determination toward it, breathing through the cling-ing vapor that collected on the inside of his face mask. Then he paused and gently pulled the sheet back, staring at the naked body on the table. So small, so battered, all those bruises from the fury it had been through. There was caked blood on the lips which swollen, slightly parted, showed some damage to the front teeth. But these details weren't important. Even with them, the boy was striking. Blond, angelic, innocent. This was the first time that the medical examiner had worked on some-one he'd observed in life, the first time he had done this to a patient. But then that was just the point. He *never* had a patient. That was why he'd become a medical examiner—to keep these feelings of regret away from him, to shun these awful obliga-tions to the memory of the living. Well, he'd brought this on himself. He *had* become responsible, and he paused to elimi-nate emotion before reaching for the scalpel that he would use to peel the hair away. He took a breath and didn't want to do this, but he leaned close to select his point of contact while the eyes flickered suddenly below him and then stared at him, but they were purged of any innocence, as old and stark as any eyes he'd seen, and they kept staring. When the boy's hand came up, the room appeared to swivel, and his own hand to his mouth beneath his face mask, the medical examiner stumbled backward, screaming.

## FOUR

Marge had stayed on duty at the police station until everything was finished at the mansion. There was nothing she could do up there to help, but she could free a man from night shift on the radio while he went up to lend a hand, and Slaughter needed every officer in town. So she had gotten the news in bits and pieces from the radio, and when she'd found out what at last had happened, she had done her best to keep from crying. Slaughter didn't need the people he depended on to break down when he most required them. Marge couldn't help it, though, and she had sat there, wiping at her tears, relaying messages. She knew the mother and the father. She had gone to school with older sisters in the mother's family. She had known this woman since the woman was a baby. Why, the woman lived just two blocks down from Marge's house, and Marge had often gone to visit, to see the boy, to bring him presents. Now the boy was dead, and partly out of sympathy for what the parents must be feeling, partly out of sorrow for the boy, she wept. But she did her job, and when the man she had relieved came back to resume his shift, she tried to hide that she'd been crying. All the same, the man had noticed, and he sat with her a while until he felt that she could drive. "You need a little sleep is all," he told her, but they both knew that it wouldn't be that easy. There were many people now who wouldn't get much sleep tonight, and she had thanked him, walking to her car. He'd asked if he should walk outside with her, but she had thought about the radio, with no one to attend to it, and she had told him that he really didn't have to. Anyhow, from five years of work with Slaughter, she had learned the value of control, and she was certain she'd be fine.

So she had gone out to her car and driven from the parking lot. Almost midnight on a Saturday. She normally would have expected lots of movement in the streets, especially outside the bars, young trail hands come in for a weekend's fun, but she was not surprised when she saw little action. A few cars and pickup trucks, a couple of men who stood outside a bar and sipped from beer cans. But in contrast with a normal weekend, this was more like a quiet Tuesday, and she wondered if the word had spread, or if ranchers, losing stock, had stayed home watching for some trouble with the cattle. But no matter what the reason, things were quiet, and that bothered her. As she drove through the outskirts, she saw lots of houselights on, and that was hardly normal either. She wished that she'd had the chance to talk to Slaughter, but he'd been so busy, and she didn't want to stay at home alone, so she drove past her house, went two more blocks, and if there were lights on, she meant to go in and console the mother and the father

There were lights on for sure, the whole house both in front and back. She saw the plumber's truck, the car before it. Both the mother and the father must be home then, and she parked her car, wondering if she would be intruding. Well, she'd come this far, and after all it was her duty, so she got out, locked her car, and started up the sidewalk. She could hear the crickets screeching. She was peering toward the lights in all the windows, wondering if anybody else had come to visit, when she heard the voices. Loud: two men it seemed, and they were shouting. Then they were screaming. Marge was paralyzed. The cool night air was still, the crickets silent now, as someone ran out onto the porch as if for help, a man she once had met from two doors down, and he was staring at her. "Jesus, she's gone crazy."

"What?"

Abruptly Marge heard the snarling. Instinct almost made her run away, but she moved slowly forward as the window in the dining room came bursting toward the porch, two figures struggling through the broken edges, falling, writhing on the porch. The mother and the father, the mother snarling, the father screaming, and the mother was on top where she was scratching, biting.

Marge ran up the steps. "You've got to help me! Get her off him!"

"But she's crazy!" the neighbor said.

Marge would later recollect how she had thought of Slaughter at that moment, wondering how the chief would try to handle this. She wanted him to say that she had done the right thing when an instant could make all the difference. She pushed at the man behind her, shouting "Go get help!" as she looked all around for something to subdue the mother. She wasn't about to grab the mother and get bitten like the father screaming there, but when she saw the thing she needed in one corner of the porch, she couldn't bring herself to grab it. Warren evidently had been playing with it the day before he died. She didn't want to touch it, but the father's screaming was too much. She reached for it. Slipping on the broken glass, she lurched toward the mother, raised the baseball bat high above her head, and thinking about Slaughter, started swinging.

## FIVE

Slaughter waited in his locked house until Rettig and Hammel arrived. He shouted out the window that they'd better look around before they left the cruiser. So they flashed their searchlights, but there wasn't anything. He went outside to meet them, staring past them, scanning all around them and then pointing. "This way."

"Well, what is it?"

"Don't you think I wish I knew?"

They stiffened. They were dressed in jeans and sport shirts, a gunbelt strapped around each waist. They saw that Slaughter had his own gun out, and they were drawing theirs as they walked toward the fence where he was pointing.

"Shine your flashlights."

The beams arced out across the field.

"But I don't understand this," Rettig said.

"Just keep your back protected. Keep looking all around you," Slaughter told him. "There was something out here. Hell, it came up on my porch."

Slaughter climbed over the fence and flashed his light while they jumped down beside him. Then he started walking with them through the field.

"Your porch?"

"That's right." Slaughter was embarrassed, determined not to admit that he'd run in panic. He felt safer with his men to help him, but he couldn't subdue the burning in his stomach, and he wished they wouldn't ask too many questions.

But they kept on. "Well, what is it?" Rettig asked again.

"I told you, I don't know. I never got a look at them."

"Your porch, though."

"I was talking to you on the phone when I heard it. When I looked, it wasn't there."

Then Slaughter saw what he was searching for and wished that he'd been wrong. With his flashlight aimed, he glimpsed the fallen objects in the field, and he was hurrying through the grass toward them. He stopped and stared. The horses were mangled like the steer that he had seen by old Doc Markle, like the other steer that he had seen by Bodine's pickup truck, except that these were worse, so mutilated that he almost didn't recognize them. He heard his men gasp.

"Some damned thing was out here all right. God, I'm sorry, Chief."

"These horses . . . They were all I . . ."

Slaughter stalked toward the gully. "I heard three of them up in those bushes, two more by the barn. I'd like to—"

"Wait a second, Chief." Rettig grabbed his shoulder.

Slaughter pulled his hand away. "These god-damned—"

*"Wait a minute.* We don't even know what we'll be up against. You say that there were five of them?"

"That's right. Like a bobcat."

*"Five* of them?"

"I know it doesn't make much sense, but—"

"I don't care about that. Sure, bobcats don't hunt in packs, but anything can happen. What I mean is, we need help to do this. We need better light."

"You want the sun to come up? Damn it, they'll be long gone when that happens."

"You can find a tracker."

"Who, for Christ sake? I already thought of that. These cowboys maybe think they're expert trackers, but I never saw one yet that knew enough to be able to trail a sick man to the outhouse. If we don't go now, we'll never find whatever did this."

"I'm sorry, Chief, but I'm not going."

Slaughter scowled at Rettig, then turned to Hammel. "What about you?"

Hammel shrugged.

"You don't have a lot to say since we saw Clifford's body."

"Well, I figure I'll just watch and learn," Hammel said.

"Yeah, I bet you will."

Slaughter spun to face the gully. Even with his flashlight and the moon, he couldn't see much in the bushes, and his anger became fear again.

"Okay, you're right. It's stupid to go in there. Looking at these horses, I just—"

"Don't you worry. We'll be sure to get whatever did this," Rettig said. "But not right now."

Slaughter's anger changed to grief. He had to get away from here.

"But what about your horses?" Rettig asked.

"Leave them. Hell, what difference does it make?"

Slaughter heard his men walking behind him as he climbed the fence, and when he stepped down, from the house he heard the phone again. Whoever kept on calling, he was thinking, livid. He would make sure that they stopped it. He was running, cursing, toward the house, but when he burst in, grabbing for the phone, he heard a voice this time, and as he listened, he mentally started running again. It seemed as if the last few days he'd never stopped.

SIX

He charged along the corridor, the nurses staring at him. Rettig and Hammel were on guard back at his house, and he was thinking of his mangled horses, hoping that the two men would be safe as he pushed through the door marked MORGUE and rushed across the anteroom to push against the second door. The morgue looked like a shambles. There was blood and broken glass and scattered instruments. The medical examiner was leaning against a table. He had blood across his gown, his face mask hanging around his neck. His face was pale in contrast with the blood. He looked as if he'd been sick, although he might have seemed that way because the neon lights reflecting off the green tiles tinted everything a sickly pallor. The medical examiner was shaking, and the man beside him, wearing street clothes, didn't look much better. Owens. Slaughter recognized him as a veterinary whom he had come across from time to time and had last seen on Friday morning when they'd looked at old Doc Markle on the floor beside the mangled steer.

The two men turned to him, and Slaughter kept glancing all around. The smell of chemicals, of sick-sweet clotting blood. He didn't understand it. He inhaled, drawing breath to ask them, but the medical examiner interrupted. "I just killed him."

Slaughter stared at him and then at Owens. He was puzzled, walking toward them. "Look, you'd better take it easy. When you called, you sounded like you'd had a breakdown."

"But I killed him."

"Yes, I know. You told me on the phone. You said that at the mansion. But you had no way of knowing that the sedative would kill him. What's this blood here? I don't understand what's happened."

"Christ Almighty, listen while I tell you. I just killed him."

Slaughter spun toward Owens. "What's the matter with him?"

"Over there. You'd better take a look."

Owens had trouble speaking. He pointed toward the far end of the room, beyond the final table where a smear of blood was trickling down the wall, and Slaughter felt apprehensive again. He started forward, although a part of him was holding back. He peered down past the corner of the table, and he saw the tiny feet on the floor. Then he leaned a little closer, and he saw the boy, his belly sliced wide open. "Christ, you mutilated him!"

"No! I told you, I killed him!"

Slaughter swung and glared. "You said that he was dead back at the mansion!"

"I was certain that he was. I would have bet my reputation."

*"Bet your reputation?"*

"Never mind that. I did every standard test, and he was dead."

"Well, then he—"

"Seemed to come back from the dead and tried to grab me."

Slaughter felt as if he'd heard some unknown language. The words made no sense. They didn't have a meaning. Then he understood what he'd been told, and he stepped back from the medical examiner. "My God, you've really had a breakdown. You've gone crazy."

"No, just listen. I don't mean that the way it sounds."

"I hope to God you don't."

"I mean the paralytic stage of the disease must have been aggravated by the sedative."

Slaughter shook his head in confusion.

"He was so unconscious that his life signs couldn't be detected."

"What the hell is *this* now?" Slaughter asked him. "Edgar Allan Poe?"

"No, please. I listened for his heartbeat. I checked his breathing. I even took his temperature when I got back here. Everything was negative."

"You did a brain scan?"

"I did *everything,* I told you. He was dead as far as I could tell. I started working with him on the table, and he looked up, and he grabbed for my throat. I—"

"Take this slowly. One thing at a time. You're saying he was catatonic. That's it? That's your story?"

"On occasion, it can happen. Rarely. There are cases where a patient has been certified as dead, and he wakes up on a slab at the morgue."

Slaughter looked at Owens. "This is true?"

"I'm not a doctor, but I've heard of things like that. It's rare, just as he said, but it can happen."

"But Jesus, a brain scan."

"Look," the medical examiner said. "Once we thought that no sign of a heartbeat proved that someone had died. Then we found out that a person's heart could beat so weakly that our instruments couldn't detect it. So we made up other tests. For body heat. For electrical impulses in the brain. The fact is, we don't know exactly when a person dies. A patient goes to surgery. He's doing fine when suddenly his heart and brain fail.

We try everything we can to resuscitate him. No success. He's dead. Then all of a sudden, on its own, his heart starts beating again. So tell me how that happened. You explain it. I can't."

Slaughter looked at them, more disturbed. "All right, let's assume your argument's correct. The sedative wore off along with the paralysis."

"He grabbed for me. We fought. I knew I couldn't let him bite me, scratch me. Never mind how small he was. I couldn't let him touch me. He kept coming at me. I was kicking, yelling for help, but those two doors muffled the sound. We dodged around the table. I got cornered. I was scared and lashed out with the scalpel I was holding, and I killed him."

They were silent, staring at each other.

"Oh, my God." The medical examiner pounded a fist on the table.

Slaughter walked close. "Take it easy."

"But I—"

"Take it easy. Everything is going to be all right."

The medical examiner trembled.

"Something else. The mice died," Owens told them.

"What are you talking about?"

"We have mice down at the lab for doing tests on viruses," Owens said. "The mice were born and raised in sterile conditions, as the parents were, and those before them, so we know they're not contaminated. We can study any symptoms they develop from injections we give them and be certain that the injections caused the symptom. It's a way of isolating what we're dealing with and finding what will cure it. Anyhow, a standard test for rabies is to inject infected tissue into mice. If they live, then we're not dealing with the virus we suspected. If they die, then we have perfect samples of the virus to examine. Well, our first tests on this virus weren't conclusive. Oh, we knew that it was deadly, but the slides we studied looked a little different than they should have, so I did more tests. Instead of looking at the dog's brain, I injected several mice."

"And now they're dead?"

Owens nodded.

"Well, that isn't news. You said that it was deadly."

"But the mice don't normally develop symptoms for at least a week. These mice died in less than four hours. It was like a spedup version of the rabies symptoms. First, a subtle difference in behavior, then hostility, lack of coordination, finally paralysis and death. The hostility was quite pronounced, although they didn't snap at one another, only at the glass enclosures. But the point is that instead of surviving for seven days, they barely lasted four hours."

Slaughter's mind raced, making jumps in logic. "Show me."

Owens frowned at him.

"I want to see them. Show me where they are," Slaughter insisted.

"I didn't have the instruments I needed. An electron microscope for one thing, so I came up here to—"

"Never mind. Just show me."

"Over there. I brought them with me."

Slaughter pivoted toward a metal case and reached to lift its clasp. "It's all right if I open this?"

Owens nodded. "Everything is sterile. You won't be infected."

Slaughter pushed the lid up, staring at the specimens in sealed glass containers. He saw the white fur of mice, and something else that he had dreaded but expected, lifting one container, showing it. The medical examiner had turned now, he and Owens staring, and the mouse in there was snarling at them. Slaughter felt the scrape of its claws through the glass.

"But they were dead, I tell you!" Owens insisted. He crossed to Slaughter, pulling out the other glass containers. In them, every mouse was frantic.

"You're certain?" Slaughter asked him.

"Don't you think I know when something's dead?"

The medical examiner added, "As certain as *I* was when I examined that boy."

They continued staring at the frantic mice.

"Then I believe you." Slaughter grimaced. "I didn't, but I do now. I don't know what's going on, but I do know that it's happening." He frowned at the farthest table. "What about the boy? The mother and the father won't believe us when they see him. I can't think of any way to tell them."

"Then we won't." The medical examiner braced his shoulders, coming toward them, color in his face now. "I'll continue with the autopsy. I'd have to do it anyway, to learn how the virus works. I'll fix that slash across his stomach so it looks like it was part of the autopsy, and the three of us will be the only ones who know."

Suddenly they looked at one another, understanding the significance of their conspiracy, ever after their dependence on each other.

They were silent. Slaughter nodded, Owens with him.

"Owens, did you bring the samples for the microscope?"

"I've got them with the mice."

"Okay then, let's get started. Slaughter, if you go up to my office, you'll find a stack of books beside my desk. Search through the master index and read everything that you can find on rabies. That's not what we're dealing with. It's close enough, though, and we can't waste time from now on, telling you what we'll be doing."

Slaughter studied him. "How long till you know?"

"At least a couple of hours."

Slaughter glanced at his watch and saw that it was three a.m. "I don't look forward to the morning."

"For a lot of reasons."

"They'll be coming to me with their questions."

"Well, let's see if we can find the answers."

Slaughter nodded. Trying to smile in encouragement but failing, he started toward the doorway.

SEVEN

"This is what a rabies virus looks like."

Slaughter peered at where the medical examiner was pointing.

"Yes, I know. I read about it," Slaughter told him.

"Fine. Now here's a micrograph from the electron microscope. The virus from the dead dog."

Slaughter watched the medical examiner put down the micrograph beside the book that they'd been looking at. He studied it.

He thought about it quite a while. "Well, this one's thinner than the rabies virus."

"Yes, that's one of several contrasts. Normally we say a rabies virus has a bullet shape, but this one looks like, I don't know . . ."

"A missile," Owens said.

They glanced at him.

"Why not? All right, then, a missile." The medical examiner pointed at the micrograph again. "A missile is in keeping with the speed of this thing anyhow. The point is that a lot of viruses are shaped in general like this. Vesicular stomatitis would be one. But this thing isn't quite like any of them. It's much sleeker, and while there's an indentation at the bottom, there's no sign of an appendage there. What's more, the nervous system of the boy was not infected."

Slaughter looked at him. He knew enough from what he'd read that rabies moved along the nervous system, fed off it, and finally destroyed it. He frowned. "But I thought that—"

"Yes, I know. It shouldn't be. This is unlike any virus I've ever studied. It did infect his limbic brain, however."

Slaughter didn't understand. He tried to recollect what he had read, but nothing on that subject came to him.

"The limbic brain," the medical examiner repeated. "It's the part around which all the other sections of our brain developed. It's sometimes called reptilian, but I think of it as animal. It causes our survival instincts, our emotions and aggressions. Infection there would help explain why that boy acted as he did. Put simply, he became an animal."

"But what about the coma he went into?"

"Just don't rush me. Wait until I get to that. It's my guess that this virus is transmitted through the bloodstream. That explains the quick communication through the body. You should know that when I looked at where the boy said he was cut by glass, I found some evidence that he'd been bitten. When the doctor at the hospital examined him, he had no reason to assume the boy was lying, and besides the wound was jagged as if from a broken bottle. But the boy was bitten, all right. There isn't any question. Not more than a day ago. The virus travels through the bloodstream. It's selective. Only certain cells appeal to it."

"The limbic brain."

The medical examiner nodded. "It produces the symptoms of rabies very quickly; passes through, let's say, a twelve-hour phase in humans, paralyzes, and produces a coma. Evidently when the brain shuts down, the virus becomes dormant. When the victim regains consciousness, the virus starts to work again. It's really quite efficient, feeding until it produces near death and then holding off until the victim can sustain it once again. Because it passes through the bloodstream, it would show up in the salivary glands, infect the spittle, and pass to another victim in a bite. But if you were cut already and you came in contact with its blood, you'd get it just the same."

The medical examiner pointed toward the scab on Slaughter's cheek, and Slaughter suddenly was worried, raising one hand to it, frowning.

"It's too late to worry, Slaughter. If you'd been infected, we'd have known about it yesterday. But next time don't be so damned cavalier."

"If what you say is true, there wasn't anything that you could do about it anyway."

"That's right. Our vaccine would be useless." The medical examiner reached up to touch his own face then, his lips scabbed and swollen. "I got lucky, too. I would have had it by now if this cut had been contaminated. As it is, I gave myself two antirabies shots. Absolutely useless. Christ, I don't know what we're going to do."

"You say you never saw a virus like this? You never even heard about it?" Slaughter asked.

The medical examiner shook his head.

"Well, I did," Owens told them.

They studied him.

"I read about it," Owens said. "Nineteen sixty-nine in Ethiopia. A herd of cattle came down with a special form of rabies, little frenzy, just paralysis. They all collapsed. The owner didn't know exactly what they had. He gave them up for dead, and then they all recovered."

"What?" The medical examiner looked astonished. "Nothing can survive it. That's impossible as far as I know."

"This herd did. The problem is they still retained the virus and in several days they manifested symptoms once again. They had to be destroyed.

"You're certain it was rabies?"

"Oh, yes, all the later tests confirmed it. And I read about another case in India two years ago, but this time it was water buffalo."

"But this thing isn't rabies. Any vaccine they developed wouldn't be of use here. Even if it would, there isn't any time to get it."

"What would cause a brand new kind of virus?" Slaughter asked.

"You tell me," the medical examiner responded. "You want to know the truth? I wonder why it doesn't happen all the time. Never mind a thing like legionnaires' disease, which evidently was around for quite a while, but no one diagnosed it. Never mind a thing like staph or gonorrhea which mutated into forms resistant to a drug like penicillin. Let's just go along with my contention that this virus is a new one. Asking what would cause it is like asking why our ancestors developed a big brain from their limbic system and turned into humans. There's no ready answer. Evolution is an accident. A cell develops in an unusual fashion. Something happens to the DNA. We like to think that everything is fixed and ordered. But it isn't. Things are changing all around us, not so quickly that we recognize the change, but it's occurring, people growing taller, dogs whose breeds are now defective, dying out. We recognize extremes, of course. We call them monsters. But the really startling changes are occurring in those simple life forms that we hardly ever notice. Cells. Their time scale is much different from our own, much faster. Evolution has sped up for them, the chance for random variants. But evolution doesn't even have to be in stages. Quantum leaps can happen in an instant. Every time a person gets an X ray, tiny bullets zinging past those chromosomes. You want a model? Let's try this one. Let's assume we've got a dog. The dog has rabies, but the symptoms haven't shown up yet. The dog is hurt, though. Let's say that it's got a broken leg or some internal swelling so the owner takes it in for X rays, and the dog is treated and gets better. But the damage has been done. The rabies virus has by chance been struck by just one X ray. Hell, it only takes one mutant cell that lodges in the limbic brain and starts to reproduce. Now the owner goes on holiday. He takes the dog up into the mountains. The dog goes crazy, and it runs away. Contagion starts."

"What you said about these dogs up in the hills. Psychopathic animal behavior," Slaughter told him.

"Sure. Just two roads from the valley," Owens said. "The mountains are around us, so the virus has been localized. But why did no one ever recognize it until now?"

"Because, so far as I remember, no one ever tested for it," the medical examiner said. "Ranchers maybe shot a few dogs and then buried them, but did you ever have a look at one?"

Owens shook his head.

"Well, there you have it."

"But you told me Friday night that people have been bitten by them," Slaughter said. "They would have come in for the rabies treatment but, in spite of that, have developed symptoms."

"And they *did* come in for treatment, and there wasn't any problem. So the dog that bit them didn't have the virus, or the virus didn't mutate until later. That's no argument against the model."

"But the virus is so virulent that everything would have it by now," Slaughter insisted.

"I don't think so. The attacks we've seen were plainly murderous. I doubt too many animals or people would survive them. Plus, the victims must be weakened by the virus. When the winter comes, it likely kills them. That's a natural control. We haven't studied any long term consequences of the virus. Maybe there's a calming process. I don't know at this point."

"So why now would the virus show up suddenly in town?"

"You know why as well as I do. All it takes is just one dog to wander in. But I think there's another reason. Don't forget the winter was a hard one. It drives victims down from where their normal hunting routes are in the mountains. That's one version of a model anyhow. I might be wrong. At least, it's something. What we do know, in addition to our tests, is that the victims are nocturnal."

The medical examiner pointed toward the case that contained the jars of supposedly dead mice that Owens had brought from the veterinary clinic. Owens had discovered that the mice were peaceful if concealed in darkness, that their rage was manifested only when their eyes were aggravated by light.

"That's another symptom this virus has in common with the rabies virus," the medical examiner continued. "Intense sensitivity to light. That was why the dead boy snarled the way he did. The moon was shining through the upper windows of the mansion. And that helps explain why so much trouble has occurred at night. The victims hide and sleep in daylight. Then they come out after dark, but now the moon is almost full, and they're reacting to it."

"One thing more. We know that they're not dangerous to one another," Owens said. "When I put some of them together in the same container, they ignored each other, staring fiercely at the light and lunging at the glass around them."

Slaughter thought about the figures he had seen up in the bushes by his barn tonight. "You mean they hunt in packs?"

"Not necessarily, although it's possible."

"But what would make them do that?"

"Look, this virus gives control back to the limbic brain and makes it act the way it once did several hundred thousand years ago. To hunt in packs is natural. It's even a survival trait. Individual behavior, at least in humans, is by contrast very recent."

EIGHT

Wheeler braced himself up in the tree and waited for the sunrise. He'd been up there all night, and his back and legs were sore and twisted from the way he was positioned among the branches. He was numb from lack of sleep, his eyelids heavy, plus his hands were cramped around the rifle he was holding, but for all that, he was satisfied. His effort had been worth the pain. He smiled toward the murky rangeland and the object lying by the sagebrush. Yes, he'd gotten what he had come for, which was something very different for him, getting what he wanted. Things had not gone well for him in quite a while. Since 1970 and that October afternoon when he had shot that hippie. On occasion when he managed to be honest with himself, he recognized that he had been in trouble long before that, with his wife and in particular his son, but if he'd helped to make that trouble, it was nothing that they couldn't have worked out among themselves. What had made the difference were those god-damned hippies who had come to town. *They* were the cause of this, their loud mouths and their garbage. He remembered how he had gone to town and first had seen them, angered by their sloppiness, their easy answers to the country's problems. Sure, drop out and act like children, more than that, like animals. Oh, that was some solution, all right. They were just afraid to go to Vietnam is all, too god-damned yellow to protect their country. He had been there when the town had forced them from the valley. He had helped to push them out. He'd kicked and thrown rocks as had others. He had shut their filthy mouths for them and hoped they'd learned their lesson. But his son had gone up to that lousy commune then, and he himself had been made to look like a fool. No son of his was going to end up like those freaks, not so that the town could make jokes about him.

Plus, those hippies might be dangerous. The drugs they took, they might do anything. Wheeler had known he had to get his son back. So he'd gone up to the commune, and of course, they tried to fight him, to hide what they were up to. There'd been no choice. He'd had to shoot the hippie who had come at him. It was self-defense. The town would understand that, Wheeler had figured. But it *hadn't* understood, and his son had turned against him as well, and he himself had gone to prison for two years. Oh, that was fine, the way his friends had turned against him. He couldn't count on anyone. He should have learned that lesson years before, but he had learned it then all right. His son had run off after that, and then while he himself had been in prison, he had gone through all that trouble with the guard. The guy just wouldn't let him alone. There wasn't any choice except to fight. By Jesus, he wouldn't be pushed around, so instead of getting time off for good behavior, he'd been forced to serve the full extent of his sentence.

What did he expect? If they were out to get him, he was powerless, and then his wife had turned against him. She'd been keeping up the ranch while he was gone. She hadn't come to see him, but he'd figured that she'd been so busy that she couldn't get away. The day he came home he found out the truth, however. She told him that she'd stayed to manage things because she didn't want to leave the place to strangers, but she wasn't going to live with him, and now that he was back, she wasn't needed, she was leaving. He had fixed her for that. She had limped out to the taxi when it came for her. He didn't help her with the bags. He let the driver do that. He just stood there on the porch and cracked his knuckles, telling her that he would never take her back, that if she tried to come back, he would beat her even worse, and that had been the last he saw of her. Well, that was fine as far as he was concerned. She'd never been good for him, always nagging at him about how much he was drinking, about the work he didn't want to do. Christ, he was better off without her and without that mouthy, trouble-making son. He didn't need them. He could get along without them.

But Wheeler had trouble, all the same. His former friends avoided him, although he expected that. They really hadn't been his friends. All they'd wanted was a sucker to buy them drinks. Sure, they'd been lying to him all the way. But he'd found *new* friends, trail hands and a couple ranchers in the valley who were not so god-damned proper that they wouldn't take a little time out to relax. A man got stale if all he did was work. That wasn't any kind of life. But then Wheeler's cattle got sick one year. The next year, there were many stillbirths. After that, the price of beef went down. There wasn't any way to get ahead once everybody turned on you. *This* year, the bank was making noises about mortgage payments that he hadn't met; the barn was close to falling down; the winter had been so bad that he'd lost more stock than he had counted on; and now the predators were moving in.

Wheeler had found the first steer Friday morning, so disfigured that he almost didn't recognize what it had been. He'd never seen a carcass like it. Not just one wolf or a coyote, but a whole damned pack had done this, in a frenzy. He heard that night about another rancher who had found a steer like this, and in the morning when he'd gone out to check his stock, he'd found three other mangled steers, and he couldn't stop from cursing. Hell, they meant to ruin him. He heard that a dozen ranchers in the valley had also found cattle like this, and they didn't know what they could do except to post some guards and maybe have a meeting. There was no sense in their leaving poison that the cattle might get into. But Wheeler knew what to do. He was not about to let this thing continue. He meant to stop it dead right now. Those predators had picked the wrong man to play games with.

In the afternoon, he chose three steers and led them to the spot where he had found the mutilated carcasses. The predators were in a routine, choosing this location each time. With the foothills so close, they just figured they could slip down for an easy kill and aggravate the man who owned their supper. But tonight he would surprise them. First he staked the cattle, leaving portions of the mangled steers to spread their odor and to hide his scent. If he had lately not been good at ranching, he was *very* good at hunting, and he'd gone back to his house to eat and get his rifle and the Benzedrine he'd been given by a trucker in a bar one night. He'd walked back toward where he had staked the cattle. That was crucial, not to drive his truck and warn whatever might be watching. When he'd come to within a quarter mile, he had eased down, crawling, inching toward a solitary tree that was between him and the three steers. From there, with the moonlight to help him, he would have a good view, and he stayed low by the tree until sunset, waiting even longer for the darkness to enclose him before slowly standing, hidden by the tree, and climbing through its branches to a cradle near the top.

He moved as silently as he was able. Then he settled back against the trunk and swallowed a Benny, staring toward his cattle. He checked his rifle and made sure that he hadn't lost the extra rounds that he'd put in his pocket, and he knew that he was ready. Even with his jacket, he was cold, but that was just because he couldn't warm himself by moving. He ignored the cramps in his legs and scowled toward the cattle as the moon rose higher and higher.

The cattle were nervous, but he saw no sign of anything coming toward them. Soon he swallowed another Benny. Abruptly he saw shadows moving and aimed his rifle, only to realize that the shadows were only in his imagination. Shit, this idea had been wonderful when he had planned it. Being here was something different, and he almost climbed down, going to his house, when what seemed several hours later, they were out there.

First he heard them baying at the moon. He tensed. Then

he saw a silhouette to one side, next another just behind it. As
he blinked, he saw the darkness filled with them. He couldn't
wait until they came so close that they would see the tethers on
the cattle, dimly sensing they were ambushed. He quickly
aimed, but he couldn't chance a poor shot that would scare
them off and make this agony of waiting worthless. He would
have to do this properly, and breath held, he was thinking of
his wife, his son, the prison guard, his former friends, imagining
that they were swarming out there. He was easing his finger
onto the trigger as one silhouette became distinct, and when he
fired, the recoil knocked him hard against the tree trunk. He
worked the rifle's bolt and fired again, but they were gone now,
although he saw a huddled figure out there by the sagebrush.
It was still and silent, and he smiled to think that he had
dropped one, maybe more if he kept waiting, and he shivered
from excitement, from the Bennies and the cold, but he didn't
see further movement in the shadows. He just heard them howling somewhere in the distance. Then the howling stopped when
the moon went down.

He waited even longer. Once he thought he saw something, but it darted so fast that he didn't know what it was, and
he wanted to go down and see what he had shot, but he'd stuck
things out this long, he might as well stay put a little longer.
For a change, he'd see a project to the finish. But his legs were
sore and twisted, and the darkness was turning gray, the sun
about to rise. At last, he climbed down the tree and hobbled
toward the figure.

From the distance, it had seemed like a wolf, but now as
he came closer, it looked more like a bobcat, smaller, with long
hind legs and a face that wasn't pointed but flat. The fur was
draped around it more than growing on it. The fur was ragged,
torn in places, and some sections of the skin were bare. There
wasn't any tail, and coming closer, Wheeler was frowning, thinking that this was his imagination, trying hard to calm himself.
But then he stopped and saw the feet and hands and nose, and
what he felt was like a replay of that instant twenty-three years
ago. God, he'd shot somebody! Not a man! A boy! The kid
looked maybe twelve. But why was this kid dressed in ragged
pelts the way he was? Had children from the town come out to
scare the cattle? Had some campers . . . ? But Wheeler knew

the answer even as he asked those useless questions. That long hair below the shoulders. Christ, he'd shot another hippie.

He pivoted, scowling around him. Had another bunch come through here? Was that first bunch still up in the mountains? He had heard that they had left, but if they hadn't, this might be one of their kids. That big hole in its back from where the bullet had burst out. That motionless, silent body. He was nudging at it with his boot, but nothing happened. He breathed, shaking. How could he explain this? First one, now another, and the town would act the way it had the first time. No one would believe him when he said it was an accident. They'd send him back to prison, and he knew he couldn't bear that. Not that guard again. He couldn't stand it. Just because these god-damned hippies came down here to take things out on him. He started digging with his rifle butt, but all he did was chip the wood because the ground out here was hard, and he needed tools, a pick and shovel. Quick before somebody found this. He stumbled from the figure, bumping against the tree, and lurching toward his ranchhouse. Then he started running. Have to hurry, get that pick and shovel, make the hole deep, make sure scavengers don't dig up the body, sprinkle it with quicklime. He ran harder. His fear had changed to a frenzy, his speed now almost manic as he saw the ranchhouse in the distance while, his stomach churning, he kept charging toward it.

# THE
## PART FIVE
# LAKE

SLAUGHTER STOOD BEFORE THE GLASS PARTITION, NUMBED BY WHAT HE SAW. CODY WHO HAD found the boy inside the mansion last night and been bitten was now snarling, writhing to escape the straps that bound him to the bed. His throat was bandaged, and the damage there might help explain the hoarse inhuman sounds he made, but Slaughter didn't think so. No, the virus was at work. The man was like a lunatic, and Slaughter thought again about the medical examiner's remark, about the madness from the moon. "It's just a guess," he told the orderly beside him. "Turn his room lights off, and maybe that will calm him. God, I wish he'd pass out."

Even with the window as a buffer, Slaughter felt the snarling touch him. He was nauseated by the foam that drooled from Cody's mouth. The snarling and writhing became more extreme. Cody tried to twist his head to bite the nearest strap around him.

"I can't watch this."

Swallowing, Slaughter glanced at where Marge waited at the far end of the hallway. She was peering through another window. Slaughter knew that the mother of the dead boy was inside there, and he took one final look at Cody before walking slowly toward Marge.

"I just hit her," Marge said, not turning to him. "There was nothing else I could do. I didn't mean to hit her so hard. She was—"

"You can't go on like this."

"But she's got a fractured skull."

"You'd rather that she'd killed her husband?"

"No, I . . ." Marge faced him.

"Then take it easy. You did what you thought was necessary. As it is, she's going to live. That's all that really counts, although I don't know what they're going to do with her. There isn't any way they know to cure her."

He peered through the window at the mother who was strapped unconscious to her bed, bandages around her skull, an intravenous bottle draining toward a needle in her arm.

"We know this much," Slaughter said. "She shouldn't be sedated, so the fact that she's unconscious from the blow you gave her might turn out to be the best thing, all considered. If she were awake, she'd be hysterical like Cody up the hall."

Even here, Slaughter heard the snarling from the other room.

Marge leaned against the wall.

"Hey, why not go home?" Slaughter suggested. "There isn't anything that you can do here. You'll be told whatever happens."

"What about yourself?"

"Oh, don't you know? I'm trying for a record. How long I can go without sleep."

He hoped that would make her smile, but she only stared.

"Marge, I know that what you did was hard."

She studied him.

"I know that if there'd been another way you would have chosen it. I think that you did fine. I wish you wouldn't feel so bad."

"You'd feel the same."

"Of course, I would. But then I'd need a friend like you to say what I just said to you. I mean it. You did fine. I don't want you to worry."

"Thanks." Marge bit her lip. "But it doesn't help."

"All the same, go home. I'll get word to you."

She nodded. Even so, she lingered.

"Come on. Let me walk you down."

He touched her arm, and she responded, walking with him along the hallway. Neither looked at Cody. At the corner, she glanced back at the windows in the wall down there, and then she went downstairs with him, and he was watching by the back door as she walked across the parking lot.

That poor, sad, lonely, tortured woman, he was thinking. When she raised that baseball bat, she must have been in agony. He waved in farewell as she drove away, then thought a moment before heading toward the phone inside the nurses' station.

He'd avoided making this call much too long, reluctantly dialing Parsons' number, and the man answered, sleepy, angry.

"Slaughter? Eight o'clock? On Sunday? Can't this wait until a decent hour?"

"No, we really have to talk."

"Well, Jesus, Slaughter—"

"This is serious. We don't have too much time."

Parsons exhaled. "All right, then. I'll see you in my office in an hour. But this better be important."

"Oh, don't worry," Slaughter told him. "You'll wish that you didn't know."

Slaughter frowned and hung up. He was thinking that in all the years he'd lived here he had never been to Parsons' house, and he wondered why just now he'd thought of that, with everything he had to keep his mind on. Then he guessed it was because of all the power games that Parsons liked to play. The man kept his subordinates away from where he lived because he wanted to dissociate them, keep them from assuming friendship. That way he intimidated them. But Slaughter didn't care much. He had never been afraid of Parsons, although in truth he didn't want to go through this with him, and needing to keep occupied, he went out, driving to the station where already, even early in the morning, there were calls about more prowlers, about mangled cats and dogs and cattle, several missing persons. Well, it's just beginning, he decided. Then he did his best to shut his mind off as he cleaned up, washing in the men's room, changing from his sweaty shirt to one he kept inside his office drawer. No, Parsons wasn't going to like this, and a half hour later, as the two men (Slaughter unshaven) sat facing one another, it was worse than Slaughter had expected. Parsons had been fifteen minutes late, and Slaughter had been forced to wait outside the locked doors of the Potter's Field *Gazette*. Then Parsons had shown up, freshly showered, wearing a suit and tie. "No, not yet. Wait until we're in my office," the man had told him, and upstairs the man had listened, then quite calmly answered, "You expect me to believe this?"

"I don't know. I wish I didn't."

"Really, Slaughter, think about it. All you're sure of is that a boy came down with some disease, or maybe he just had a breakdown. Then his mother got hysterical and fought her husband. Cody is in shock. He's got a raging fever. There's your explanation."

"You've forgotten Clifford's body."

"No, I haven't. Clifford was attacked all right and likely by a wild dog as you say. But were there any tests performed?"

"Just to find out what attacked him. At the time, we had no reason to suspect a virus."

"So the only tests were on that sick dog, and the evidence was very close to rabies."

"But the medical examiner—"

"Look, Slaughter, I don't want to disillusion you, but everybody knows that he came back here because no one else would have him. He broke down in Philadelphia, and it wouldn't surprise me if he made a crisis of this just so he'd seem important. As I interpret what you told me, there's been no time to test the dead boy for this so-called virus. Granted that his brain had been infected, if what the medical examiner says is true. But that could be because of many things. To do a proper slide for the electron microscope takes at least a couple of days. I gather that some steps can be eliminated if a person's in a hurry, which explains how Owens had his samples ready, but I know this much—the slides from that dog's brain were made so quickly that we shouldn't put much faith in them. I'll need a lot more to convince me. Think about it as I told you. Which makes more sense? Rabies or a brand-new virus?"

"You weren't there to see the boy."

"But I heard all about it."

Slaughter straightened.

"Sure, what's the matter, Slaughter? Did you think I didn't know? I run the god-damned paper. I'm the mayor. I have all kinds of people watching for me. If those parents choose to prosecute, the medical examiner is in shit to his eyebrows. He administered a sedative without the proper cautions. Now of course he's going to say a virus killed the boy. He surely won't incriminate himself. His word on this is hardly what you'd call objective. And that's something else I want to talk to you about. We'll leave aside for now the issue of this woman you employ who hit the mother with a baseball bat, although I wonder why you haven't charged her and I'm positive there'll be a lawsuit. Let's just think about the medical examiner. He was the last man I'd have chosen to do tests on that boy. He—"

"It's not important. If you'd seen the boy, you'd know he wasn't acting normally."

"That's exactly what we pay you for. To deal with things like that. To stop trouble, not cause more of it. You've had it fairly easy, Slaughter. Not too much goes on here. Now the first time something unusual happens, you come waking me on Sunday morning with your crazy notions about sealing off the valley and exterminating all the livestock."

Slaughter scowled. He kept his fists gripped tightly by his legs where he was sitting, and he felt his face go warm. He tried to control his breathing. "I said if it came to that. I don't know if it's necessary. I'm just asking your opinion."

"Well, it isn't necessary. Let's relax a minute, Slaughter. Let me talk about my job a little. I was mayor for many years before you came here. I was mayor when all those hippies came to town, to name an instance, and I knew that there'd be trouble, plus I knew that all I had to do was flex my muscles and arrange to move them out of town. I didn't, though, because there would have been complaints about that, people saying that, sure, no one liked those hippies but maybe we should have let them have a chance. And so I waited for the opportunity. Their foul mouths and their dope and garbage got extreme, and still I waited because I knew people shortly would come begging me to move them, which precisely is what happened. Now I got what I intended, but I did it diplomatically. Does all that make some sense to you?"

Slaughter's gaze intensified.

"The truth is that the people always know what's best for them. A proper leader only goes along with what they tell him," Parsons said. "That's why they've kept me as their mayor all these years. Because I understand that. All I want is what they tell me. So you say there's going to be an epidemic. Well, that's fine. Let's wait and see. The evidence is inconclusive, but I'll keep an open mind about it. Even so, the steps that you suggest are inadvisable. Exterminate the livestock, all the animals in town? Now really, Slaughter, what if there's no epidemic, what if this is just a case of poor tests and a biased medical examiner? The people would come for our heads. They'd want someone to pay for all the cattle that were killed, and you sure as hell don't earn enough for that. Even sealing off the valley. Christ, this valley's livelihood is cattle. If a rumor starts that all our cattle are diseased, we might as well destroy them anyhow. There won't be any way to sell them. No, we'll wait and see. If there *is* an epidemic, we'll hear from the people what to do. They'll tell us, and their choice will be the right one, and we'll all survive this with a conscience, just the way we did with all those hippies."

"But the difference," Slaughter said, "is that nobody died because you waited. On my desk right now, the messages are piling up, and there'll be more until the valley's in a panic. Not just mangled cattle. Not just Clifford and that boy. We're going to wade through corpses before long, and nothing's going to help those people."

"But you haven't listened to me, Slaughter. There's no other choice. Okay, you want to argue. Here's the end of it. You'll go on as if everything is normal. You will quarantine whoever's been exposed, if indeed there is a virus, which I doubt. You'll pick up any dogs or cats or even chipmunks if they start behaving strangely. But you'll stay calm and tell the people that the situation's in control. And listen to me, Slaughter. If you even hint about an epidemic, your ass won't be worth the nail that stakes it to the courthouse door. Is that clear enough? Is that an order you can understand?"

Slaughter stared. "Can I at least get on the radio and tell the town we've found a case of rabies?"

Parsons thought about it. "Yes, I see no problem. After all, we do have evidence of rabies, and the town should be informed for its protection. But don't dare mention cattle. That's a different issue. Now I have to get back home. I'm late for church, and I have relatives coming home afterward for brunch."

He stood, and clearly Slaughter was expected to go with him. "Oh, yes, what about that magazine reporter from New York? That man named Dunlap?"

"I cooperated as you told me," Slaughter said.

"Well, don't let him find out what you're dealing with. That's all we need is for the rumors to get printed. Have him leave this afternoon."

"But he's not finished with his story yet."

"He's finished, all right. He just doesn't know it. Make sure he leaves town, and while you're at it, get yourself cleaned up before too many people see you. Really, you don't look so good. The job is maybe too much for you."

Slaughter almost laughed. You bastard, he was thinking. You don't miss a chance to stay on top of people, do you? They walked toward the door, and Slaughter waited until Parsons went out before him, thinking this would be the way to handle things: he'd better keep his back protected.

TWO

Slaughter was in a phone booth, but the line was fuzzy, and the noises from the other end distracted him. "Look, Altick, I can't tell you why I need them, but I—"

"Just hold on." To someone in the background, "Put them over there. I'm going with you. I don't want that chopper taking off without me. Good. I'm sorry, Slaughter. Everything is frantic here. I'm listening."

"I need some men," he responded louder. "I can't give you reasons, but I'll maybe have to borrow help."

"There isn't any way." The voice was much too final.

"But—"

"No, listen to me. I need everybody I can muster," Altick said. "I sent five men with dogs to look for Bodine, and there isn't any word from them. They've disappeared."

"But Bodine—"

"It's my men. I mean my *men* have disappeared. The chopper flew up where they'd camped, but they were gone, and they're not answering the radio. I don't like what I'm feeling. If you'd called five minutes later, I'd have been up in the chopper."

"Maybe they're behind a ridge that's muting signals to the radio."

"The chopper flew up anywhere they could have gone to. No, they're missing, and I can't waste time. I've got to look for them." More noises in the background. "I said wait until I'm ready. Yeah, we'll need that medical kit as well. Just take them to the chopper. Slaughter, there's no way for me to help you. I'll call you back when I have a chance."

"But—"

There were other noises in the background. Then the line was disconnected.

Slaughter put the phone down, staring at it. Sure, another escalation. By now, he'd grown accustomed to the burning in his stomach, but he hadn't yet adjusted to the way his mind was nagging at him. Everything was moving too fast. There was hardly any time to think. His talk with Parsons. Five policemen missing. Things weren't bad enough, he had to worry about Parsons.

He hurried from the phone booth, moving toward the hotel desk. He knew that he had planned this since he'd said good-bye to Parsons, although he wouldn't have admitted it. But why else would he have come directly here? He could have used the phone back at the station.

"Gordon Dunlap," he told the desk clerk.

"What about him?"

"Damn it, tell me where to find him."

The clerk was fumbling through cards to find the number.

Slaughter started up the stairs as he heard the number. He ran to the balcony and scanned the arrows showing which rooms were on which side, darting to the left and down a hall-way, studying the arrows once again. The halls were twisting, turning. He came around a corner, and he saw the door along a dead-end corridor and raced past the pictures on the wall. He knocked, but no one answered.

"Dunlap. Wake up. This is Slaughter."

No answer.

"Dunlap." Slaughter knocked again. He tried the door-knob. It wouldn't move. But as he leaned against the door, the catch gave way. The door swung open.

Dunlap hadn't even shut the door completely. He was sprawled across the bed, his clothes wrinkled, soaked with some-thing. On the floor there was an empty whisky bottle, papers, cigarette butts, a broken ashtray, a toppled chair.

What the hell had happened here? He smelled the sick-ness, stepping back, then going forward. Dunlap didn't seem to breathe. He wasn't moving. Slaughter grabbed him. "Dunlap, wake up. It's important."

Dunlap didn't move, though. Slaughter shook him. "Come on, you bastard. Wake up." Slaughter felt to find a heart-beat. Then he had it, and at least he didn't have to worry about that. "For Christ sake, Dunlap." He shook him again. Dunlap groaned and tried to turn, but Slaughter wouldn't let him. "This is Slaughter! Wake up! We've got problems!"

Dunlap moaned. His breath was putrid. Too rushed to mind that, Slaughter hefted him across his shoulder and stum-bled down the hallway toward the bathroom. When he set him on the toilet, he started to unbutton Dunlap's shirt, but that was taking too much time, so he just ripped the shirt off. Dunlap tilted, almost falling, and Slaughter eased him onto the floor, then got his pants off, his shoes and socks and underwear. The underwear was soiled. Nostrils flaring, Slaughter threw it into a corner. He slid Dunlap into the bathtub and turned the shower on to cold. Dunlap woke up, screaming.

"Take it easy."

Dunlap wouldn't stop screaming.

Slaughter slapped his cheeks. "Hey, it's me. It's Slaughter."

Dunlap blinked at him. His eyes were red. The vomit that had caked around his lips and chin was rinsing off, and he was frowning, his head to one side. He looked as if he might begin to cry, and then his body heaved.

"It's all right. I'm with you," Slaughter told him. "Get it out of you."

He studied Dunlap, water spraying onto the both of them, as spasm followed spasm, and then Dunlap sighed and leaned back, coughing in the bathtub. He was crying.

"What's the matter? Nightmares?"

Dunlap nodded.

"Well, I've got work for you. I need you sober. While you're stunned like this, I need some answers. And I think right now that you won't lie to me. I need to know if I can trust you."

Dunlap closed his eyes and shivered as the cold water sprayed at him. "You know already what you want to hear. You don't need me to answer."

"Listen, buddy." Slaughter dug his fingers into Dunlap's shoulder. "You're not quite so drunk as you pretend. I want to hear the answer."

"Sure, all right, I'll say that you can trust me."

"If you screw up, you'll wish you'd never met me."

"*You can trust me.* Hey. My shoulder."

Slaughter noticed the way the skin was turning purple and eased his fingers off. He leaned back, sitting on the toilet seat. "I need a man to cover me," he said at last. "A man from outside who has no involvement in this. I want you to watch me every second, check out everything I do and keep a record. There'll soon be trouble, major trouble, and I want to know that I'm protected."

Dunlap had his eyes shut as he shivered in the cold spray of water.

"Do you hear me?" Slaughter asked.

"Is it that bad?"

"It's that bad."

"Hell, I'd be crazy not to go along with you."

"You'll be crazy if you do. There's just one stipulation. All I ask is that you wait until I say that you can publish the story."

"Now I—"

"I don't want to have to worry about you. I have lots to watch for without that."

The water kept spraying. Slaughter felt his wet shirt clinging to his skin.

"All right, so long as no one else is in on this," Dunlap said.

"It's you and me."

"A deal then."

Slaughter sat back on the toilet seat. He didn't know exactly where to start. "You said you wanted a story. Here's the damnedest thing you ever heard."

### THREE

Altick scanned the trees and ridges as the helicopter swooped over them. He watched for some flash of movement, some odd color, anything, but there was nothing to attract him, just an endless sweep of forest rising sharply, boulders, dead-falls, streams and canyons, farther ridges, everything but what he wanted, and he rubbed his eyes to clear them, staring harder. There were three of them in the chopper, the pilot, Altick, and a state policeman wedged in back. They had rifles, binoculars, a portable two-way radio, and several knapsacks filled with food, water, and medical supplies. The helicopter was outmoded, small, ideal for two persons, suitable for three if absolutely necessary. With the added weight of their gear, it was unsteady, slow, and hard to keep above the trees. It burned fuel too rapidly. As they swung up the contour of these rising ridges, there were moments when they held their breath, and Altick wished that there had been another way to get up here as soon as he required.

On the ground the other team would have already started, five men as before but this time primed for trouble, clutching their rifles, watching all around them as they used their maps to find the best way to the lake up in the mountains. There were no dogs, no way to get any soon enough, but this search team had a specific destination, and it didn't need any dogs for guidance. Altick thought about them somewhere down below him, thought about the hard job they would have to push up through the forest toward the rendezvous up here. But he had made several phone calls, and there hadn't been any other helicopters he could commandeer. He was thinking that he might wish he had more than just two men with him. There was no predicting what he might find when the helicopter touched down.

He kept staring. Then he saw some movement, but as he pointed at it, he realized that what he'd seen were elk below him among the trees. He saw one bound across an open space, and normally he would have taken pleasure, but he had to keep his mind on his objective. More than that, he now was bothered that he hadn't seen more elk before this, deer, other signs of life down there. He should have, this high in the mountains, but the forest seemed deserted, and he wished the helicopter could go faster.

It was roaring, straining. Even with the plexiglass, the noise came rushing at him, and he kept peering down, and the whole scene was like everything he'd been through back in Nam in 1969. While the radicals had looted campus buildings, while the marchers had converged on Washington, he had been going on patrols, his team in a chopper, staring at the wilderness below them, and the trees of course were different now, the weather, and whatever waited for him down there, but he felt the tightness in his stomach, felt the cramps around his heart as he fought to restrain his nervousness. He remembered all the shit that he had gone through, all the friends that he'd seen killed, the blood, the disease, the suffocating jungle, believing that he served his country while the demonstrators back home had weakened the country's resolve. He had come back from his tour of duty and had signed on with the state police. The valley at least had responded to him with some pride, and with his military bearing, he'd done well. Indeed he sometimes acted as if he were still in the service, and he talked about the people in the valley as civilians, building pride and character among his men, reminding them that they were different. And they all were loyal to him, as he was to them, afraid now for the officers he'd sent up and were missing. He was staring at the forest, reaching absently to touch his mustache and the scar across his lip that it disguised. He grabbed the microphone and spoke abruptly, "Chopper to patrol. Report."

The hiss of static.

"Chopper to patrol."

"Yeah, Captain, everything's fine. We're moving fast. We should be up there before noon."

"They might have headed back already. Let's hope we didn't have to do this."

"We'll just call it exercise."

"Some exercise," Altick answered, smiling. "Ten-four. Out."

His smile dissolved, though, as he stared down from the helicopter. He was more and more reminded of those choppers back in Nam, the tension solid in him as the helicopter rose up past another ridge, and suddenly he saw it.

"There's the lake," the pilot said.

Altick nodded, studying the landscape. It was formed a basin, ridges sloping all around, then forest spreading inward, then the clearing that went all around the lake. There were few trees beside the lake itself, but Altick knew his men would have gone toward them. He pointed toward one tree by the lake, and they swept closer.

"This was where they camped," the pilot told him. "When I couldn't find them, I went back to get some help."

The knapsacks were in sight now and the black pit where their campfire had been. Nothing else, and Altick tapped the pilot's shoulder. "Swing around the lake. I want to check those trees beside it on the other shore. I want to check the edge of the forest as well."

"I did that when I first was up here."

"Yeah, well, just for me, let's do it once again."

Altick continued staring downward. They moved around the lake, the wind whipped by the rotors causing patterns on the water. But the other trees had nothing there of interest, and the clearing all around the lake was quiet, and he saw no sign of anything around the forest's edge.

"Okay, then, take her back and set her down."

"I told you we wouldn't see anything."

Altick only looked at him. He spoke into the microphone. "Chopper to patrol one. Charlie, do you hear me?"

Static. He waited. "Chopper to patrol one."

"I already did that, too," the pilot told him. "But I never got an answer."

They set down, the long grass bending from the wind created by the helicopter's rotors, and back in Nam, Altick would have been in motion by now, jumping out before the chopper hit the ground or more often hovered and then swooped away, and he'd be scrambling with his men to find some cover. Abandoned. At least this way the helicopter would stay with him, and he waited for the rotors to stop before he unhitched his harness, shoved at the hatch, and stepped out, holding his rifle.

He hurried toward the trees beside the lake, then straightened as he stared at what he'd been afraid of. Never mind the scattered remnants of the fire. Kicking at it would be one way to put it out, sloppy granted, but there was no dismissing what he found beside the charred wood. Blood. A lot of it. Huge patches of it, dry now on the mountain grass and earth. He glanced around and saw the leashes on the tree, more blood where once the dogs must have huddled. He noticed the glint of an empty rifle cartridge. In the grass, he found a flashlight, and the knapsacks had been torn, their contents missing, and a rifle butt was smashed beside a tree—the little signs he couldn't see from the air, but now he knew that there had been a fight all right, and no dog, no wolf, no bear ever smashed a rifle. At once, he saw the barrel in the shallows of the lake.

"My God, what happened here?" his deputy blurted.

Altick swung toward the pilot. "Can you use that rifle we brought for you?"

"Sure, but—" The pilot looked pale.

"Five men and five dogs, and this is all that's left of them. I don't think we can wait for help. We've got to spread out, searching," Altick said.

"Not me. I'm not going anywhere alone," the pilot told him.

From the right, a wind rushed toward them, tugging at their clothing, bending grass, and scraping branches in the tree. The deputy looked up at the scraping branches and pointed. Altick looked.

"Another rifle."

It was wedged up in the branches where it must have been thrown.

"We'll do this together," Altick said. "These tracks in the grass. I thought they might be from our men. Now I'm not so sure. Let's follow them."

They soon found a state policeman's shirtsleeve in the grass, the edges bloody. No one said a word or even touched it.

They kept walking. Farther on, they found the other sleeve and then the shirt itself. The forest loomed. They studied the grass, then the forest. The wind kept tugging at them, scraping branches. All the trees were moving.

"I'm not going in there. We have no idea what we're up against," the pilot said "It could be anything."

But Altick continued walking.

*"Hey, I said I won't go with you."*

"I heard you. Stay back then."

"But you can't just leave me."

"If there's trouble, you can use the chopper."

"I don't like this."

Altick kept walking. When he looked back, he saw the pilot running toward the helicopter.

"Just as well," the deputy said. "I don't like nervous civilians near me with a rifle."

Altick nodded. "He was sure excited at the start. But once there's danger, he's a weekend cowboy. He was right, though. We don't know what we'll find in there."

They followed the tracks in the grass, noticing more dried blood, and when Altick parted some branches, he saw four piles of guts among the fir trees. Altick swallowed something bitter, the taste of fear, and scanned the forest. He thought of corpses he had seen in Nam, their ears and balls cut off, and he knew he had only one choice now. "We're going back."

The deputy beside him was ashen. He shook and made a retching sound.

"Don't be ashamed if you get sick," Altick said.

The man clutched his stomach. "I'll be fine. It's just that—"

"Take deep breaths. I saw a lot of things like this in Nam. I never did get used to them.

"My God, they disemboweled them."

"Who or *what?* For sure, no wolf or dog did this. Come on. We'd better head back toward the chopper. I don't know what's out here, but it's more than we can handle." Altick kept thinking, *four.* There were *five* men, so why only *four* fly-speckled mounds of viscera, and then he reached the helicopter, fighting for his breath, and he found out. The pilot wasn't looking at them. Instead he faced the lake, his mouth open, his finger pointing, and when Altick got there, he saw the headless body floating in the water. His deputy moaned. The wind kept blowing fiercely. On the ripples of the lake, the head bobbed to the surface.

*"Jesus, won't those reinforcements ever get here?"*

## FOUR

It was twenty-three years since Lucas had left. Now he was coming home. He peered out from the window of the car he'd thumbed a ride from, seeing new homes on the outskirts, then a shopping center, and the street here hadn't been paved back then, but he recognized more buildings than he didn't, and he thought that he might recognize some of the people, but he couldn't. Over there, a house that had been blue was now painted white, and up ahead, trees that had been saplings now were tall. He saw front yards he once had played in, but their spaces now seemed smaller, as indeed the houses did, and everywhere he looked he had the sense of things diminished. Well, what else had he expected? Did he think that twenty-three years would leave the town and him unchanged? Or had the town been really this small all along and he too young to put it in perspective? Well, he'd seen how big the world could be. Now Potter's Field was welcome.

The driver looked at him. "If you're hungry, you'll have to wait. I don't plan to stop here. I have half a day to drive yet."

"No, this town is good enough."

"You want me to pull over?"

"In a while. The road goes straight through to the other mountains. When we reach downtown is where I'll leave."

"You know this place?"

"I used to. I was raised here."

"Been away long?"

Lucas nodded, his cheek muscles tense. "Yes. I'm coming back to see my father."

He stared toward the courthouse up ahead and pointed. "There is fine. If you don't mind, I'll get out on that corner."

"No problem. It was good to pass the time with you."

The car veered toward the curb and stopped. Lucas got out. "Thank you."

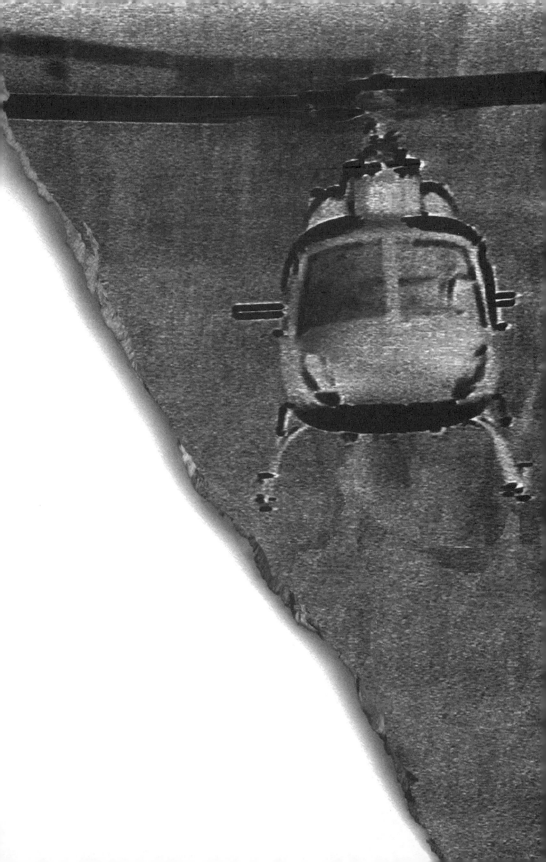

"*I* thank *you*. You know, I don't pick up many hitchhikers. Mostly they look, well, I guess, a bit too rough to handle. But a nice, clean-looking, young man like yourself. It's rare. I've got a lot of driving yet to do, and you helped break the time for me. Thanks again. I know your father will be glad to see you."

"Well, I'm sure he'll be surprised, all right." Lucas reached for his suitcase and shut the door.

"Take care now."

"Yeah. The same to you." He watched the car pull away from the curb. He watched until he couldn't see it anymore. Then he turned to face the courthouse. In the distance, he heard church bells. He saw people in their best clothes standing, talking in small groups along the street. Except for what seemed lots of traffic heading out of town, the scene was just as he remembered it when he and his mother would come into town to go to church. Another peaceful Sunday morning. But the last few years before he left had gradually stopped being peaceful, his father angry, his parents shouting. He had asked the man just now to let him off before there were too many questions. Then he'd understood that stopping here was maybe for the best. He hadn't seen this courthouse since those late October days in 1970, and he could still recall the way his father sat beside the lawyer, staring at him in the witness chair. Lucas shook his head and wondered where the cars and trucks were going. Some big fair out in the valley? Then he picked up his suitcase, crossed toward the building beside the courthouse, walked up past the trees on either side, and climbed the front steps, going in.

The place was cool and shadowy, and the first things that he noticed were the tall plants in their big pots all around the edges of the hall. They hadn't been here back in 1970, and more than any other detail he had seen, they signaled to him how much everything had changed since then. He faced the office to his right and saw the sign on top—POLICE CHIEF, NATHAN SLAUGHTER—and that sign was different too, the old chief wasn't here now. People might not understand what he wanted to tell them. He almost didn't go in, but he was too committed now to change his mind, and he stepped through the doorway.

There were half a dozen people. Phones were ringing. To his right, a policeman he didn't recognize was talking to a microphone. Beyond him, men were answering the phones and writing notes. In a glassed-in office at the back, a tall man in a uniform was talking to a gray, wasted man in a wrinkled suit, and everyone was loud, and none of them looked happy.

"Yes, sir, may I help you?" The man who'd been talking to the radio looked tensely at him.

"I'm not certain. My name's Lucas Wheeler. Someone here might know me."

"Just a second." The policeman spoke into the microphone again. "That's right. A woman and a dog. It's a hell of a mess. The animal control van should be hooked up to our frequency. It's probably waiting for you. Get over there."

A staticky voice that Lucas couldn't understand responded.

"Roger." The policeman glanced up, his expression stark. "I'm sorry. Things are crazy here. You'll have to tell me that again."

"I said my name is Lucas Wheeler, and I need protection from my father."

The policeman's eyes narrowed. "Has he threatened you? He isn't acting strangely, is he?"

"No. I haven't seen him since the fall of nineteen seventy."

"But I don't . . . Just a second." The policeman spoke to the microphone again. "That's right. For God's sake, don't go near it. Keep it locked in the basement. If it breaks out, use your shotgun."

Lucas squinted around and heard other bizarre conversations. He didn't understand it. What was going on? At first he'd thought that he had looked suspicious to this man. But he had made a point of cutting off his beard and trimming back his hair, of buying clothes as conventional as he could tolerate. Hell, he was even wearing cowboy boots, but the reaction he'd received was due apparently to what was going on, whatever that was, and he waited, and the policeman stared at him again.

"What's all—?"

"I'm sorry, but you'll have to see the chief."

"What's going on?"

"I said, you'll have to see the chief." The policeman gestured toward the glassed-in office.

"Can I leave my suitcase by the door?"

The policeman waved him impatiently away and spoke again to a staticky voice on the radio. "If he's been bitten, get him to the hospital. Keep him in the back seat of the cruiser. Don't go near him."

Lucas set the suitcase by the door and crossed the room, hearing the urgent voices around him, staring at the troubled policemen, then reaching the entrance to the glassed-in section of the office.

"Quarantine won't work now. I don't care what Parsons says. We've got—" The big man stopped and looked at him. "What is it?"

"Well, I guess I picked the wrong time, but the man out there said I should see you. I've been out of town for quite a while. I've come to see my father, but I think he might make trouble for me."

"Trouble?"

"Yes, my name is Lucas Wheeler."

The big man only shook his head, puzzled, as if the name meant nothing to him.

In contrast, the wasted man in the wrinkled suit snapped to attention. "Wheeler? You're the rancher's boy?"

"Thank God. I was afraid no one remembered or would help me."

"Rancher's boy?" the big man asked.

"The murder back in nineteen seventy," the wasted man said. "He's the kid who testified against his father."

"And my father said that if he got the chance he'd kill me," Lucas said. "I need protection."

But the big man only leaned back in his chair and wiped his face. "Look, can't it wait a few days? We've got trouble here."

"My father wasn't kidding," Lucas said.

"But I don't have the men. Just wait a while, and I'll go out with you myself."

"A few days? I don't have enough money to stay in a hotel that long."

And the big man sighed as he glanced toward the ceiling.

"Never mind. I'll handle this," the wasted man said.

"No. I want you with me."

"Nothing's going to threaten you while you're here. I just need to talk with him. You like some coffee, Lucas? Have you got a little time to talk with me?"

"I want to see my father."

"And you'll see him. But I have a couple of questions."

"About what?"

"The commune."

And the horror of it all returned to him.

## FIVE

The thing came struggling down the street. It crawled on its hands and knees and tried to shield its eyes from the sunlight, but the pain was too intense, and all it did was crawl on blindly. It was snarling, foaming at the mouth, although it didn't do that willingly. The broken white line stretched before it, and it wavered to one side and then the other as in agony it tried to move directly down the center. Objects angled past it, beeping. It heard voices, sensed the people crowding near it, and it snarled at them and bared its foamy teeth and kept on crawling. How it reached here, it could not remember. Trees and grassland it remembered. But this hot black surface and this white line, it could not recall or understand. It just kept struggling down the white line. Someone screamed. More objects inched past, beeping. And the pain. The awful pain. It fell, face cracking on the hot black surface. It squirmed forward on its stomach, the white line stretching forward from its nose. It pawed at its skull. It jerked its head from side to side. As the murmurs gathered closer, it snarled to defend itself.

## SIX

Rettig stopped the cruiser, puzzled by the crowd that filled the main street. He saw cars and trucks stopped, drivers getting out, people on the sidewalk pointing, others coming from the side streets, from Sunday brunch in restaurants. He was stepping from the cruiser, putting on his hat, and with his hand near his revolver, he moved forward. What the hell was *this* about? He'd seen so many bad things in the last few days that he had no idea what worse could happen. And this morning. Word had gotten around so fast that even for a small town it was startling. People in a panic, leaving town or gathered in small groups and talking wildly. He had seen three traffic jams this morning, forced to waste time clearing them. He'd shot a frenzied dog, had helped its bleeding owner to a doctor. He had found a mangled woman by a laundromat. But now a mob that filled the street. He didn't like where this was heading.

Weak from lack of sleep and scared because the town would shortly be in chaos, worried for his family, he had phoned his sister down in Denver to make arrangements for his wife and daughter to go there. They were packing right now, and he knew that many others had made plans to leave the town as well.

But all the same, he thought he knew what to expect—more of this but surely nothing worse. Yet even as he walked up to the crowd to part it, he was sensing something that was far beyond his knowledge, something that when he reached out to shift the crowd would show him some dark final truth that ever after would change everything.

He heard the words but didn't understand them, couldn't make them out, a snarled fog-throated muttering. He pushed on through the crowd and stopped and stared, and it must once have been a person, but its trunk was cloaked with furs. Its arms and legs were bloody. It was snarling, drooling, jerking, its hair down to its waist and falling all around it, a beard down to its stomach, its face dark from dirt and scabs, and bugs were crawling on it as it leered up, blinking. "Own oom," it was choking. Rettig didn't understand the sounds. He stumbled back against the crowd, his heart beating faster. Then he understood the choking, rasping, barking. "Throne room," it repeated. "Throne room, throne room, throne room."

<u>SEVEN</u>

They were standing in the hallway, staring through the window at the figure on the bed in there. The figure wore a gown now, the collar of it showing just above the sheet that covered him. His beard was trimmed, his hair was cut, an intravenous bottle hung beside him, leading to the needle in his arm. Although he was unconscious, straps restrained him.

"Do you recognize him?" Slaughter asked.

Lucas Wheeler concentrated. "I'm not certain. It's been lots of years. I mean, I doubt many people could identify *me* after so long. How can I be certain about *him?*"

"But is there anything at all familiar?"

"Oh, a little. That thin nose and mouth. The thing is, I knew several people like that, but the commune had a couple hundred members, and I wasn't up there long enough to meet them all. Plus, no one was as gaunt as he is. Let's say he was twenty back then. Now he'd be forty-three. A man can change a lot in that time."

Slaughter glanced at Dunlap. Then he scratched his wrinkled brow and turned to Lucas once again. "Well, would it help if you were closer to him?"

"I don't think I want that."

"He's unconscious. Those straps are secure. He isn't any threat to you."

"I know that. But you have to understand how much that commune scared me."

Slaughter narrowed his gaze. "What do you mean?"

"Look, I never said this back in nineteen-seventy, but when my father came to get me, I'd been praying all along for something like that. I was scared I'd never get away from there. When that policeman found me in the ditch for the latrine, I wasn't hiding from him. It was Quiller I was hiding from."

"You know about this?" Slaughter said to Dunlap.

"Yes, he told me when we went to get some coffee at your office. They were evidently—"

"Let me tell it," Lucas said. "I should have told it long ago. You've got to understand how young I was. Eighteen, and I thought I'd figured everything. The way my father acted toward my mother and me. Hell, he was actually convinced that she was cheating on him. He was certain that I wasn't even his. I mean I couldn't stand it anymore. I felt there had to be a better life, and when those hippies came through town, I knew they'd found it. So I hung around with them. Can you imagine? No guilt. Freedom to do anything that you're inclined toward without fear of what somebody else will say. I'd never had that, and I loved it. But the trouble started then, and soon the town turned on the hippies, and the ranchers forced them from the valley. I was worse off than before because I thought I knew then what I wanted, so I struggled through the summer, but my father and I kept arguing, and I snuck out late one night to join the commune. But I didn't know that they were crazy, see. I figured they'd be like the hippies in the town. But these were different. Quiller had selected them. That's why he wanted several thousand at the start. To pick and choose the special types he wanted. Every freak who'd tripped out once too many times. Every nut who was almost psychotic. Every radical whose idea of protest was to plant a bomb or set fire to a building. Hell, they didn't need the drugs. A lot of them were scrambled to begin with. And they took one look at me and said that I would be their first new member. Well, I should have known. The hippies in the town had warned me. 'Very bad,' they told me, but they never explained what they meant. I suspect they only sensed what was the matter. All the same, I should have known. Because the summer had been time enough for Quiller to control the commune, to make it even more extreme. You want to talk about hypnotic people? Quiller had a way of looking in your eyes and making you agree to anything, and he had crazies working with him who would make you go along with him. I'd grown a half-assed beard. I'd let my hair grow long, but if I stood out from the people in the town, I stood out equally from Quiller and the commune. They had let their hair and beards keep growing longer. They had started dressing even weirder than the hippies who had been in town. Quiller used to sit in his Corvette—"

"The red Corvette? He kept it?" Dunlap asked abruptly.

"Oh, hell, yes. He rigged up a grotto for it off in the woods. He parked it there beneath a shelter made from tree boughs, and he used to sit in it to hold his meetings. But the funny thing is that, while all the others let their hair and beards grow, Quiller shaved and kept his hair short. When he didn't wear his robe, he walked around in patent leather shoes and expensive slacks and custom-made shirts that he'd brought with him. In the context of the commune, he looked twice as weird as anyone, just sitting in that car and staring toward the forest. You'd have thought he was on the freeway. God knows where his mind was taking him. And there I stood before him in my jeans and workshirt and the stubby beard I'd tried to grow, and he was saying that he'd let me be their first new member. He was smiling, and I didn't understand till later that if I'd refused, I wouldn't have had a choice. I didn't understand that I was a prisoner."

"It's like Jim Jones," Dunlap said. "Or David Koresh.'

"Or Charles Manson," Slaughter added, and they frowned at one another.

"I need a smoke," Lucas said. "Has anybody got one?" His hand was shaking as he took the cigarette that Dunlap offered. A nurse going by frowned at them. She slowed as if about to tell them that smoking wasn't allowed in the corridor. Then she saw the look in their eyes and kept moving.

Lucas drew the smoke in. "Anyway, they had these barracks like in the military, and they put me in one, watching me. By then, I understood enough to be afraid, but there was no way I could run, and they were talking about my initiation. I don't know what I thought would happen. I saw that many of them had a scar across their chests, two wavy lines that intersected. When they brought me food, I wouldn't eat it, and I wouldn't drink the water. They kept smiling, though, as if that's what they wanted. 'That's right. Stay pure,' they told me. I don't know. They had this thing about a state of nature. Quiller's notion was to purify them, to free them from the outside world. He made them pledge their loyalty, then put them through this secret ritual. Their goal was to escape the bonds of society and act upon their instincts. But the place was set up like the military, and I didn't understand how Quiller's dictatorial attitude was compatible with freedom, or how drugs had anything to do with purity. The scheme was crazy, schizophrenic, and I sometimes wonder if he didn't get some kind of voyeuristic thrill from watching them behave like animals. The second day at sundown, they were going to have the ceremony, but my father showed up that day, shooting. When they ran to find out what had happened, I escaped the men who watched me. The policeman found me."

"But you never mentioned anything about this," Slaughter told him.

"That's right. I was too afraid. I felt that Quiller would come after me. You said yourself that Quiller seemed a lot like

Manson. He terrified me. I didn't want to go against him. If I told the town, the town would turn against the commune, and I knew who the commune would blame. Besides, you have to realize how much I hated my father. If I justified what he had done, he might have been released. I didn't want that. Hell, I knew that he'd come looking for me, too. As far as I could see, a guilty verdict was the best chance for my mother and me. Don't bother saying I was wrong. At eighteen, that's the way I saw things."

"But you're back now."

Lucas nodded. "And the whole damned thing is starting again. I don't mind telling you I'm scared. I figured that the commune would have scattered by now, that my father might be different. Last month I was with my mother when she died. She'd been staying in New Mexico. The last thing she said was 'Make sure your father doesn't cheat you. Half that ranch is mine, and now it's yours. But he'll try to keep it from you.'" Lucas straightened. "I'm finished running."

"Well, I guarantee you'll be protected."

"Don't underestimate my father."

"That isn't what I meant. I mean in there. I want you to look closely at the man in the bed. Tell me if he's really from the commune. We still have no proof of that. If the commune still exists, we don't know where it is. They moved it."

Lucas shuddered. "Oh, that's fine. That's fucking great."

The medical examiner stepped from the room where he'd been attending to the bearded figure.

"Well?" Slaughter asked.

The medical examiner looked troubled. "He's very sick. Apart from showing symptoms of the virus, he's undernourished and dehydrated. If he hadn't wandered into town, he'd have died by sunset. As it is, I still don't know how long he'll live. I'm feeding him intravenously."

"Can we have a look at him?"

The medical examiner debated. "I don't think that's a problem, but that cigarette will have to go."

He pointed toward what Lucas held, and Lucas nodded, dropping the cigarette, stepping on it.

"Pick it up now."

Lucas stared at him, then picked it up. He glanced at

Slaughter. "Fine. Let's get this finished."

The medical examiner opened the door, and they went in. They peered toward the figure, then at Lucas.

"I don't know," Lucas told them.

"Make a guess," Slaughter said.

"I can't."

"You've got to try."

"But what if I identify him and he comes for me?"

"Does he look as if he's going to live? For Christ sake, be responsible for once."

Lucas scowled at him. The veins in his temples throbbed. Then slowly they subsided, and he studied the figure. "Maybe . . . Maybe I once knew him."

"Have you got a name for him?"

"I'll tell you when I'm ready. Did you notice if he had a scar?" he asked the medical examiner.

"Two wavy lines that intersect across his chest. They remind me of a swastika."

"And what about a—?"

"Tattoo on his shoulder. It's an eagle."

"Let me see it." Lucas watched the medical examiner tug at the sheet and gown. They looked at a purple eagle.

"Yes, I knew him." Lucas exhaled. "Pollock. All I ever heard him called was Pollock. He was Quiller's second in command. That eagle's like some kind of military symbol, like a captain or a major. If he wakes up, don't go near him. He's insane. If you could see his eyes, you'd understand what I mean."

Slaughter sighed. "Then the commune still exists."

"But where the hell did they go?" Dunlap wondered.

Now the figure squirmed beneath the straps. He shook his head, unconscious, flaring his nostrils, moaning, "Throne room."

"What?" The medical examiner shook his head.

"He said 'throne room'," Slaughter told him. "I don't understand it either. He was moaning that when Rettig found him." Slaughter didn't like the smell in here. Although the figure had been bathed while he was strapped down in the bed, he stank of rancid meat and sweat and mildew, and the pungent smell of medicine mixed with those other odors nauseated him.

"Where has he been living anyhow?"

"The throne room," Dunlap told him.

"Very funny."

"No, the place clearly has some importance to him. Maybe if we asked him."

"He's unconscious. You can see that."

"I don't care. Let's try it."

Slaughter looked at the medical examiner.

"It might work. I don't think that it could hurt him."

"But it's pointless," Slaughter said.

"What difference does it make? Let's try it." Dunlap bent down by the figure. "Pollock."

"Careful," Slaughter told him.

Dunlap nodded, moving slightly away from the figure. "Pollock, can you hear me?

There was no response. Dunlap waited. Then he said again but softer, "Pollock, can you hear me?"

The figure squirmed. He hissed once. Then he settled.

"Pollock, you're with friends now. Can you hear me? Talk about the throne room."

"Throne room." That was croaked, but they could hear it.

Dunlap glanced at his companions, then spoke more softly to the figure. "That's right. Talk about the throne room."

"Red room."

Dunlap frowned toward the others.

"It could be blood," the medical examiner suggested.

"Maybe," Slaughter told him. "Or it could be something he remembers from when he was just a kid. There isn't any way to know."

Abruptly the figure on the bed started screaming. They flinched as the scream swept louder around them. It rose higher, strident, the figure twisting, agonized, and then as suddenly as it began, the scream diminished. The figure settled, moaning, on the bed. They continued staring.

"Is there nothing you can give him?" Slaughter asked the medical examiner.

"I'm not about to risk a sedative. The only thing that we can do is watch to see what happens."

"What about these lights, though? Can't we dim them?'

"He's unconscious, so they shouldn't bother him. But why not? I don't see a need for them." The medical examiner walked to the door and switched off the lights. The room became shadowy.

But the figure didn't stop its moaning. It jerked its head from side to side. Then gradually it seemed calmer.

"What about the red room, Pollock? Tell us about it," Dunlap said.

There wasn't any answer.

"Red room," Dunlap said again.

And then in answer, "Red room, red room, antelope."

"I told you this is useless. He's just babbling," Slaughter said.

"Or else he's saying what's important to him," Dunlap answered.

"Then you tell me what it means."

"You know I can't."

"Of course you can't. We have to find out where they've gone. If there's some kind of red room, I sure want to know what's in it." Slaughter turned to Lucas. "Can you tell us where they might be living?"

Lucas shook his head. He studied Slaughter and then everyone, their faces in shadow. "No, they never told me much. But now that I think back, I can understand why Quiller would have moved. My father and the state police were proof the compound wasn't safe for him. He'd want to find a better place."

"But where?" Slaughter asked. "Those hills are used for camping, fishing, hunting. Someone would have found them."

"Could be someone did," Dunlap said. "You'd better check your missing-persons file and any inquiries you might have gotten from other sections of the country. You never know how far back this might take you."

*"Slaughter, would you mind explaining what this means?"*

The new voice thundered through the room. They stiffened, turning toward the doorway, Parsons braced there, looming over them, and then they turned toward Slaughter.

"We don't know yet. We were—"

"In the hallway."

"What?"

"I'm waiting, Slaughter."

Parsons stepped back out and let the door swing shut. The room was silent as they looked at Slaughter.

"Well, I guess I knew this would happen."

*"What* would happen?"

"He objects to the company I keep."

"He what?"

"It's nothing. I'll explain it later." Through the window, he saw Parsons stalking back and forth in the hallway. "Well, I guess I'd better get it settled." Slaughter faced the door and pulled on it.

Parsons waited until Slaughter shut the door behind him. "You were told to keep that reporter away from this, to make sure he was on a bus the hell from town!"

The nurses at the far end stared at them.

"I don't think I can do that."

"If you want to keep your job, you'll—"

"Parsons, look, we really should have gotten to know each other. It's too late now, but I'll try to make you understand. I've been through situations like this many times. Back in Detroit, when there was trouble and pressure was put on our supervisors, they'd look around for someone to blame. We learned early how to come out looking squeaky clean. Now there's about to be a *lot* of trouble, and you're going to need a fall guy, but I'm damned sure it won't be me. That reporter in there is closer to me right now than my jockey shorts. Except for this conversation, I don't go anywhere, not even to the men's room, without bringing him along. Because I want to guarantee that I'm protected, that he writes down every move I make, so if you have any accusations, any tricks you want to pull to keep your lovely reputation, there'll be someone else's word besides your own."

"I'll have you—"

"Listen to me. I'm not finished. So you want to sit back and let things happen. Well, that's not the way I plan to do this. If I have to, I'll declare martial law. I'm not sure I have the power, but when this is over, there'll be plenty of time for us to argue. In the meanwhile, I'll at least be doing something which is more than I can say for you. It could be I'll make mistakes. Okay then, I'll take blame for them. But there is no way in this life that I'll take blame for your inaction."

Parsons glared. "You'll wish you'd never come here."

"Maybe. But just think about your options. If I'm right, you'll reach out and take the credit. If I'm wrong, you know who to point blame at. But that reporter is my insurance that I've got a witness to protect me. I'm in charge now. Don't forget it."

Parsons looked through the window at the medical examiner and Dunlap and the young man who were watching him. "Oh, I'm not known for my forgetfulness. Years from now I'll still remember you, but you won't be around to realize it." Parsons studied him a moment longer and then stalked along the corridor.

EIGHT

Altick raced up through the bushes. He had waited with the two men by the helicopter until the ground patrol had finally arrived. He told them what had happened, and when he was finished urging them, when he had shown them first the body in the lake and then the piles of viscera in the forest, he had succeeded in his efforts to enrage them. After all, the one thing he had always emphasized was loyalty to one another. The members of the patrol knew all the men who had been killed. They'd been close friends, and the grisly evidence of how the first group had been killed had been enough to change their fear into anger. They weren't certain what had done this, but they all agreed that someone or some *thing* was going to pay. They edged up past the viscera, and they were cursing as they found a gametrail that led higher, blood along it, which they followed. High above, the helicopter hovered. That way, they would have a lookout who could warn them of a trap he saw ahead, and if they were indeed attacked, the pilot could pick up the wounded. At the least, the pilot would survive to tell what he had seen down here, but no one liked to talk about the chance of their all dying. They were rushing up the gametrail, concentrating to insure that *their* side didn't do the dying. They found more blood on the gametrail, and they were so angry, and it was so easy to follow this clear a spoor that no one thought until later that the blood had maybe been left for them.

# THE JAIL

## PART SIX

T HE MAP WAS SPREAD OUT ON THE DESK, AND SLAUGHTER STARED AT IT. HE GLANCED UP AT THE five men grouped around him: Rettig, Dunlap, Lucas, Owens, and the medical examiner. "I wanted you to be here because each of you has been involved in this and I need your opinions."

They were silent. Outside, traffic was unusually dense for a Sunday.

"Good," Slaughter said. "I'm glad you want to help."

"There isn't any choice."

And Slaughter looked at Owens who was scowling out the window. Slaughter waited, then continued.

"As I see it, we've got two main problems, although they're really both the same. The first thing is to keep the people in town safe."

"By this afternoon, there won't be anybody to protect."

Slaughter looked again at Owens, then at where the man was scowling, at the cars and trucks that filed past toward the main road from the valley. "Okay, so word spread fast and lots of people are leaving. That can help us."

"To do what? Protect a ghost town?" Owens asked.

"That's exactly what I didn't want to hear. You've worked hard on this. I thought I could depend on you."

"But what's the use?" Owens demanded. "You know we can't beat this."

"We can try."

"Well, you don't have a family. My wife and kids are packing right now."

"So are mine," Rettig said. "That doesn't mean I'm going with them."

Owens stared at him and then at everyone. His gaze was disbelieving. "You still don't get it, do you? Everything we've found out, the way they don't like light and how they come out in the darkness, how the moon affects them, how these incidents have been increasing." He pointed toward a calendar on the wall.

Slaughter shook his head. "I don't understand."

"It's the moon. The moon is getting fuller. We've got just today and Monday and then Tuesday. When the moon is at its fullest, this whole valley's going to be a madhouse."

They looked startled.

"What he says is in a way correct," the medical examiner added. "There's a kind of logarithmic pattern to this."

"Will you please make sense?"

"The numbers, Slaughter. They're increasing at a faster rate. What you told me, all the calls that you've been getting, all the incidents your men are investigating. We start with one thing. Next it's two, the next night four, and eight, and sixteen. As the moon gets fuller, all the incidents are doubled in proportion. After sixteen, thirty-two. You see the kind of ultimate it's leading toward."

"Then that can help us."

"If it can, I don't see how."

"The moon will start to wane then, and the incidents will be reduced. The stimulus won't be as strong. If we can get through Tuesday, then we've got a chance to gain control."

"Except that it's not just a full moon," Owens said. "Look at the calendar. Tuesday. What's the date?"

"June twentieth."

"That's right, and what's it say about the next day?"

Slaughter leaned close to the calendar. "It says the twenty-first, the first day of summer."

"And you still don't get it?"

Slaughter frowned, confused.

"The summer solstice," Owens told him. "Christ, you're a cop. When you were back east in Detroit, surely you noticed how the crazies started acting up when the moon was full or when the seasons started changing. You don't even need to be a cop to notice it. Just talk to doctors or to me about the way my animals begin behaving. Talk to people at complaint departments out at Sears or Ward's or K-Mart. The moon does crazy things. And now the full moon and the summer solstice will be coming together. All those ancient stories about pagans losing control and worshiping chaos on Midsummer's Eve. Chaos. Think about it. We've got a virus that affects the limbic brain and makes us act the way we did when we were animals. Tuesday night, you're going to see hell."

They gaped at him, their faces drained of color.

"Jesus," Dunlap said.

"Yes, you've scared me," Slaughter said and looked down at the map, then at the window, then at him. He took a breath. "Yes, I admit it, and I guess after what I've seen, you're likely right that anything can happen now. But I don't know what I can do about it."

"Leave before you don't have a choice," Owens said.

"I can't allow that."

"Why?"

"Because I have a job."

"That's just as crazy as the things you've seen," Owens said. "You won't do any good, and even if you do, who's going to thank you? Parsons? He looks out for himself. You think the people in the valley will be grateful if you die for them? Don't believe it. They'll just say you didn't have control, that you were foolish. Take the chance and get out while you can."

"But I'm not doing this for the town. I'm doing it for me," Slaughter said. "If I run now, I couldn't tolerate myself. And I don't think you could run out either."

"No? Just watch me."

And they did. They waited, staring, and Owens returned their stares, and for a moment, it seemed certain that he would walk away, but then he didn't.

"Something wrong? You're bothered?" Slaughter asked.

Owens kept looking at him.

"Maybe you had something more to say?"

But Owens only swallowed.

"I tell you what. It's daylight. Things won't get too bad until tonight. Just stick around a little. Tell your family to leave, that you'll catch up. And in the meanwhile, keep helping us the way you did just now. You've given us more information than we had. I don't know how to use it, but you're really quite important."

Owens kept staring. "Until tonight at sunset."

"That's no more than I could ask for."

And then Slaughter did an unexpected thing. He reached close to shake hands with him, and Owens seemed a little better, and the other men relaxed then.

"We're a team again. Let's do it."

## TWO

Parsons pulled the roadblock across the two-lane highway. It was like a sawhorse, only bigger, longer. He had found it by the roadside where a highway crew had been repairing asphalt, and he pulled the second one across so that both lanes were barricaded, and he faced the backed-up traffic. His intentions were uncommon to him. All his life he'd learned to occupy a still point, to let power channel through him rather than be active and pursue it. He had earned his station simply by agreeing to what everyone already was committed to. That government is best which governs least, he always said. A public servant's job is not to lead, instead to follow. And for twenty-five years of being mayor, he'd found that notion was successful. Now it failed him. From his house on the outskirts of town, he'd seen the people leaving. He had begged his friends to stay and trust him, but that moment when, if he had only acted, now was past him, and he saw the town dissolving, saw the power he had passively received dissolving with it. For the first time in his life, he was a failure. More important, he would never occupy his same position. If the town were ever saved, if the people ever came back, they would surely not be loyal to him. They would change things, choose a new mayor, want to do things differently, and he would be like presidents who once were influential, leaders who were set aside and even an embarrassment. He knew that these analogies were grandiose, but this had been his country, this town in this valley. He had ruled it absolutely, and he couldn't bear the thought that he'd soon be deposed and useless.

It was Slaughter's fault, he told himself, Slaughter who had screwed things up and let the situation get so out of hand, Slaughter who now with that reporter was determined to abuse him, to publish stories that would damage him, hell, ruin him. Slaughter maybe had ambitions. Parsons hadn't thought of that, but maybe Slaughter planned to claim that Parsons had been weak and ineffective. Slaughter then would show how he himself had taken charge and he would soon become the mayor. Like hell. Parsons would be damned if he let anybody take his power away. Who did Slaughter think that he was dealing with, and what made Slaughter think he could suddenly take charge? This valley wasn't ruled like that, and Parsons was determined to instruct him.

He had both his roadblocks set up, and with his shotgun in his hand, he stalked ahead toward where the first car waited. He was bulky, towering above the car. That was the first thing he had learned: to use his size, his presence. "Turn around. We have to work together on this."

"Get those roadblocks out of there before I ram right through them."

"And what then? If everybody leaves, there won't be anybody left to stop this."

"Look, the guy next door was mangled by his German shepherd. Two doors down, the husband went berserk. I know of twenty people who've been missing since last night. Something's going on, but it's been covered up, and I don't plan to wait around to find out what it is."

"I'll shoot your tires out."

"And what about the other cars behind me? You don't have enough ammunition. Just clear those roadblocks. Let me on my way."

"I can't permit that. We don't know what this thing is, but if I let you from the valley, you'll be spreading it. This valley, starting now, is quarantined."

Parsons knew that he was being contradictory, that what he'd said to Slaughter went against what he was doing now, but he was in a fight with Slaughter, and if using Slaughter's tactics meant success, then he would use them. What was more, the situation was so uncontrolled now that this tactic really was the best way, and besides, as he was saying to the driver, "If you leave now, if this valley goes to hell, you won't be coming back. There won't be anything you want here or can trust here. Take a stand, for God sake. Go back into town and fight this."

All the cars were lined up, honking, drivers getting out and swarming toward him. He was ready with his shotgun. "If you'll trust me, I can show you how to beat this."

They were yanking at his roadblocks.

"It's those hippies. Don't you see it?"

Yes, he knew about that too. He had informants everywhere, and he'd been talking to them since he'd been with Slaughter. There were still a few things that he didn't understand, but he knew just enough that he'd found a scapegoat. Plus, the hippies really were the enemy, and if he'd worked this angle back in 1970, he could work it once again.

"Those hippies?" The drivers paused with the roadblocks in their hands. "But they're long gone."

"I'm telling you that they're still in the mountains. Oh, they moved to some place else, but they're still up there, and they're crazy. God knows what all they've been doing, using drugs and living like a bunch of animals. They've picked up some disease now, and they're coming to the valley. Oh, sure, I know dogs and cats have got it too, but we can handle them. Those hippies are the ones I'm afraid of."

It was a prehistoric argument that took advantage of their tribal instincts, conjuring the image of some hairy foreign thing that no one understood and hence that everyone feared. Parsons was almost ashamed to use it, but he nonetheless believed it, all those hate-filled recollections of those hippies, latent, ready to be triggered, and his anger was intense enough now that he wanted to get even. Damage Slaughter. Kill those hippies. Get his town back as it was for him. Oh, yes, by God, the way Slaughter had spoken to him, he meant to see that someone paid.

He waited as they stared at him. "You don't remember nineteen-seventy? Hal there lost his boy in Vietnam while those damned hippies crudded up our town. And now those hippies are on their way back. They're going to come down from the mountains and kill us unless we make plans to stop them."

The crowd kept staring.

"I don't even need you. I'll go see the ranchers. *They* know what's important. *They* know how to keep what they've worked hard for. I'll go find some *men* who aren't afraid!"

Now Parsons felt emotion stirring in them. In a moment, he would ask if anybody knew the people who'd been murdered. He would tell them that the state police were heading into the mountains, that they needed help—yes, he had heard about that too—and he would tell them about Slaughter, how their chief was so inept that he himself, their *mayor,* was forced to come down here and take charge of his people.

### THREE

Slaughter scowled down with the others at the map. They'd made arrangements for their message to be broadcast on the TV and the radio, for everyone to stay inside, to keep away from animals, from strangers, to report a bite or any odd behavior, then to call the police station for assistance, and to watch for the cruisers that were out in force along the streets. He himself had called the state police, but there was only one man on duty at the local barracks and no word had come from Altick. He had called for help from Rawlins, Lander, Sheridan, and Casper. If he had to, he would call in the state militia. But right now, his main objective was to find the commune. "You men know these mountains more than I do. Tell me where the commune is."

"It's too much area to figure," Rettig told him.

"Yes, but . . ." Slaughter paused and rubbed his forehead.

He'd been having pains there for several hours, from lack of food and sleep, the tension building in him, and his argument with Parsons. He was hoping he could handle this, but he was overwhelmed by what he faced, gradually more doubtful. "Yes, but there must be a couple places you can think of, caves or canyons where a group of people could live undetected."

"If you want to think about it that way, there are hundreds," Rettig said. "I remember when I was a kid there weren't even terrain maps for those mountains. Hunters, fishermen, oh yeah, they go up through there, but I used to know an Indian who lived there as a hermit for three years and never came across another person."

"What you're telling me is that we won't find any answer."

"What I'm saying is, we don't have the time for trial and error."

"Look, there has to be some logic to this," Dunlap said.

They turned to him, the city man who planned to tell them about mountains.

"Logic? Where the hell is logic?" Slaughter demanded.

"You'd know the way to do this if you were still in Detroit. Think of everything that's happened as a group of crimes you're plotting on a grid of city streets. Diagram it for the pattern."

"But there *isn't* any pattern," Rettig said.

"Of course, there is. Don't think about what's happened in the town. Just concentrate on incidents near the mountains. I've been here only since Friday, but I spotted right away that everything has happened on the western section of the valley."

"Don't you think I know that?" Rettig said impatiently.

"Use it!"

Slaughter shifted his attention to the map. "Okay, if you're so confident. Why not? It's worth a try. We haven't anything to lose." He drew an X. "That's Bodine's ranch, pretty close to where we found the abandoned truck. Here's the lake where Altick's men were lost."

"And here's the deserted compound."

"Don't forget your own place," Rettig told him. "It's obvious those weren't bobcats. You live near that section, too."

"Can you think of any other things?"

"The ranchers who reported mangled cattle live over

there, and that hippie staggered into town from that direction."

There were X's all across that section of the map.

"I don't see what that accomplished," Slaughter said.

"I do," Lucas answered. "Draw some lines up toward the mountains. Intersect them."

Slaughter did, and the men grouped around the table, frowning toward the map.

"Well, it's high up. That's what you expected," Slaughter told Rettig.

"High enough that people don't go up there much. You see that there aren't any trails marked."

"What's this broken line here?" Slaughter asked.

"That's the railroad that went up to where they used to mine the gold back in the old days. It's all broken down now."

"Mine the gold? Mine *what* gold?"

"This was once the richest section of the state. Back in eighteen ninety-five. There used to be a town up there."

And Slaughter felt the chill begin.

"Dear God, the answer's been there all along, and we were just too dumb to see it," Owens said.

"The ghost town," Rettig said. "They called it Motherlode. It's hard as hell to get there now that we don't have the railroad up there. I mean, there's no wagon road, no trail. That's why they built the railroad in the first place."

"Motherlode, and there are shafts that cut in through the rock walls. If you knew what you were doing, you could live up there a long time. All those miners did."

"And now the hippies," Slaughter said.

"And now the hippies," Owens echoed. "There's no telling what we'll find up there."

*"I'm sorry, Slaughter."* Parsons' voice came strong across the room. They whirled and looked beyond the glass partition at the group of men with rifles who were hurrying through the main door, standing in the middle of the larger office. Parsons was ahead of them, looming huge and staring toward the glass partition.

"You keep barging in. It's not a habit I admire," Slaughter said.

"Well, this will be the last. You'll have to come with us."

The room was silent. The shuffling feet had stopped. The

officer on duty at the radio was frowning. The three men who'd been answering the telephones halted in mid-sentence. They made brief remarks and set down the phones. At once, the phones started ringing again.

"Pull the jacks on those things," Parsons said. "I don't want to hear them."

They were looking first at Slaughter, then at Parsons.

"Pull the jacks, I told you."

They leaned down quickly, pulling out the jacks.

"That's better. Now we won't be interrupted. Well, you heard me, Slaughter. Let's get moving."

"Where? What for?"

"I just declared emergency conditions."

"I don't—"

"This is what you'd call a citizen's arrest."

"You're joking."

"Am I smiling? Move before we make you."

"But you can't be serious."

"I'm not prepared to argue. It's a known fact that you wouldn't follow orders."

"That's because you didn't want to deal with this."

"Do I appear as if I'm not prepared to deal with this? Your logic's not convincing. You've been acting on your own without authority. Your methods have been irresponsible. You've let this thing get out of hand while you, the medical examiner, and Owens were conspiring to hide evidence of murder."

"What?"

"The boy the medical examiner slashed open in the morgue. The boy was still alive. You think I don't know about that? Once I figured that the parents would be suing us, I had a second autopsy performed. That slash is hardly what you'd call professional. Oh, sure, the medical examiner worked hard to make it seem a part of his procedure, but he didn't do it well enough. We're holding all of you until we learn the truth about this."

"Not including me." Dunlap stepped ahead. "I don't know anything about this."

"But you've seen enough to be a circumstantial witness. Slaughter bragged about that. And this fellow here. I don't know how he's involved in this."

"I'm passing through," Lucas said.

"You're Wheeler's son. I know that much by now. You used to chum with all those hippies, and we can't afford to trust you. How much money do you have?"

"I don't see—"

*"How much money?"*

"Ten, maybe twelve dollars."

"Not enough. You're a vagrant, and we'll likely find a record on you once we start investigating. All of you, I'm tired of waiting."

"What about me?" Rettig stepped forward.

"I have nothing I can claim against you. Actually I'm putting you in charge, although I'm still suspicious of your friendship with Slaughter. Make one move to help him, and you'll join him. This department's been in bad shape for too long. I mean to put some muscle in it. *I won't ask you anymore,"* he told them. "Rettig, take his gun."

But Rettig hesitated.

"It's all right," Slaughter told him. "Every second we argue, there's more trouble outside. Do what he tells you. I'll make good on this."

Parsons laughed. "Sure you will. In your own jail. Let's get this finished."

Rettig looked at Slaughter, then took Slaughter's gun. The men with rifles stepped ahead to form a cordon, and the five men went out, guards around them.

Rettig watched as Parsons remained in the office and studied the map.

"How much help did he call in?" Parsons asked.

"Sheridan and Lander, places like that."

"Well, I think that I can keep them quiet, keep the word about this strictly in the valley. I don't want those ranchers ruined. Did he call in the state militia?"

"He wasn't sure yet." Rettig had troubled speaking.

"Good," Parsons said. "I stopped him just in time. Slaughter meant to ruin everyone."

"I hardly think so."

Parsons tapped his fingers on the map. "Rettig, what I need now is cooperation, someone who can do the job. Are you prepared to help, or aren't you?"

"Yes, I want to help."

"Then there isn't any problem, is there? You stay, and you work to keep the town safe. I have people who'll be downstairs watching Slaughter."

"But that reporter. Surely you don't think you can muzzle him. Eventually he'll write about the valley."

"What, a drunk, a common lush? When I'm through smearing his reputation, there won't be anyone who'll listen to him. Plus, there won't be anything for him to see. He'll never have the story."

"He can try."

"But he'll need evidence, and if you think your chief was good at cover-ups, you haven't seen what *I* can do. When I'm finished, this place will be happy valley. We'll have had a small exaggerated rabies scare."

"And Slaughter—"

"He'll be on his ass in jail or on the road to nowhere. He can't take charge of a town the way he planned and not get punished for it. We still have laws, you know."

"I guess it all depends on how you look at it."

"You're learning, Rettig. I might have a place for you. Let's get these phones in order."

"Tell me how much force you'll let me use."

"Enough to get the job done."

"That's too vague."

"I mean it that way. Walk the line. It keeps you careful. This town's economy is based on animals, on livestock. If you have to shoot, take time to get permission. Get in touch with anyone who owns a cat or dog. The court house has the license records. If you see a hippie—"

"Yes?"

"Well, I think you know how to handle it." Parsons looked at him, then slowly walked across to where he paused in the doorway, looked again, then went off down the hallway.

Rettig stood there, silent, stunned by what had happened. Glancing toward the window, he saw people in the front yard, mostly men, and they were angry, holding weapons. He felt suddenly exhausted.

"Tell me what that bastard thinks he's going to do," the officer beside the radio said.

"I don't know. He saw the pattern on the map. He heard us talking. It's my guess he plans to go up to the ghost town, pick a fight with them, and kill them all."

"But that's crazy. He can't get away with that."

"Oh, can't he? If those hippies have the virus, they'll attack for certain, so the killings will be justified. And even if they aren't, if Parsons takes enough men with him, we can't prosecute the whole town."

"But he's instigating them."

"No, he's just doing what they tell him. That's what he'll say later, and that's always been his pattern. Oh, he'll get away with it all right, and he'll come back with twice the power he started with. We're going to see some bad times, and I don't know how to deal with them. I wish Slaughter were in my place."

"Go downstairs and spring him."

"Do it for me."

"No, thanks."

"Then you see what I mean. We'd only end up in there with him."

Rettig turned to face the window once again. Outside, the crowd had shifted so that Parsons could go through, haranguing them. The phones were ringing. Officers were answering.

"I hate to say it, but no matter how you look at it, we've got some bad times coming, and God help us, there isn't any way to stop them."

FOUR

He was feeling strange now. They had warned him this might happen, but the bite had not been deep across his finger. Lots of scratches on his face and neck, but just the one slight bite where he had reached up to defend himself against her. When she'd started last night, he'd assumed that she was crazy from her grief. Their only child and he was dead now. Then he'd vaguely understood that even grief could not account for how she acted, and he'd tried to get away from her. She wouldn't let him. If that woman hadn't clubbed his wife, he doubted that he would have had the strength to fight her

311

off much longer. Now more grief. His wife unconscious. Although grateful, he was sorry that his wife had needed such strong force to be subdued. He wondered if their lives would ever regain normalcy. He worried that his wife might even not survive.

And now the knowledge of the virus she and Warren had contracted, of the virus he himself might harbor. They'd explained to him that, if he had the sickness, he would demonstrate the symptoms in the next full day, and they had put him in this chamber. Locked him in the chamber really. It was padded, floors and walls and ceiling, without windows. It was for hysterics, and the thought of what he might become was reinforced by these conditions.

He glanced at his watch. They'd let him keep it, which to some degree was comforting. He saw that it said three o'clock— fourteen hours since he'd been bitten. Maybe he'd survive this, but he felt the strangeness in him. Only grief? Depression? Was it something else? Was this the way it started?

Angered, suddenly he punched against a padded wall. He kicked it, cursing. Yesterday his life had been perfection. Driving home with Warren from the doctor, he had felt relief and happiness, togetherness. Now everything had been destroyed for him. His son was dead. He punched the padded wall again. He growled at it. So easy to imagine how this day could have been different. Then he understood that he had growled just now.

He stood immobile, startled. No, he'd merely been angry. It was nothing. But the sharp salt smell of sweat in here was powerful. He sniffed. It came from the walls. He stepped close, sniffing harder. This was how it started then, he guessed. There wasn't any question. Although he should have felt more fear, his grief and anger had wearied him. He didn't at last care. And maybe that passivity was part of this thing too. He didn't have a choice. It forced him to accept it.

And that sharp salt smell of sweat. He leaned close, sniffing. He was licking. Then he realized that he was licking, but he couldn't stop himself. The urge was irresistible. His tongue scraped against the rough canvas. For an instant, he could recognize his double personality, but then analysis was past him. When they came ten minutes later, he was raving.

FIVE

Parsons waited in the field beside the fairgrounds. There were many who were here already, but he knew that soon there would be more. He had sent messengers to all the ranchers in the valley. Other men from town were driving in now. He saw ranchers whom he knew well just behind them. It was almost time to start. He climbed up into the Jeep and stood and raised the bullhorn.

"Listen to me." Amplified, his words boomed stridently toward them.

They stopped talking, checking their weapons, or organizing gear in the back of their pickup trucks. They turned to face him, tense from expectation. Small motions rippled through them. Then the group was still, and they waited.

Parsons stood straighter, using his weight and size to gather their full attention. "Everybody knows the risk." His voice blared through the bullhorn. "Second thoughts? You'd better say so now because we won't turn back once we get started. If you want to go home, we won't think less of you, but make your minds up now before you don't have a choice."

They didn't move or speak. They just kept watching.

"Good. I knew I could count on you. Now there'll be outsiders who don't like what we're doing, who'll call us vigilantes. They don't understand the spirit of this valley, how our fathers' fathers got this land and more important how they kept it. These outsiders sympathize with weakness. If they had their way, we'd all have nothing. But I don't intend to give up what I've worked for, and it's plain that you don't either."

The group nodded forcefully.

Parsons watched as more Jeeps and pickup trucks drove in. "We have to look ahead to what they'll say against us. And I want it understood that we're no lynch mob. Our only goal is to defend ourselves. We'll go up, and we'll face them, and we'll make them stop what they've been doing. If they want to fight, they bring it on themselves. But we're not looking for that. What we want is peace. Remember that. If anyone accuses us, you know what our intentions are."

They murmured in agreement.

313

"Understood?"

They murmured louder.

"All together on this?"

They shouted, "All together!"

"What's that?"

"All together!"

*"Now you sound like you deserve to live here!"*

He gave instructions. They obeyed, getting in their trucks and Jeeps, starting motors, moving out to form a line. Others followed. Parsons slid down in his seat beside the driver. Other engines started. Other vehicles moved out. He heard the roar of motors, the crunch of tires. They headed across the rangeland, one long caravan of trucks and Jeeps, dust cloud rising.

## SIX

Altick slumped exhausted on the gametrail. "This is no good. There's no time left," he gasped.

"But it can't be very far now."

"We'll need cover in the darkness." Altick squinted toward the dimming sky. The helicopter had gone back to town a while ago. It needed fuel. Besides, in the night, it would have been useless as a lookout. Altick had explained the places where they might seek shelter, and the helicopter would return at sunrise. They were on their own now, and although angry, Altick was hardly foolish. He studied the gametrail. "On that level up there. Grab some dead branches, bushes, anything. We're going to make a barricade."

They ran up, taking turns, some working while the others aimed their rifles toward the forest, then exchanging jobs so everybody had a chance to rest. They built the wall in a circle, a thick barricade made of fallen tree limbs with pointed branches sticking out. It was like the makeshift outposts he had sometimes helped to build in Vietnam. There were pointed branches projecting from the top as well, and anything that tried to breach them would soon be impaled or scratched damned bad for certain. Meanwhile, Altick and his men had their flashlights and their rifles and their handguns, lots of ammunition, seven men all told, forewarned this time and

scared and angry and determined to put up a fight.

"There'll be no fire. I don't want to draw attention to us. Not until I'm ready for them. Let's find out tomorrow where they're hiding. Then we'll stop them. Help me make these torches. If we need them, we can light them."

They hurriedly gathered dead pine-tree branches, tying their needles into packets for torches. Their shirts were soaked with sweat as they worked breathlessly, others watching with their rifles as the sun sank behind the mountains. At once they entered the barricade, blocked off the entrance, and huddled silently in the darkness.

## SEVEN

Wheeler had never worked this hard in his life. After he had buried what he'd shot, he'd led his bait to water. It was no good if his three steers fainted when he needed them. He brought them back and staked them again, and then he dug a trench around them, not deep, just five inches. He brought five-inch plastic drainage tubing from the barn, cut it into manageable sections, sealed one end with a screw-on, glued plastic cap, filled each section with gasoline, then sealed the other end. He was almost ready.

He'd been careful not to fill the tubes near where he planned to use them. Fumes from gasoline would only scare his targets away. His only compromise was that he drove his truck to the trap he was preparing. There he struggled with the tubes as he made several trips from truck to trench, but then he had the tubes in a circle, and he drove the truck back to the barn.

A trigger now. He needed something to ignite the gasoline. He doubted that a bullet would do the job, but for sure a dynamite cap would. He had the plunger and the wires from when he'd been blasting boulders that blocked the stream to his pond. When had he been doing that? Two years ago. He'd never finished that chore, but at least he had a use for his equipment now, and he rigged the dynamite cap between two sections of the tubing, and he strung the wire and plunger to his vantage point up in the tree. He sprinkled dirt across the tubing and the wire. He glanced sternly around in search of anything he'd forgotten. Then he slung his rifle across his shoulder and climbed the tree. Jittery from Benzedrine, he stared at the darkness. When the moon came up, he knew he'd have no trouble seeing. It was brilliant, even brighter than last night, almost full. He wouldn't have to strain to see their movements out there. He would hear them as well, hear his cattle, because this time he intended to permit the steers to die. He wanted to catch as many of those hippies as he could, to trap them as they swarmed upon his cattle.

At first he thought that the cattle fidgeted and lowed strangely because they were tethered. Then the night was suddenly in motion out there, figures crouching, darting forward from all angles. Jesus, this was going to be much better than he'd hoped.

He waited until he couldn't tolerate it any longer, until the cattle were sprawled on the ground and bellowing with madness. When he pushed the plunger, night turned into roaring day. A circle of tall flames entrapped the figures. He shot repeatedly. Through the whooshing flames, he couldn't see his targets precisely, only fire-enshrouded movement.

He kept shooting. Abruptly he was out of bullets, and he frantically reloaded. Laughing, he shot again. His shoulder ached from so many recoils. He shot and shot. He heard the screams. He smelled the burning flesh amid the roaring circle of flames. He shot, reloaded, and shot again, laughing.

The fire diminished. He scanned the mounds of lifeless bodies and continued shooting at them. Then his rifle clicked on empty, and he fumbled in his pocket for more cartridges. Finding none, he tried the other pocket, but that was empty as well, and then he heard a noise below him. Staring down, he saw a figure. No, several of them, clawing at the tree trunk. In the brilliance of the moon, the dying flames around the charnel mound, he heard them climbing, their bearded faces looming toward him, and he kicked. He jabbed with his rifle as hands reached up to grab him. He was screaming.

EIGHT

Five men in the cells downstairs, two other men with rifles

watching them. The guards were leaned back in their chairs against the wall. There was a desk, a door that led out to the stairs up to the main floor, and a second door that led through to the tunnel toward the courthouse. That way prisoners could be escorted to the judge without their ever going outside, and the tunnel was both dank and fetid, odors that came underneath the bottom of the second door and filled the cell room. Slaughter had been down here only when he was required. Certainly he'd never been a prisoner, and he was understanding the humiliation, vowing that he'd make things better if he ever got the chance, although that didn't seem too likely. He was finished in this town. He knew that. Parsons had been much too clever for him. He was sickened, and the damp oppressiveness around him didn't help things.

He at least had gotten some sleep. At first he had been anxious, pacing back and forth across his cell. He'd even tried to reason with the guards, but they just looked at him and didn't answer, and his friends who were imprisoned with him, when the arguments had lagged, exchanged diminishing complaints, then gave up, sprawling in defeat across their bunks and finally were silent. Slaughter gave up with them. In his weariness, he slept.

The cells were in a row, five units with a prisoner per unit.

Lucas, who had come back after all these years to see his father, only to discover that the wheel of time had swung around to trap him. He had stayed a prisoner down here when he had testified against his father at the trial. The prosecution had been worried that he'd flee town before telling the jury about his father's temper, so he'd been jailed for what was jokingly described as his protection. He had thought he'd never come back, but his dying mother had been forceful. She'd wanted him to claim the birthright she had worked so hard for. Plus, he intended to make amends. He knew that he'd been wrong, that if he'd told the truth about the compound there was every chance his father wouldn't have been punished. He had stolen two years from his father. With the passage of too many seasons, hate had turned to pity, and with one remaining parent, he was determined not to lose the father he'd never had. He wanted to get to the ranch, to make peace with his father, to warn him, to see if he needed . . .

The medical examiner, who was puzzled how he'd let himself become committed to this. All his life, he'd tried to keep a distance from other people, and now he was close to being prosecuted for his rare social behavior. If only he'd persisted in his concentration on the dead and not the living. Yesterday when he had found the virus-ridden dog, he should have phoned the police station and been done with it. Instead he had become involved, and now he surely would be forced to . . .

Owens, who was worried about his family waiting for him. He'd been denied a chance to call them, and he wished that he had left the office upstairs when he said that he was going. But he'd stayed for stupid reasons, loyalty to people other than his family, to this group of men who'd said that they had need of him when his first duty was toward home. Now he would maybe face a jury because Slaughter and the medical examiner persuaded him that they all would lie about the boy's death. What had he been thinking of? What power did these men have over him? Did he want that much for them to like him? He'd be punished for protecting people whom he had no obligation to, and he was wishing now that with his family he had fled to some new place beyond the . . .

Dunlap, who a while ago had dreamed about that antlered figure, turning, staring past its shoulder at him. He had never dreamed it with such vividness, as if each visitation were more real, more clear until he'd wake up one last time and see it there before him. But it wasn't in his cell when he awakened. Just the memory of what had happened, and beyond the bars the two guards who leaned, chairs against the wall, and held their rifles. He was sweating from the dream and from the absence of the alcohol that gave him strength. His hands shook as they had all day and yesterday, and he was thinking that if he could only have a drink his troubles wouldn't be so fierce and he'd be able to handle this. But in a way he was delighted. In his agony he at last had gotten his story, and if Parsons thought that his imprisonment would keep him from the truth about this, Parsons didn't know how good this loser once had been, although he was not a loser any longer. He would find the truth and neutralize the nightmare and save himself. He clutched at every instant, wondering what . . .

Slaughter, who was thinking of five years ago and old Doc

Markle and the secret they had shared. Slaughter was a coward. If the others had their secrets, that was Slaughter's own grand secret. He had walked too many darkened alleys in Detroit. He'd faced too many unlocked doors and silent buildings. He'd chased too many unseen figures.

The grocery store. A February snowstorm. At midnight, Slaughter had finally completed his shift. It had been exhausting, the fierce weather making people feel on edge, causing him to be sent on more assignments than usual, mostly to settle violent domestic disputes and drunken arguments in bars. While doing his best to drive home without having an accident on the slippery streets, Slaughter had suddenly remembered that his wife had left a phone message at the precinct for him to pick up some milk, bread, breakfast cereal, and orange juice. The schools were closed, and his wife hadn't been able to leave the apartment to do her weekly shopping because she was busy taking care of their nine-year-old twins.

He'd skidded around a drift and glimpsed the snow-obscured glow of an all-night convenience store. Braking, fishtailing to a stop, he'd quickly left the car and entered the store, where he'd been surprised to find two boys in their early teens standing behind the counter, one of them munching potato chips while the other pocketed money from the cash register. The next thing he'd noticed were the legs of a man, presumably the clerk, projecting from the side of the counter, a pool of blood spreading around them on the floor.

His chest cramping, Slaughter had fumbled to unbutton his overcoat and grab his revolver, but the kid eating potato chips calmly dropped the bag and raised a shotgun, his eyes expressionless when he pulled the trigger. Slaughter had groaned from the blast's impact against his stomach. The stunning force had lifted him off his feet, thrown him past a rack of magazines, and hurtled him backward through the store's front window. Hearing glass shatter, he'd walloped onto the snow-covered sidewalk, in agony, unbearably cold, but worse than that, paralyzed from shock. No matter how hard he had strained to reach for his revolver, his arms refused to move. Snow lanced at his face, and he kept struggling, but he was powerless. Jesus! His hands felt like slabs of wood. Steaming blood gushed from the wound in his stomach, snow landing on it and turning red.

Christ! Oh, Christ! But his pain, as excruciating as it was, couldn't compare to the intensity of his fright.

The two kids ambled out of the store, paused before him, and looked bored as the one with the shotgun raised it, aiming at Slaughter's face. No! Slaughter had mentally begged, unable to speak, fighting for breath. He'd narrowed his vision toward the shotgun's barrel and inwardly winced, panicked, dreading the blast that would blow his head apart.

Then, absurdly, the kid who'd been eating potato chips had asked the other if he thought Detroit would beat Toronto in the hockey game tomorrow night. Still aiming the shotgun, the second kid had answered matter-of-factly that Detroit would. But the first kid responded that he thought Toronto had a better chance, and that had started an argument about being loyal to the local team. Through gusting snow, Slaughter had blinked in terror at the shotgun aimed at him.

Abruptly the shotgun wasn't there anymore. The kids had become so involved in their argument that they walked away, contemptuous of him, indifferent to whether he lived or died. As they disappeared into the storm, the kid with the shotgun rested it against his shoulder, the barrel projecting upward. And for a moment, just before they vanished, Slaughter—in his delirium—saw the shotgun turn into a hockey stick.

A passing patrol car happened to find him. Slaughter spent a week in intensive care, then four more weeks in the hospital while he recovered from two excruciating operations. His physicians told him that he'd nearly died from shock and loss of blood. The only reason he'd survived, they believed, was that his overcoat had provided a buffer against the full force of the blast. Otherwise, they concluded, he'd have been disemboweled.

After Slaughter was released from the hospital, the police department had given him a month's leave and then a temporary desk job to ease him into his regular, hazardous duties. All the while, a department psychiatrist had counseled him. But the counseling didn't help. Although Slaughter tried to hide his nervousness, the truth was that he'd had a breakdown. A nightmare kept haunting him, making him afraid to go to sleep because of the horrifying, snow-obscured image of the two kids aiming the shotgun at him—except that the kids would suddenly be wearing skates and goalie masks and the shotgun would be a hockey stick. With equal suddenness, the hockey stick would blow his head apart. Several times every night, Slaughter woke up screaming. When the department finally decided to see how he would perform if they sent him out on patrol, Slaughter flinched each time he heard the voice from the two-way radio sending him and his partner to a crime scene. As Slaughter's breakdown worsened, he finally had to take another leave of absence, and his nerves weren't all that had broken down.

So had his marriage. He was to blame, unwillingly, unable to control his temperament. At last, his wife couldn't bear the strain of his outbursts and had asked him for a divorce. Bitter, but not at her, instead toward himself, Slaughter had agreed. Why not? he'd gloomily decided. I'm no good to her. I'm scaring the children. I can't be any good to my family if I'm not any good to myself. Soon afterward, confused and desperate, he'd made the decision to put his past behind him, to go to Wyoming and the arbitrarily chosen town of Potter's Field. His horses were a therapy for him, but he was terrible at raising them. The only thing he knew was being a policeman, and the day that old Doc Markle told him to apply for this position, Slaughter had been shocked by something in the old man's eyes. The old man understood that Slaughter was a coward. Slaughter would have bet on that. "Go on. Try again," the old man's eyes had told him, and the old man had convinced him. Slaughter, with no option, had applied and gotten the job, and he had worked so hard at it because he meant to prove himself.

The bad part was that he had then ignored the man who saved him. Slaughter always told himself that he was just too busy to go see the old man, but the motive, he suspected now, was that he didn't want to face the man who knew he was a coward. Oh, he was a coward, all right. Seeing Clifford, walking through that moonlit field, trapping that dead boy, and running from the figures near his house, he'd felt the old fear rising in him. Hell, he'd *panicked* in the field and at his house. He'd lost complete control. He didn't understand now how he'd come this far. His bluff of manliness to all these friends, his arguments with Parsons. They were overcompensations, last attempts to keep his self-respect, because the one thing that he wanted was to get the hell away from here, to free himself from any need for strength and courage. Five years he had coasted. Parsons had been right. In fact the mayor had done him quite a favor. By imprisoning him, Parsons had relieved him of this burden. Slaughter silently was grateful. He had argued with the guards to let him free, but he had known there wasn't any chance, so arguing was easy. But the dream of old Doc Markle had enlivened ancient guilt, and he was caught between conflicting notions. Stay here. It's the safe place for you. Or find a way to get out. Prove that you're still worth a shit. He told himself he didn't have a choice. Regardless of his shame, he was imprisoned. Sublimate the shame. Get rid of it.

The night was deep upon him. Through the tiny windows high along one wall, he heard the howling and the shouting and the screaming outside. Thank God that you're in here, that you're safe. But he was growing angry at himself, at Parsons, at this trouble. He was just about to argue with the guards again. Although useless, that would help suppress his tension. Then the door swung open at the far end, and he stared as Rettig stepped in.

Both guards stood now, careful.

"Take it easy," Rettig told them. "Watch out for those rifles, or you'll maybe shoot your mouths off."

They looked puzzled, shifting nervously. "You're not supposed to be here," one guard said.

"Oh, really? Well, I'll tell the woman here to take the food back." Rettig turned.

"Wait a minute. What food?"

"For the prisoners. They haven't eaten."

"No one fed us, either."

"Well, I'm sorry I didn't think of that."

"Hey, you just bring the food in."

"I don't like this," the second guard said.

"It's only food, for Christ sake. What the hell, I'm hungry."

"Yeah, but they might pull a trick."

"We've got the rifles. Bring the food in."

"If you're certain." Rettig shrugged.

"Bring it in."

"Okay then." Rettig went toward the door and gestured.

Marge came in. She had two baskets. She looked at the five men in the cells and in particular at Slaughter. Slaughter tried to smile, but she seemed nervous, and the last few days had aged her. She had always borne her weight with pride, but now it sagged around her, and he couldn't stop his sorrow for her.

"Hi, Marge," Slaughter told her.

She just looked at him. "I thought you'd maybe like some food." She sounded weary.

"Something wrong, Marge?"

"It's the woman I hit."

"What about her?"

"She died half an hour ago."

Slaughter pursed his lips, glanced down at the floor, and nodded. Then he peered up at Marge. "I still think you did the right thing."

"Do you? I wish I could be as certain. Nathan, I *killed* her."

Slaughter didn't know what to say.

"What's in those two baskets?" the first guard asked.

"Sandwiches and coffee," Rettig answered.

"That's just fine. You bring them over to this table."

"Hey, there's plenty to go around. Don't eat it all."

"Who us? Why, we'll be sure to throw them scraps from time to time. Don't worry."

Rettig frowned.

"I told you, don't worry," the guard said. "They'll be fed. I promise."

Rettig debated, then nodded, motioning for Marge to set the basket on the table.

"No, I don't like this. Something's wrong," the second guard said. "They're giving us this food too easily. What is it, drugged?"

"It's only coffee and sandwiches," Rettig said.

"And in a while we'll be sleeping like babies. Hell, no, they eat this first. We're not dummies."

"If you say so." Rettig picked up the two baskets, moving toward the cells as the second guard stopped him.

"No, we check it first."

"You think we've got a hacksaw in the meatloaf?"

"How about a rifle up your nose, friend? First we check the basket."

So they sorted through the sandwiches and looked inside

the thermoses and shook them. Everything was fine.

"Okay, you stand back here while I distribute them."

The first guard walked past Rettig, left some sandwiches before each cell, set down plastic cups, and then the thermoses.

"All of you listen. Just as soon as I step back, you can reach out for them. Since you've only got two thermoses, you'll have to pass them to each other, but the moment you're done pouring, put the thermoses back out in front where I can see them. I don't want somebody throwing them."

Slaughter kept his gaze on Rettig. "What about outside?"

"Don't ask. All the animals are going crazy. Everybody's got their doors and windows locked. There's random shooting. Prowlers. Two of our men have been wounded."

Slaughter shook his head.

"We found two hippies by the stockpens."

Slaughter waited.

"They'd been clubbed to death."

And Slaughter made a gesture as if he didn't want to hear any more. He glanced at Marge, then at the sandwiches and plastic cups and thermoses. He cleared his throat. "Well, listen, thank you, Marge."

She didn't answer, only started from the room.

Slaughter looked at Rettig. "Hey, take care of her."

"You know it," Rettig said, and then the two guards scowled at Rettig. "Yeah, okay, don't get excited. I'm already gone." Then Rettig scanned the cells and paused, and he was leaving. "See you, Chief."

"Take care now."

The door was closed. The room became silent.

The group studied the guards.

"Get started," the first guard told them. "Let me see if the food's been drugged. I'm hungry."

Slowly they crouched. Slaughter was the last to reach out for the food. He chewed, his mouth like dust, the meatloaf sandwich tasteless.

"Here, I'll pour the coffee." Troubled by the shooting outside, he reached through the bars and unscrewed the cap on the thermos. He poured the coffee into several plastic cups and passed the cups along.

But one cup he was careful to keep only for himself.

Because as he had poured, a slender pliant object had dropped with it, splashing almost imperceptibly, so soft and narrow that it hadn't rattled when the guard shook both the thermoses. He didn't dare look around to see if anyone had noticed. He just went on as if everything were normal. Then he stood and leaned back on his bunk and chewed his sandwich, stirring with his finger at the coffee. This he knew. He wasn't going to drink the damned stuff, although he did pretend to, and then his finger touched the object. It was like a worm. He felt it, long and slender, pliant. But what was it? For a moment, he suspected that it was an explosive, but that wouldn't do much good because there wasn't any way to set it off. Besides, the noise would draw attention. Rettig wouldn't give him something that he couldn't use. This wasn't plastique then, so what else could it be? He leaned to one side so that no one saw him as he picked the object from the coffee, glancing at it, dropping it back in the coffee. It was red, just like the worm he had imagined. But he couldn't figure what it was or how to use it.

"Christ, this coffee's awful," Dunlap muttered.

"Just shut up and drink," the first guard told him. "I was right," he told the second. "The food's been drugged. They'll soon be asleep."

"Or worse."

"That's all we need. Well, they can throw up all they want to. I'm not going in to help them. You remember that," he told the prisoners. "If anybody's sick, he's on his own."

They set down their plastic cups.

"It's true. This coffee's rotten," Dunlap said.

"Don't drink it then," the medical examiner said.

The first guard started laughing.

Slaughter stood and walked to the bars. "Well, I don't know what's wrong with the rest of you, but this coffee tastes just fine to me. If you don't want it, pass the other thermos down."

"Be careful, Slaughter," Owens told him.

"I know what I'm doing. Hell, I'm thirsty."

"Suit yourself." From the far end, Lucas passed the thermos down. They moved it, hand to hand, along the cells, and Slaughter set it by the thermos he had poured from.

"I'll save this for later."

"If you're not too sick," the second guard told him,

grinning.

"You don't know what you're missing."

"I think you'll show us soon enough."

Slaughter shrugged and went back to his bunk, pretending that he sipped and liked the coffee. "All the more for me." And he was yawning. As he lay back in his bunk, he wondered if another worm was in the second thermos and if he would figure out what it was and how to use it. On the wall, the clock showed half past midnight.

<u>NINE</u>

In the barricade, Altick waited. He and his men had been hearing noises for some time, but that was normal. Night sounds in the forest. Animals come out to hunt or graze or simply wander. Coyotes howling. Nightbirds singing. There had been no evidence of danger. They had formed a circle within the barricade and stared out toward the darkness, reassured by what from all signs was another pleasant night spent in the mountains. Then the noises stopped completely, and the men inhaled, their stomachs rigid.

Silence in the mountains was something to be afraid of. One man jerked. An antelope or something big like that was suddenly charging down a wooded slope, its hoofbeats thundering, as if in panic to escape what chased it. There was scurrying through bushes, branches snapping, and abruptly the night became silent again, and they were sweating.

Altick tapped the man beside him. In the almost perfect fullness of the moon, the other man could see Altick pointing. Over to the left, a sound so vague, so indistinct that maybe it was only their imagination. Over to the right, another sound, and now there wasn't any question. Something cautiously approached them. From the forest on the far edge of the barricade, leaves brushed. Then a twig broke, and whatever was out there had encircled them.

Now take it easy, Altick thought. Three things out there can't encircle you. But then he heard a subtle fourth and then a fifth and howling.

"Jesus."

The howling wasn't like wolves or coyotes. It was unlike anything Altick had ever heard, first from the woods before him, then behind him, then no longer singly but in concert all around him. He remembered how the enemy had tried to spook him with their noises like this back in Nam. They'd shout or laugh or play rock and roll. Sometimes they'd talk in English.

But this howling. He'd never heard anything like it. Hoarse and crusty. At the same time, high-pitched and strident. Altick told himself that in Nam he'd endured about the worst thing that a man could live through. This could surely be no worse than that.

You hope, Altick thought. Again he tapped the man beside him. While they'd worked to build the barricade, Altick had explained the significance of each tap and gesture so they could understand each other without talking. Now he passed the sign that emphasized the need for silence. They would have their guns and flashlights ready, and he passed another sign, reminding them to hold their fire until whatever might be out there reached the barricade. He wanted to be certain of a target, but the howling was persistent and unnerving. Lord, it wouldn't stop.

It must have hidden other noises because suddenly he felt the pressure on the barricade. He heard the snap and scratch of something climbing. As he switched on his flashlight, he was slammed aside, his gun went off, and he was struggling with a thing that clutched him. All around him, he saw flashlight beams and muzzle flashes, diving bodies, heard the shots and screams and gasps of struggle.

The scene was a swirl of chaos as he rolled and punched with his gun and pulled the trigger at the obscene thing that grappled with him. He was suddenly in Nam again, and that remembrance was familiar, helped to give him courage, but the thing that faced him, swinging with its club, was more grotesque than anything he'd survived in Nam, and for an instant he was fearful that his shock had slowed his reflexes. The club swooped toward him, and the angle of his flashlight showed the spike at one end, streaking toward his eye, as he stumbled to avoid it, firing again. Abruptly something struck his back. Oh, Jesus! He swung to fire. Too late. Shadows swarmed, and he was falling.

TEN

"What's that?"

"Your imagination."

"No, it's shooting."

"It's just thunder or a rockfall."

The ranchers and the men from town went back to their drinking.

They had their Jeeps and trucks parked in a circle on an upper mountain meadow. They had posted guards who watched the darkness, and they'd built several campfires which they sat around. They ate and drank and checked their rifles. They were anxious, glad to be enclosed in something, and with that accomplished, Parsons sat among some hunter friends, pretending to be one of the guys.

So far he had taken chances, inciting a mob, imprisoning those five men back in town, particularly Slaughter. There'd be trouble about that, he knew, but not as much as he could make for Slaughter. After all, so many people had gone along with this that few were left to make accusations.

But Parsons couldn't keep the pressure on. If for a brief time he had taken charge, he'd have to self-efface now, ease off, let inertia carry forward. Because the men had come this far, they'd keep going, and he'd have to make it seem as if from now on he just went along with what they all intended. That had always been his method, and he knew that it would work again. They'd solve this problem; he would still have power; and the valley would continue. With the precedent of 1970, he didn't see how clearing out these hippies could be anything but good for him. He'd have to do this with some care, though. He would have to stay in the background.

What was more, he'd have to take care that these men weren't drunk when they went up to face the hippies. Image was important. There couldn't be any accusations that this group was just a drunken mob. He whispered to a few subordinates, and acting as if on their own, they went around to tell the men to stow the whiskey. Anyhow, the night was well upon them. They'd need sleep if they expected to wake up by sunrise and start moving. There was plenty to do tomorrow, a lot of miles to cover yet, a long trek through the high, thick, twisted mountain ridges.

## ELEVEN

They were waiting. They had crept up to the forest fringes, staring at the once familiar objects in a circle, at the fires and figures near them, hearing voices, watching shadows.

They were nervous, glancing toward the moon and trembling. On occasion, they couldn't resist the urge to howl, but the men across there only turned in their direction as they spread their blankets by the fires. Then the forest fringes were deserted. They were backing toward the high ground, moving deeper through the forest. They were eager for the taste which, although it sickened, they nonetheless craved, but this was not the moment or the place. Higher, deeper in the mountains where the quarry would be less protected—that was what they wanted. So they shuffled through the underbrush, and far beyond the upper ridges, they heard rumbles that rolled down like thunder. The echo of gunshots. They moved toward it.

## TWELVE

Slaughter waited in the darkness. He was lying on his bunk, pretending to sleep as through his half-closed eyes he glanced out through the bars toward where the two guards, having dimmed the lights, were tilted back in their chairs, their heads against the wall. He knew he had to move soon, but if *too* soon, he would rouse them.

He was cursing to himself. He had been safe. A cell to keep him occupied while everything went on without him. Now the force of choice was on him once again, and if he didn't act, he knew that Rettig then would understand him. Did it matter? Yes, he finally decided. He would not relive his past humiliation. He had come here for a fresh start, and if he ignored this opportunity, he would never feel whole again; he would have chosen a progressive pattern of defeat; he'd just keep moving pointlessly. Of course, he could pretend to Rettig that he hadn't understood the objects in the coffee, but he didn't know if he would be convincing. Even so, he wouldn't be convincing to himself. He had to do this.

Cursing to himself, he studied both guards. Then he sat up slowly in his bunk. Because he finally had understood these objects in the coffee. They were obvious, so much so that he wondered why he took so long to realize their purpose, that he wondered how much smarter Rettig was than he had ever guessed. The plan was simple to the point of genius. Perhaps that was the reason Slaughter took so long to figure it. The objects in the coffee were pure phosphorus. The liquid kept them from igniting. That had been the word that solved the puzzle for him. Still thinking that these things were explosive, he had wondered how to detonate them. Detonation made him think of fuses, a bright light burning. But the blast would warn the guards. These things must have a silent function then, but if they were indeed explosive, how the hell could he ignite them? Since he didn't smoke, he didn't carry matches. Bright light, matches and their phosphorus, ignition, and he had it, suddenly in high school, watching as his teacher drew the worms of phosphorus from jars of water, waiting as the worms, exposed to air, abruptly were on fire. Later he would think how close he'd come to missing the significance, but now he understood and didn't have a choice.

He got up slowly from his bunk and walked with caution toward the bars. He saw that all his friends were sleeping. He stood motionless and waited for some action from the guards. There wasn't any, and he knelt to reach through toward the second thermos. Then he slowly opened it and poured the coffee into plastic cups. Another red worm slid out, dropping. So there *was* another one, and he was reaching in the cup to grab the worm and drop it quickly into the cup that held the other, the coffee safely over them. There was one thing that still bothered him. He knew that phosphorus was poison. If some portions had dissolved, the coffee might make them sick. But then he thought that its foul taste might not be from the phosphorus but from the way the coffee was prepared to make it taste so bad. Rettig hadn't wanted anyone to drink it. So they all had tried a sip and spit it out. They maybe would be fine.

He watched the guards and guessed that there wasn't any

point in waiting further. He dipped his finger into the coffee, grabbed the worms, and as they dripped, he pressed them around the bolt that locked his cell. He wouldn't have attempted this if he'd been in a new and well-made jail. But this place had been built in 1923. When he had first come down here, he had been appalled. Oh, sure, the locks would hold if someone lunged at them or tried to break them, but the metal wasn't pure enough or thick enough for him, and he had asked permission to revitalize the jail which the town council had denied him. What did he expect? they asked him. Hacksaws or a bomb. There had never been that kind of trouble here, and if he did his job right, none of that stuff would get in here. Well, he had a trick to show them now, and he was grateful that they hadn't acted. Phosphorus burned at high temperatures. Although not sufficient to melt steel, the heat would weaken this poor metal, and the lock seams weren't that good to start with. Hell, he didn't have a thing to lose. He had to try.

He stepped back, but the phosphorus remained inert. Or maybe he was wrong, and these things weren't what he had figured. No, the coffee still was dripping from them. They weren't yet exposed to air. The coffee had to dry, as suddenly he saw what seemed to be a spark, and in a flash the phosphorus was burning. White hot, sparks, a thick cloud rising. He was staring toward the guards. The hiss was louder than he'd expected, like a thousand sparklers blazing on July Fourth, and one guard moved a little in his chair as Slaughter lunged against the cell door.

But it held. The phosphorus kept blazing around the bolt and lock seams, and he lunged again, and this time he could see the seams begin to part. The guard was shifting in his chair and in a moment would be fully wakened. Slaughter lunged against the door again, the metal clanging, and abruptly he was weightless, stumbling forward, almost falling as he realized that he was out, the cell door swinging free, the phosphorus still hissing, blazing. He kept stumbling, his arms out for balance, as the guard was sitting upright in his chair, and Slaughter lunged against him. While the guard fell, upsetting his chair, Slaughter grabbed the rifle, and he swung to grab the rifle from the second guard who now was sitting up as well, his face grotesquely startled, wincing from the rifle blow against his shoulder, falling. Slaughter dropped one rifle, aiming with the other, and the two guards paused where they were halfway to their feet now, and the worst part had been managed.

"Stay exactly where you are. Don't move or even fidget," Slaughter told them.

"How the hell . . . ?" They stared from Slaughter toward the dimming remnants of the phosphorus.

"What's going on?" the medical examiner asked.

In the cells, the men were moving.

"Nothing. We're just getting out of here is all. Remember," Slaughter told the guards. "Don't even scratch your noses."

He was shifting toward the table, pulling out the drawer and grabbing for the keys. He watched the two guards all the time he edged back toward the first cell, Lucas waiting.

"Here. The big key," Slaughter told him, and he moved again to watch the guards while close behind he heard the scrape of metal as the key was turned. The cell came open. Slaughter glanced at Lucas coming out. He concentrated solely on the guards then as the cells were in their sequence unlocked and the men came out.

"But how did . . . ?" Owens said.

"I'll tell you later. You two, get on in there." Slaughter pointed toward the guards.

They hesitated.

"Damn it, move, I told you." Slaughter started toward them, and they raised their hands.

"Okay. We're moving."

"You get in the first one. You get in the fourth."

"But why . . . ?"

"No reason. Just do what I tell you. I just want you separated. Move, for Christ sake."

And they did, and Slaughter told the medical examiner to bind and gag them, using belts and strips of cloth torn from the bunk sheets. Slaughter watched them, aiming the rifle. Then the medical examiner stepped out, and Lucas shut the doors and locked them.

"Bring the keys. The other rifles."

Dunlap was already halfway across to reach one door.

"No, we're going this way," Slaughter told him. "That way leads upstairs. This other one is where we're going."

Dunlap was puzzled.

"You'll see."

Slaughter went across and took the keys from Lucas. He unlocked the second door and swung it open. Then he flicked the light switch in there, and they saw the damp, slick, brick-lined tunnel.

"It leads toward the courthouse. There's no time."

They hurried through. Slaughter stared back at the two guards in their cells. He waved and stepped inside the tunnel where he shut the door and locked it. Then he turned, and they were running.

It was slippery in here. Condensation on the ceiling dripped down on them, and the tunnel echoed from the clatter of their footsteps. Slaughter saw the vapor from his breath and felt the damp brick chill and kept on running. He was forced to stoop as he ran underneath the lights that hung from the ceiling. Then the tunnel curved a little, and they reached a second door.

"It's locked. I have to use the key."

But when he fumbled with the key, it didn't work. The door stayed locked.

"What's going on here?"

Then he realized the door had not been locked at all. What he had done just now was actually to lock it. He worked the key and turned the handle. Slowly, wincing as the door creaked, he pushed at the door, and they faced darkness.

"There's a hall. Just follow it. You'll reach some stairs."

Now Slaughter flicked the lights off.

"But we—"

"I don't want to be a target. Feel along the hall."

They inched through the darkness. Here the floor was tiled. It echoed from their halting footsteps. Owens struck an object, cursing.

"Quiet," Slaughter told him.

"There's a table."

*"Quiet. People might be in here."*

So they kept inching forward. Slaughter felt ahead. We should have reached the end by now, he told himself, and then his boot struck wood, and he gripped the staircase bannister.

"We made it," Owens said, and Slaughter didn't take the

time to caution him. He just continued up the stairs, and everything was dark up there as well, except that from some windows moonlight spilled in, showing the front door and the big main hallway.

"Shush," he told them, and they stopped while, breath held, Slaughter listened. "We'll use the back. For all we know, there are guards in front."

He moved down the murky hallway, and the layout in here was the same as at the police station. He passed silent offices and reached the back door, staring out, then looking at the others, pulling the door open, stepping into the moonlight.

"My car is in the lot behind the station. If we're careful, we can take it."

He shifted from the sidewalk toward the grass, concentrating on the parking lot as a man stepped from the bushes beside the courthouse. Slaughter, thinking of the two kids in the grocery store who'd shot him, almost raised his rifle, firing. But he managed to subdue his fear and resist the impulse. There wasn't a reason to kill this guard. The most he could hope for was to overcome the man before he could shout to warn other guards. Slaughter shifted his grip on the rifle, about to club the man, as Rettig came up close to him.

The other men sighed.

"Christ Almighty," Owens said.

Rettig stopped in front of Slaughter. "It took you long enough. I almost gave up waiting. So you figured what that stuff was."

"How come you're so smart to think of that?" Slaughter asked, relieved.

"I didn't. Marge did. She remembered what you said about the cells downstairs, how you complained that they were weak." Then Rettig explained what had happened while Slaughter was in jail, and Slaughter wished he hadn't heard.

"I think Parsons is going to kill those hippies," Rettig said.
"What?"

"He's going to pick a fight and kill them. He'll arrange it so it looks justified, but he'll kill them just the same, and he'll have so much help that no one'll say it wasn't self-defense. It's nineteen seventy again."

"But those hippies," Owens said. "Everything they've

done. Why should *we* care what he does to them?"

From the farthest sections of the town, muffled gunfire echoed. Slaughter looked down at the ground, then turned to Owens. "Because they're people, or have you forgotten that?"

The group was silent.

"Oh, I know the townsfolk used to call them animals. But you more than anyone ought to know the difference," Slaughter said.

Owens stared. "It isn't worth it, Slaughter. *They* aren't worth it."

"Maybe not to you. So go on. Look out for yourself and your family. But I've got my own obligations. Those damned hippies don't mean anything to me, but I'll stake everything to help them."

Owens stared a moment longer. "If I didn't have a wife and kids."

"There's no need to explain. Go on. We'll talk about it some time."

"Sure."

Except they both knew that they wouldn't.

Owens lingered.

"You stayed until sunset. You made good on what you promised."

"Sure."

Owens hesitated, then backed off and turned, walking along the courthouse, disappearing into the shadows.

Slaughter watched him.

"Here, Chief," Rettig said. "Take my gunbelt. I'll get another one from the station."

The weight of the gunbelt was satisfying. Slaughter strapped it on. "Your family?"

"My brother's with them. They left this afternoon."

"That's all that Owens wanted, too, I guess."

"But he intends to leave with them. We need him, but he doesn't plan to stay. That makes the difference."

Slaughter stared off toward the sound of the gunshots. "Well, we'd better get moving."

"Be careful when you reach the parking lot. Parsons has men inside the station."

"I don't plan to advertise." Slaughter turned to face the

medical examiner. "You coming?"

"I have work to do."

"Yourself?" he said to Lucas.

"No. I have to see my father."

"Without help?"

"I've had a chance to do more thinking. If there's trouble, I know where my place is."

"Yes." Slaughter studied him. "I understand that, I suppose. I'll see you." He started toward the parking lot.

"Hey, wait. I'm going with you," Dunlap said.

"You'd better not. I don't know how I'm going to stop Parsons, but tomorrow will be rough."

"You need a witness."

"Is it me, or just your story?"

"I'm not certain any longer."

"Just so you know the risks. I'm going to need a friend up there, that's certain. Rettig, you stay here and watch the town. I've got to count on someone."

"But you don't have any men," Rettig said.

"How many would I need? Ten? A hundred? If I take the men we have, this town will be defenseless. Even then, we wouldn't be a match for Parsons and what I assume must be an army. No, if Dunlap and I can't do it, then it simply won't get done. The numbers are against us if I try to beat Parsons on his terms. I'll have to beat him on my own terms."

Rettig studied him. "Take care."

"I mean to. I'll see you in a couple days."

"Sure." But Rettig didn't sound convinced.

Somber, they shook hands. Then Slaughter moved toward the parking lot.

The group was disbanding. Lucas went one way, the medical examiner another. Rettig watched as Slaughter reached the parking lot, scanned the police station, and walked toward his car. Slaughter had the rifle and the handgun. Dunlap got in the cruiser. Slaughter slid behind the steering wheel. The engine started, and they drove from the parking lot. Rettig waited until they disappeared. He frowned as the rumble of gunfire rolled across town.

# THE
# MOUNTAINS

*Part Seven*

PARSONS AND HIS MEN WOKE HALF
AN HOUR BEFORE SUNRISE. THEY CRAWLED FROM THEIR SLEEPING
bags, squinting, shivering in the morning dampness. There was
hurried cooking, hunters packing their gear and squatting by
the camp's latrine, then scuffing out the cookfires, pouring
water on the coals, checking that the embers died before the
Jeeps and trucks were started and the caravan moved out. A
few men were reminded of Quiller's caravan when he first
crossed the valley. Now a different kind was heading up to stop
him, and they thought about their families, their businesses, the
cattle dying, and they meant to put a stop to this as soon as they
were able. Parsons didn't talk much now. If there had been a
way to go back to the town, he would have, not because he was
afraid, but he was wishing they would do this on their own. If it
went wrong, he could avoid the blame then. Otherwise he still
could take the credit. But he'd come this far, and he'd be

noticed if he left, and so he stayed with them, silent, letting
their determination carry them forward. They would drive up
through this meadow, take another loggers' road up to a second
meadow, then a third. After that, they'd move on foot. By five
o'clock, they'd reach the start of the escarpment, and if not
today, then tomorrow, everything would be completed.

As the column passed rockfalls, cliffs, and ridges, there
were unseen caves that shut out the sunlight, and for now, what
hid in there slept uneasily.

TWO

The helicopter was anchored near the runway. Slaughter
crouched behind oil drums near a shed and stared at the damp,
chill, post-dawn mist that shrouded the chopper. He dimly saw
the rotor blades that stretched out from the top, their long ends
partly sagging, saw the bubble of the nose, the insect-resembling
tail, the smaller rotors at the back. He felt the wind shift,
swirling mist so that the helicopter now was thoroughly
enveloped, and he turned to Dunlap who crouched beside him,
shivering.

"It can't be long now."

"That's what you keep promising," Dunlap said. "What I
wouldn't give for a shot of rye to warm me up."

"You want to back out?"

"Try to make me."

Slaughter frowned. Dunlap was in bad shape, more than
Slaughter had realized when they had left the jail. But there had
been so much to do, so much to think about back then that
Slaughter hadn't argued with him. Anyway, what Dunlap had
said last night was true—Slaughter did still need a witness,
although Dunlap shook so much now that Slaughter wasn't sure
how useful the reporter would be. There wasn't any choice,
however, Slaughter reminded himself. Events were in charge,
and he was compelled to move with them. He could tell himself that, if he wanted to, he could run. But given who he was, he
couldn't allow himself to run. His life had trapped him.

When he'd left the jail, his first impulse had been to go

after Parsons in a Jeep, but Parsons and his men were too far ahead of him. Slaughter needed something quicker, and he'd thought about the helicopter that Altick had been using. Because it couldn't search the hills at night, the pilot would have set it down until the morning when he would take off again. The hard part was to find it. Slaughter didn't think the pilot would have gone back to his home base in a neighboring valley. Given the emergency, the pilot would have saved time, staying here. Slaughter drove out to the state-police office on the highway, but the helicopter wasn't there. He checked the park, the fairgrounds, and at last settled on the obvious, the simple airfield from which ranchers flew to reach their cattle in the worst of winter, dropping bales of hay. There was just one airplane that the ranchers leased in common, a gravel runway, one hanger, and a few equipment sheds, but there the helicopter was, anchored near the runway.

After that, Slaughter had risked driving home. He doubted that with so much trouble in town, guards would have time to search for him. Nonetheless he'd been nervous when he reached his house. Relieved to find it deserted, he'd quickly packed two knapsacks with food, canteens, woolen shirts, sleeping bags, lots of ammunition, and a first-aid kit. Dunlap didn't have his camera anymore, so Slaughter had lent him one. If there'd been time, Slaughter would have made coffee, but dawn was approaching, and they returned to the runway just before the sun rose.

Now the mist was thinning. Slaughter glanced at his watch. The sun had been up for half an hour.

"Maybe he's not coming," Dunlap said.

"No, the helicopter's too important. He'll be here. I'm sure of it."

At once, Slaughter heard footsteps crunching on gravel. He tensed as the footsteps came closer. Then the footsteps paused on the other side of the equipment shed.

Slaughter frowned. He glanced at Dunlap, then out toward the helicopter. When the footsteps went back toward where they had begun, Slaughter didn't understand. Who was here? A patrolman?

"So this is where you are."

Unnerved, Slaughter swung to face the voice. He found

himself staring at Lucas.

"Christ, don't sneak up on me," Slaughter told him.

"He's not here yet?"

"Who?"

"The pilot."

"No, we're waiting. How'd you find us?"

"Process of elimination. Yesterday you talked about a heli-copter that the state police were using. I drove around until I found it."

"Where'd you get a car?"

"A truck. It was my father's. Look, I'm going up there with you."

Slaughter noticed the rifle Lucas held.

"What's happened?"

Lucas didn't answer.

"Something with your father?"

Lucas gazed out toward the helicopter. Then he looked at Slaughter.

"They killed him." Lucas squinted. "He was evidently hunting them. He had some cattle staked out for bait, and he was going out at night to shoot from a tree. He must have killed a lot of them. There was so much blood."

"You found the bodies?"

"Only his. As much as I could recognize when they were finished with him." Lucas wiped his mouth. "They disembow-eled him for a start. They—"

"You don't have to talk about it."

"But I want to. Then they ripped his arms and legs off." Lucas spoke without expression. "When I got to the ranch, I didn't find my father. But I smelled this stench that drifted toward me from the foothills. Roasted meat and burning hair. I drove my father's truck out. There was something burning, all right. I could see the flames, mostly from range grass when I got there, and I saw the mangled cattle and the blood, and then I found my father in a half a dozen places. From the empty car-tridges around the tree, I'm sure he must have killed a lot of them. Even drunk, he never failed to hit a target. They must have taken the bodies with them. As I said, I'm going with you."

"But you didn't even like him."

"I don't care. I owe him. I took two years from his life,

and if I hadn't, maybe everything would somehow have been different."

"I don't know what good you'll be up there."

"I'll be your eyes behind you. Right now you need all the friends you can find."

Lucas said the right thing, that was certain. Slaughter stared at him and nodded. "If the pilot ever comes."

Then Slaughter heard other footsteps crunching on gravel. No, a double set of them, and he motioned for Lucas and Dunlap to crouch with him beside the oil drums next to the shed.

The footsteps crunched past the opposite side of the shed and then moved into the open. With the mist almost gone, Slaughter glimpsed two men who crossed to reach the helicopter. One man rubbed his hands together and blew on them. The other unhooked the helicopter's mooring cables.

Slaughter straightened, walking toward them, Lucas and Dunlap following. "You've got some passengers," he told the two men, who swung in surprise.

Slaughter recognized the pilot. The other man he didn't know, but they were rigid, and he wondered if they'd heard about his jail break.

"Who's that? Slaughter? Hell, you scared me."

"We'll be going with you in the chopper."

"There's not enough room."

"Then we'll leave this other guy behind."

"And what about the rest of you?"

"They're coming with me."

"Sorry. I can't do that. One man with me isn't any problem. I took two men with me yesterday." The pilot shook his head. "Three men with me, and I guarantee we'd never make it. This thing wasn't built for that much weight."

"We'll have to try it anyhow," Slaughter said.

"That's impossible."

Slaughter pointed toward the western mountains. "You don't understand the trouble up there."

"Maybe. But there'll be even more trouble if we all try to go up in this thing."

"We'll have to chance it."

"Without me to fly you. Choose less men or none of us

gets off the ground."

They scowled at each other. Slaughter turned toward Lucas and Dunlap. Which man could he choose? He really needed both of them, and more important, neither of them would agree to be left behind.

"I can't do that," he said, and his first mistake had been to think that they knew nothing about how he'd broken out of jail, his second had been to turn toward Lucas and Dunlap. Because suddenly he felt the pilot's arms around him, grabbing for the rifle. At the same time, Lucas was struggling with the pilot's companion. Dunlap faltered, blinking.

"Well, if you boys planned to have a dance, I would have bought some tickets," someone said, and everybody stopped then, pivoting toward the shed as a policeman stepped into view. He had his handgun drawn, and Slaughter didn't know if this was help or more trouble as he recognized Hammel, the new man on the force whom he'd disciplined when they had looked at Clifford's body on Friday.

"Now then, everybody step clear of each other. Keep those rifles down."

They didn't move.

"I mean it." Hammel walked sternly forward, and they parted.

"You two." Hammel pointed toward the pilot and his friend. "Step over to the left there. Don't you know enough to stay away from men holding rifles? In particular our fine police chief here. He might get angry and shoot your toe off. My God," Hammel asked the pilot, "what did you think you'd accomplish by trying to capture Slaughter? Did you think the town would make you a hero?"

"I don't care about his jail break. I don't even know why he was arrested. I just don't intend to go up with three other men in that helicopter."

"Well, you're honest. That's a credit." Hammel smiled and waved his handgun. "Okay, clear out. You're no use to us."

"But—"

"Hey, I'm giving you a break. Clear out. Don't try my patience."

Slowly they moved toward the shed, and then they started running.

"'No use to *'us'* you told him?" Slaughter asked.

"That's right. Let's keep this in the family. When Rettig told me what had happened, we sat down to figure where you might turn up."

"I must be obvious as hell."

"Well, a few of us aren't quite as stupid as you think we are."

"You call it smart to chase off my pilot?"

"We don't need him. Rettig told me to keep a watch on you, to use my judgment."

"And your judgment—"

"—says I'm going with you. Do you remember when we found Clifford's body? I said something about what had killed him being obvious. You called me on that. Oh, not much. Enough, though. Hell, you made me feel like an idiot. And it turned out you were right. So, fine. But now it's my turn. I can do a few things you'd give anything to do. I'm going to fly your helicopter for you."

Slaughter thought back to the file he kept on every man.

"I see that it's coming back to you," Hammel said. "I spent three years in the Air Force. My specialty was choppers. And I was damned good. Just this once you're going to shut your mouth and watch somebody else who's good at what he does, and when I'm finished, you had damned well better step up, face me straight on, and say, 'Thank you.'"

"More than that, I'll say I'm sorry for the other day."

"It's too late for that, Slaughter. Shove your friends inside. Let's get this party started."

Slaughter touched his beard stubble. "There's only one thing."

"What is it?"

"If we crash, I'll say we should have kept that other guy to fly us."

Hammel started laughing.

<br>

## THREE

"You can see that something happened here."

Parsons and his group looked at the barricade.

"The question, though, is what."

There weren't any bodies, but they saw the blood, the state police hats, the ripped discarded knapsacks, the empty bullet casings.

"So there really was a fight up here. That wasn't thunder we heard."

"It wasn't thunder. No, it wasn't thunder."

They walked around the barricade. Several of them glanced nervously toward the forest.

"I don't like this."

"Why? You think those hippies would be stupid enough to attack this many men?"

"We don't know anything about them."

"We know that they've likely killed more people."

"I don't mind admitting I'm scared."

"So what? You think we ought to go back for more help? You think that we don't have enough already?"

"I can't tell you what I think."

"Let's leave it that way. Altick is in trouble. That's all anybody has to know."

"Or *was* in trouble."

"It's the same. We're here to put a stop to them. If Altick still needs help, we're here to give it. If he's long past help, we're here to make them pay for that."

The odd part was that Parsons didn't have to say a word. The group had formed a common personality, and for a time as they had driven up the loggers' roads, he had been satisfied that he would not be blamed if things went wrong. But as they drove higher, he had gradually felt uneasy up here, and when at last they'd left the Jeeps and trucks to continue on foot, he started feeling scared. For one thing, he had never liked the mountains. Oh, he'd gone up hunting with his friends, but that was part of his position. Hunting was expected from him. But he'd never really liked it or the wilderness up here. His best surroundings were his office and the town-council chambers. These men were at home up here, however, and for several hours they had grown in strength as his diminished. They had used terrain maps, plotting which direction was the best way to the base of the escarpment. They had hiked up past the lake where Altick's men had disappeared. They'd traveled Sunday afternoon and evening, then today through Monday morning. All told, they'd been ten hours on the move now, mostly in the trucks and Jeeps. Considering how poor the loggers' roads were and how hard it was to hike up through these mountains, sixty miles was some achievement, although they had another fifteen yet to go.

The things behind them traveled only in the night, so they would not catch up until tomorrow at midnight if they moved as fast as they were able. In the hills above the group, however, there were many others sleeping, waiting, although of course that information came out only later. In the meanwhile, there was nothing in the forest near the barricade to indicate what finally had happened to the men within the barricade. The sun was high above the forest, and the group was tightening their knapsacks, taking time to eat some beef jerky or to urinate. Then they were moving higher. As one member of the group would later say, it was like climbing toward another country.

### FOUR

Slaughter flinched from every treetop they scudded over. "Jesus, go down any lower and you'll have us pulling pine needles from our asses."

Hammel grinned. "If you want a smooth ride, call United Airlines. Did I promise anything except to get you off the ground?"

"But . . . Watch it! Look out!"

The helicopter tilted, its rotors nearly colliding with a tree. Slaughter clutched his harness as Hammel worked the controls, and the helicopter tilted on a different angle. Frantic, Hammel fought to gain altitude. Abruptly the helicopter was steady again. Slaughter realized that he'd stopped breathing.

"It's the wind. I didn't count on this much wind," Hammel said.

*"Can you get us there, or can't you?"*

"If you want to take your chances, I can keep on trying."

"Hey, you didn't talk about taking chances when we were back on the ground."

"Well, that was easy, talking."

As Hammel grinned again, Slaughter said, "Oh, I get it now. You're crazy."

"Sure. I'd have to be to try this. You're a little nuts yourself."

"Well, you're not far wrong about that."

Slaughter heard a noise behind him. When he turned, he saw that Dunlap had his hand up to his mouth as if he might be sick. Lucas was ashen, staring at the treetops.

"I think *everybody* in here's crazy," Slaughter said.

They were past the treetops, swooping across a meadow. Slaughter briefly felt relieved. At least there wasn't anything for them to hit, although the wind was tugging at them again, the helicopter twisting. Then the trees loomed before him, and the helicopter struggled to rise above them. Slaughter thought he heard a branch scrape on the landing struts. He closed his eyes and swallowed. When he looked again, the trees were thick a few feet underneath him.

"I don't see a sign of anyone," he shouted to be heard in the roar of the engine and the wind.

"We don't know which way they came," Hammel shouted back. "I'm simply heading straight toward the escarpment. Once we get there, we ought to have a good view of the ridges below us. But we've got another problem. This thing isn't any Honda. Look at how much fuel we're using."

Slaughter did. The gauge was just below the halfway mark. "But we've been gone just a couple of hours."

"Overloaded in a wind that's stronger than I figured. That's the reason I've been flying low. To avoid the wind and save on fuel. With this much weight, if we were higher, the wind would hold us back worse than it is. The chopper would have to work harder. We'd have even less fuel."

Hammel paused between each sentence, drawing breath to shout more.

"Then we can't go back," Slaughter said.

"Right. We'd never make it. I'll keep flying until we're using fumes and I have to set her down. I don't know if we'll manage the escarpment."

"You mean get above it?"

"It's too high for all this weight. I'll have to set down at the base." Hammel paused. "If we have fuel to get that far."

Slaughter's temples throbbed.

The landscape was wild below them, ridges, hollows, rock-falls. Struggling in the wind, the helicopter narrowly missed trees. If we crash now, Slaughter thought, we're finished. Then something flashed ahead of him, and he was pointing. "There. I see them."

Hammel aimed the chopper toward the flash. "No, it's the vehicles they used. I don't see any people."

They swooped toward the surreal image of a parking lot across this distant mountain meadow, Jeeps and vans and trucks all parked absurdly in a pattern of straight lines as if at a super-market or the K-Mart. Then they were past them.

"Sure. I understand now what they did," Hammel said. "They moved up the long way through that chain of loggers' roads and meadows you see on the map. They must be hiking toward the base of the escarpment. If we keep on a straight line toward the mining town from here, we'll have to see them."

"If the forest doesn't hide them."

"They'll move through as many clearings as they can. That many men. We'll see them, all right. We might wish we hadn't, but we'll see them. Right now, that's the least of our worries."

The helicopter swayed again, and Slaughter gripped his harness, sweating. "Everybody feeling all right back there?"

"Oh, yeah, fantastic." Dunlap groaned.

"Just think about your story."

"What I'm thinking about is straight ahead of me."

Dunlap pointed. The land curved up past wooded ridges, higher, past the cliffs and rockfalls, far beyond to where the snow-capped peaks loomed hazily in the distance. Where two peaks were close together, in the pass between, a cliff glinted in the sunlight. It was massive beyond belief. Slaughter saw that even from this far away. The cliff was like a dam or a huge stone glacier, and on top somewhere the mining town had been estab-lished. Slaughter felt a chill pass through him as he saw it getting larger, as he gradually came near it, and he knew what Dunlap meant. He really didn't want to go there.

#### FIVE

Parsons and his men stumbled through the forest up a gametrail that they'd discovered. Past an open ridge before them, far off, they could see the high cliff they were heading toward. The wind was fierce, but it failed to moderate the force of the sun, and as they sweated, working higher, one man slumped off the trail to lean against a boulder.

"This is wrong. I have to rest."

A few men stopped beside him, scowling with contempt. "When you were riding in the Jeep, you thought this was great."

"That was then. Now I have to rest." The wind shrieked through the trees. "This god-damned wind. What difference does it make how soon we get there?"

"Because everyone agreed to reach the cliff by sundown."

"Why? We can't do anything at night. We'll have to wait till tomorrow morning anyway."

"He's right," another man said. "So what if we spend the night down here? We'll end up sleeping in the woods no matter where we are."

"Because I don't like knowing they might be around me. You guys saw how well that barricade was built. But it didn't do any good. I don't intend to sleep until I know that this is finished."

As a branch snapped in the forest, they pivoted, startled.

"It's the wind," the first man said. "I'm telling you. I have to rest."

"Well, damn it, rest then. But you'll do it by yourself. The others are ahead of us now, and I don't intend to stay behind." The man hitched his knapsack tighter to his shoulders and proceeded along the gametrail. "You must be stupid, hanging back like this."

"Hey, wait for me. I'm coming with you."

They hurried to reach the main group, which was out of sight among the trees. But the first man didn't have the energy to push himself away from the boulder. As another branch snapped in the forest, he looked all around in panic and suddenly did have the energy.

"Hold it. Wait." He stumbled up the gametrail.

At the crest, he saw the main group filing through a wooded hollow, angling up the other slope. He ran to catch them, seeing the men whom he had talked to join the main group. He lurched toward the hollow, then up the other side, and at the top he swung around a lip of rock before he saw the men stopped so closely before him that he almost bumped against them.

"What's the matter?"

"We don't know yet."

The overweight man breathed hard as he glanced toward the group before him. They had left their single-file formation, spreading out to stare ahead. Some were slumped against fir trees, and then the words came drifting back through the wind. "They found something up ahead."

"What is it?"

"I don't know yet."

The men who'd leaned against the fir trees straightened to stare past the heads and shoulders of the men before them.

"It's a uniform." The words were muffled by the wind.

"What kind?"

"A state policeman."

There was no way that the overweight man could see from where he was. He veered to the side to get around his companions. He climbed a slope of fir trees, looked down toward the men on the gametrail, and saw Parsons plus two members of the town council searching through blood-stained clothes.

"The shirt has a captain's insignia," the overweight man heard Parsons say. "This was Altick's."

"But what happened to him?"

"Do I have to draw you a diagram? This gametrail leads up to the mining camp. What do *you* think happened?"

Apprehensive, the wind-blown men flinched and raised their heads, directing their gaze toward the rockwall miles above them. Even that far away, it dominated.

The overweight man stared at it, wishing that he hadn't come here. This was wrong. The notion had been fine as long as he was in town, but up here, everything was strange and different. You're just a little scared is all, he told himself. Just keep your eyes on Parsons. He knows what he's doing.

All the same, he didn't understand why there were no

policemen here. He'd heard about the trouble Slaughter was in, about Slaughter's holding back, not acting until it was almost too late. Even so, that didn't sound like Slaughter, and he wondered if the rumors were true. It could be that we shouldn't be here, he thought. But he knew that the group could not turn back now, that he'd be considered a coward if he went back on his own. He had to stay, to go with them, although he wished desperately that he had stayed in town.

Then he heard the helicopter. Peering up, he saw it roaring toward him. It was just above the trees. It must have used the gametrail as a line to follow, and it swooped up past him, Slaughter's grim face distinctive through the canopy. The helicopter's rotors added to the wind. The overweight man saw the chopper's belly and the landing struts. The other men stared up, frowning, pointing. Parsons stared up as well. The bloody clothes he held were contorted by the wind.

On the slope, the overweight man stepped higher, peering through an open space between the trees at where the helicopter roared past him, getting smaller, and he strained to catch a final look. He lost his balance. He slipped on the slick mountain grass, thrusting his arms out to grab a branch. But he missed the branch and rolled. When he hit, the slickness beneath him muffled his impact, and he felt the slickness soaking through his pants and shirt, and he gaped beneath him, seeing mashed lungs, bowels, liver, and kidneys. He screamed. But it wasn't just the guts that made him scream. It was also the bones, ribs and legs, arms and pelvis, shoulders, and most of all the skull, its lipless tongueless teeth bared smiling at him. Throat raw, shrieking, the overweight man tumbled down the slope.

SIX

In the helicopter, Slaughter pointed. "There they are."

The men were bunched out on the gametrail, wearing red-checkered shirts and khaki hunting jackets, examining an object they had found. At first the trees obscured them. The men were small, then growing larger as the helicopter neared them. Then they must have heard the rotors, and they peered up, and Slaughter saw one man on a wooded slope above the group. The man was squinting up at him. The helicopter roared past, and as Slaughter looked back, he had lost them. He was glancing forward at the final rising sweep of ridges, disturbed by the rockwall looming miles ahead.

"Just as well we found them. We've got less than a quarter tank of fuel," Hammel said.

"Take her down. My business isn't on the escarpment. It's with Parsons."

"Well, I don't know where to land this thing."

They stared ahead. There wasn't any clearing. All they saw were wooded ridges stretching toward the mountains and the rockwall far above them.

"Look, there has to be a way for you to land. A few more minutes, and we'll be too far ahead of Parsons for me to walk back and reach him before sundown."

"There were open spaces behind them."

"*Far* behind. I still wouldn't be able to reach him before sunset."

"Well, I don't see a clearing, so you'd better sit back, relax, and enjoy the ride."

The wind tugged at them, buffeting.

"I don't think we'll have a chance to find a place to land. The wind will choose it for us."

"I don't understand."

But then he did. He saw the higher ridge of pine trees they were heading toward. He felt the helicopter jolt to one side, felt the snap of branches underneath him. "Jesus, I don't think you've ever flown a helicopter until now." He braced himself as green obscured the sky. Metal scraped against wood. The helicopter tilted. Slaughter's head slammed back. Through the canopy, down among the trees, his stomach swooping, he saw granite rush toward him.

SEVEN

Slaughter crawled from the wreckage, stunned, moving slowly. There were broken branches in the boulders all around him, and his shoulder throbbed, and there was something he'd forgotten. Then it came to him. "Is she going to blow?" he blurted to Hammel.

"More than likely!"

Hammel squirmed out on Slaughter's side. The far side was impassable, the helicopter wedged among boulders and shattered trees, the broken rotors adding to the chaos. Slaughter stood and slumped against the helicopter. He was dizzy. "We have to get these men out."

He leaned in, feeling off-balance until he realized that the helicopter had tilted when it hit the trees, falling head first, its tail in the air now. He wiped at his eyes to clear their double vision, reaching in for Lucas who was slumped above him, hanging from his seatbelt, dangling across the seat that Slaughter had been in. He had snapped ahead, then back, then forward again, and Lucas now was moaning.

"I smell gasoline," Hammel said.

"Hurry."

Slaughter unhitched the seatbelt and pulled at Lucas, bracing himself to take the weight, but even so he stumbled backward, nearly falling in the rocks and broken branches as he felt support behind him and Hammel clutched at Lucas.

"Have you got him?" Slaughter asked.

"He's mine. Go back for Dunlap."

Slaughter struggled back into the wreckage. Dunlap was slumped behind the pilot's seat, and Slaughter had to climb up to reach him. He stretched, his stomach hard against something, and gripped Dunlap's suit coat, tugging.

"Dunlap, can you hear me?"

Dunlap moaned.

"We have to get you out of here." Slaughter's chest was pressed so hard against the top part of the pilot's seat that he almost couldn't muster enough breath to talk. He tugged again. "You hear me?" He gasped. "This thing's leaking fuel. We have to get you out of here."

Slaughter tugged again, and this time Dunlap moved a little.

"Good. That's good. You're going to make it," Slaughter told him. "Unhitch your seatbelt. Try to climb down toward me."

Dunlap peered groggily toward Slaughter, and his face

was bloody. "What?"

"Unhitch your seatbelt. Let me grab you."

Dunlap nodded, but his eyes were stupid, and he didn't move.

"You've got to—"

"Yes, I heard you. Can't you see I'm trying?" Dunlap murmured.

"Jesus, try harder. This thing's going to blow."

Dunlap nodded again. He blinked, fumbled to release his seatbelt, and tried to push himself toward Slaughter. Then Slaughter had him, tugging, and they both slid downward, tumbling low against the instrument panel on the upended helicopter. Slaughter felt Dunlap's weight upon him, gasping. "Dunlap, I can't breathe." Slaughter's voice was muffled by Dunlap's chest against his face.

"I'll get him off you," Slaughter heard. He felt Hammel reaching in, and then the weight was off him.

Slaughter inhaled deeply. "Get moving."

"What about—?"

"I'll bring the rifles and equipment."

"Leave them."

"Can't. We'll need them. Get away."

Hammel almost argued. Abruptly he lifted Dunlap and stumbled through the boulders.

Slaughter strained to raise his head, and then he stood and stretched up to grab the knapsacks, which had fallen behind the seats. He threw them out. Then he grabbed the rifles. He was just about to leave when he saw the camera he had lent Dunlap. Gripping it, he lurched from the helicopter. He fell, gasped, wavered to his feet, hoisted the knapsacks and rifles, and he was running. The odor of fuel was everywhere. He stumbled over a branch, but he managed to keep his balance, and he kept running although he didn't know where he was going.

"Over here."

He saw Hammel on a slope above him, tugging Lucas and Dunlap, fir trees thrashing in the wind. Slaughter struggled up the slope, but they were moving higher, cresting, disappearing down the other side. He rushed to catch them, smelling fuel. He slipped and almost fell but kept surging higher. Then he reached the crest and lurched across it, saw them and tumbled toward them, falling. He fought to breathe, huddled among sheltering boulders.

"Those packs weren't worth the risk," Hammel said.

"The rifles are, and anyway we're stuck up here, we have to eat."

"I still say—"

"Are you hurt? Is anybody hurt?" Slaughter asked.

"Well, *he* is."

They frowned at Dunlap who was propped against a boulder, his eyes closed, blood across his forehead.

"Dunlap, can you hear me?" Slaughter asked.

"Let me rest a minute."

"Hold still while I check your head."

Dunlap's hair was bloody, matted. Slaughter saw the gash above his hairline.

"Is it deep?" Hammel asked.

"I don't know. There's too much blood."

"Oh, Jesus," Dunlap muttered.

"You're all right. The blood is clotting."

"Jesus, Jesus."

"Take it easy. Lucas?" Slaughter turned to him. He saw that Lucas was awake at least. The eyes were cloudy, narrowed, but nonetheless open.

"I hear you," Lucas said.

"This knapsack." Slaughter tossed it to him. "There's a first-aid kit. Some bandages and disinfectant. Help me." Slaughter could have done it by himself, or he could have asked Hammel, but he wanted Lucas to get moving, to regain control, and now he turned to Dunlap. "Just hold on. Apart from your head, does the rest of you feel okay?"

"I'm sore, but nothing's broken. At least, I don't think so. Jesus." Dunlap winced, and Slaughter watched as Lucas found and opened the first-aid kit. Slaughter took a bandage. Then he fumbled in the second knapsack for a canteen, wet the bandage, and swabbed at Dunlap's face.

"You're looking better."

Dunlap shook his head and grimaced as Slaughter dabbed the gash above his hairline.

"There's no more dirt that I can see. I don't see any bone.

These head wounds can be awfully bloody, even when they're nothing."

"Slaughter, you don't need to lie to me."

"I'm telling you it's deep but not too bad. We'll make sure you don't go to sleep. We'll watch for signs of a concussion. If you get afraid, though, you'll only make it worse. Now hold still while I do this."

Slaughter opened a tube and squeezed disinfectant onto the wound. He put a square of gauze on top, then wrapped a bandage around the head and tied it. "Don't touch the bandage. It might slip off."

Dunlap nodded, slumping lower against the boulder. "Jesus, Jesus."

Slaughter opened a canteen. "Here. These pills will help the pain."

He watched as Dunlap took the pills, drank, and swallowed. Then Slaughter turned to Lucas and Hammel. "Both of you are sure you're all right?"

Both men thought a moment, felt themselves, and nodded.

"What about you?" Hammel asked.

"A little dizzy."

"Let's hope that doesn't mean you're going into shock."

"At least the chopper didn't explode," Lucas said.

Slaughter leaned against a boulder, wincing. "Well, I guess things could be worse, although right now I'd hate to think exactly how. We'll rest a little. Then we'll look for Parsons."

"Better make it soon. The sun is heading down."

They all looked up then, and the sun was dipping toward the rockwall up there. The wind thrashed the forest.

"How soon?"

"I don't know. A couple of hours."

"And if we don't find Parsons by then," Slaughter said, "in the dark we might *never* find him."

EIGHT

The gruesome discovery of the mutilated organs and the

dismembered skeleton had not been anything that they'd expected. They'd anticipated the possibility of finding corpses, yes, but not organs that had been chewed and bones from which the flesh had been gnawed. No one had imagined that further degree of horror. For a time they were distracted by the need to calm the man who'd fallen onto the guts and the bones. Then they directed their troubled attention toward the rockwall and were forced to decide if they intended to go farther.

"Look, in nineteen seventy I helped kick out those hippies, but I'm telling you that this bunch isn't like those others."

"Sure, that first bunch, they were pacifists."

"What do you mean 'pacifists'? They fought us."

"But they didn't want to. They knew they were whipped before they started."

"Christ, what's wrong with you guys? We just found—"

"I know what we just found. Don't talk about it."

"But they—"

"*I don't want to talk about it!* Did you think we'd just hike up, kick their asses, and chase them down the mountain?"

"Hey, you were as eager to come up here as the rest of us."

"Yeah. And now I wish to God I hadn't."

They were silent as the wind howled.

"Well, we have to make a choice. We either go on or go back."

"They'll catch us in the forest."

"What?"

"We don't have a choice. You saw the barricade, the blood. Hell, you saw Altick, what was left of him. They'll trap us, and they'll kill us."

"We've got too many men for that."

"You think so? There were—what?—five hundred hippies in that commune."

"There could be less," a man said, hoping.

"Or a shitload more."

The hopeful man frowned.

"Why not say *two* hundred? That's still more than we have, and they know these hills, they live up here. We haven't got a chance."

"Then what—?"

"I say we go up and get them before they come down for us."

Again the group was silent.

Parsons stood to one side. He listened, careful not to add his comments. Because he was frightened almost to the point of panic. They would hear his fright, and they would lose respect for him. If he had his way, they'd all be running down the mountain to reach the trucks and Jeeps. He'd assumed that this expedition would be 1970 revisited, but now he saw the truth, and he was terrified. He tried to calculate how to turn them back without revealing his fear. He saw the sun dip toward the mountains, and he knew that, even if the group left now, they would still have to spend the night away from their trucks and Jeeps. But anything was better than the implications of the rockwall they were facing. Going back, at least they had a chance.

The men continued talking.

"Pete makes some sense, you know that?"

"What? To finish them before they finish us?"

"It's better than just waiting for them."

"Sure. It's what we started out to do."

"But you're not listening."

"I heard you. Now shut up. I'm going on. At least this way we've got a chance of surprising them. Anybody coming with me?"

They stared.

"If we split our force, we don't have any chance at all."

"I'm going with you," someone said.

"Count me in as well,"

The rest were nodding.

"But I don't mind telling you—"

"You think the rest of us aren't scared?'

And that was good enough. They all frowned toward the rockwall.

"Let's get up there."

"No, I can't," the man who'd found the dismembered skeleton said.

"Stay behind then."

"You can't leave me."

"It's your choice. I'm sorry you found it. But you have to

get control."

The two men glared at each other, and the weak man swallowed. Looking at the ground, he nodded.

The group walked up the gametrail. Parsons joined them near the front, still maintaining the pretense that he was their leader, but he needed all his will power to keep from screaming, "You're all crazy! Let's get the hell away from here!"

## NINE

Slaughter waited, ready with his rifle, as he heard the noises in the forest. He glanced toward the wooded slope on his right where Hammel, Lucas, and Dunlap huddled, where Hammel had the other rifle ready, where Slaughter would have to run if there was trouble. They had left the area of the helicopter and climbed toward a higher ridge to find a vantage point. On one side, the rockwall had towered, cast in shadow by the lowering sun. On the other side, ridges had descended toward the valley. Straight below, close and vivid, was the gametrail. They had worked down through the forest, choosing a spot on the trail where slopes came down on the right and left and the trail itself was wide, and there they had planned their tactic, and they waited.

Slaughter didn't like his back exposed. He didn't know what thing might creep behind him. The light dimmed with every moment, and the noises in the forest now were louder, even in the wind. He thought he knew what was approaching, especially when he heard the voices, and he felt slightly more at ease, although not much. Then he saw the men in red-checkered shirts and khaki hunting jackets, Parsons near the front, and when they saw him, they slowed, then halted.

"Slaughter?" someone asked in surprise.

He didn't answer, just stood straighter, his rifle ready.

"Where'd you land the helicopter?"

"We heard you were in jail," another man said.

But Slaughter only pointed rigidly toward Parsons. "You and me."

"I don't—"

"We can do this in the open and let everybody hear, or else—"

"Yes, I want to talk to you." Parsons amazed Slaughter, stepping readily from the group.

Slaughter glared as Parsons reached him. "I should jam this rifle—"

"Keep your voice down," Parsons said.

"What?"

"These men are crazy," Parsons whispered. "No, don't look. I'm telling you. They want to go up to that mining town."

"For Christ sake, that's exactly what you wanted."

"Not any longer. Not after we found . . ."

Parsons explained.

And Slaughter's face went cold.

"Look, we've got to get down out of here," Parsons said.

"In the dark? How? And to where? We're not safe as long as they're around us."

Parsons stiffened. "Have you seen them?"

"You stupid . . . I ought to hit you over the head and call it a kindness. First, you bring them up here. Then you whine the second there's trouble."

"But this isn't like the hippies back in nineteen-seventy. They're going to—"

"Kill you? That's right," Slaughter said. "Now it's turned around. You're going to find out what it felt like. And I hope to God you suffer."

"You don't mean that."

"Almost. But I'll fix you in my own way. Listen to me. All of you. Get over here."

The group hesitated, then approached.

"Our fine mayor here made a slight miscalculation. It seems he thought that this was open season, that he'd bring you up to do a little hunting and then grin as you went back to town. Well, this is how it's going to work. We're going to find a place to camp. We're going to spend the night, and if there's trouble, we'll defend ourselves. In any case, we'll head back in the morning, and we'll calculate exactly what we're dealing with. We'll get the trained men we need."

He paused then. "Hear me? *Trained* men, not a bunch of weekend heroes, and we'll bring in all the gear we need, and we'll do this properly. My guess is, a few planes dropping some kind of sleeping gas up there will be enough to let us move in safely. We'll use straitjackets as restraints, and then we'll take the commune back to town and help them. But we're not about to shoot them if we've got another choice. It's one thing to defend ourselves, but I'm the law here, and what you men planned is murder."

"If the word gets out, if our buyers discover there's an epidemic, business here is finished," one man said. "We'll never sell our cattle."

"I can't take one side against the other. All I know is what the law is."

"Well, you came here from the East."

"I'd say the same no matter where I came from. You'll have to kill me before I let you kill somebody else without a reason. Have you got that?"

They glared.

"Anyhow, I think you'd like a graceful way to stop this. You don't have the vaguest notion what you're up against."

"We saw the—"

"So you know enough to want to quit now," Slaughter told them.

He felt their tension start to ease as he took the burden from them.

"I'm in charge now, and you'll all do what I say."

They brooded and nodded.

"Good." Slaughter studied them before he signaled to his companions up on the slope.

The group turned toward where Lucas, Dunlap, and Hammel stepped from the trees and bushes. Dunlap still had the bandage wrapped around his head.

"Why were they hiding?" someone asked.

"So they could be my witnesses if you made trouble. One of you was in Hammel's rifle sights."

The group frowned at the rifle.

"There's no time. The sun is almost down. We have to move. That ridge up there. At least we'll have the high ground."

"Christ, this wind will tear at us up there."

"I prefer the wind to whatever else might be in this forest," Slaughter said.

TEN

The wind persisted. Slaughter hunkered by some boulders on the ridge. The place was barren, just a razorback above the treeline. Here and there, mountain grass had caught hold, but the ground was mostly bare, and the men had either crouched among other boulders or else dragged dead trees onto the ridge and lay behind them, waiting, shaking from the cold.

Or so they told themselves that they were shaking from the cold. Hunched low to escape the wind, Slaughter was reminded of the cold in Detroit, of when he'd walked into that grocery store that winter night and found those two kids and been shot and how his world had changed. For the past five years, he'd lost his nerve. What puzzled him as he hunched waiting here now was that he wasn't afraid any longer. Oh, he was apprehensive. That was to be expected. But he wasn't frightened, and that puzzled him.

Pride, he guessed. Once his pride had started to grow, it had smothered his cowardice. Exactly when the pride had started, he didn't know. Perhaps when he had broken out of jail. Perhaps before that when he'd gone against what Parsons thought was best. Some moment in the past few days had been a turning point for him, and if this night would be his last, at least he knew that he would acquit himself with dignity. He wished his ex-wife could see him now, but then he realized that he was thinking too much. Memories like that were bad ones, and he shut them out and concentrated on the forest.

The night was thick, eerily so inasmuch as the sky was bright, the stars sharp, the moon an almost perfect brilliant circle, glowing coldly in the wind. The moon seemed extra large also, as if it had been magnified, and Slaughter felt its brooding power. Once he thought he heard a howl down in the woods, but in the shrieking wind he wasn't sure, and clutching to the woolen shirt that he'd taken from his knapsack and put on, he continued to study the forest.

Someone moved beside him. When he looked, he saw that it was Hammel, and he nodded, then redirected his gaze toward the trees below him.

"There's something I want to tell you," Hammel said.

"What is it?"

"That big speech you gave."

"I know. I'm embarrassed."

"No, listen. What you said about those hippies, about wanting to protect them . . . I admire you for standing up to Parsons."

Slaughter shrugged. "I watched a lot of kids get pushed around back in Detroit, and this is one place where it isn't going to happen. I don't care how sick those things up there might be, we're not about to kill them unless we're forced to. They once were people, still are if we find a way to help them, and I mean to try my best to do that." Slaughter shook his head. "I've seen enough hate. Some of it I felt against myself. I think it's time this town looked ahead instead of backward."

"Unless they come for us."

No reply.

"Slaughter?"

He was silent, staring toward the forest, and he groaned then.

"What's the matter?"

"Something hit me."

He rubbed his shoulder.

Something cracked against the boulder next to him. Something whipped hard past his head.

"It's stones."

"Get down! They're throwing stones!" a man nearby him shouted.

Slaughter winced and crouched low by the boulder, but the stones kept falling, pelting all around him. He held up an arm to shield his head. He heard the men around him shouting and felt the rocks crack down upon him.

"Well, it looks like they don't feel the same as you do, Slaughter. We'll soon have to fight."

"But there's a difference."

"I don't scc it."

"We're not looking for a fight. They're forcing us. This town's getting back what it gave out. They called these hippies 'animals,' and now their words have turned to fact and with a vengeance."

Slaughter gripped his rifle, and the stones abruptly stopped. He swung toward Hammel, puzzled.

"Hear it?"

Even in the wind, he couldn't help but hear it. Far off in the woods, Slaughter heard the howling. He saw the flash. He heard the blast. It came from a ridge above him, a massive fire-ball blossoming into the darkness. "The helicopter. That's where we left the helicopter."

Whump, whump, whump. In the opposite direction, the valley exploded. Whump, whump, whump. Pivoting, staring down, Slaughter saw more fireballs, dozens of them, the valley reminding him of a battlefield. Even at a distance, he felt the shockwaves.

"The Jeeps! The trucks!" a man nearby him shouted.

"They set fire to them!"

"The gas tanks!"

*Whump, whump, whump,* a steady sequence of explosions, mushrooming fireballs lighting up the night, and Slaughter, even with the ridges that obscured his vision, sensed the wider blaze, the parched mountain grass now burning, and he turned to peer upward toward the blaze from the helicopter again, shocked to see how far and fast those flames were spreading, torching trees and bushes, becoming a fire storm.

"The wind. It's fanning everything."

The blaze consumed the upper ridge, illuminating the faces of the men, revealing the rocks and ground quite clearly.

"We're a target now."

Even as Slaughter said that, more rocks pelted on them.

"Get down!"

"It's the wind. The wind will push the fire toward us. It'll sweep down across this ridge to reach the other trees and scorch us."

Slaughter clutched his injured shoulder, dropping. Men were screaming, shouting. In the lowland, burning mountain grass had led up to the underbrush and then the trees. The hills below were all ablaze now. And the howling was around them, and the rocks kept pelting them. Now the roar of flames blended with that of the wind, and Slaughter struggled to his feet to scan the slope above and behind him, where the blaze was tree-high, looming toward them.

When the next rock struck him, Slaughter made his choice. Some of the men were shooting toward the bottom of the ridge.

"Stop it!" he shouted. "You can't see your targets. There's no chance. We have to get away from here."

The flames below them roared closer.

"Everybody get over here! We have to move along this ridge, stay away from *that* ridge"—Slaughter pointed toward the burning slope above them—"and get around the fire to higher cover!"

No one listened. They were shooting, screaming as more rocks struck all around them. Slaughter glanced frantically from the flames on the upper ridge toward the burning lowland on his opposite side. He could see hills for miles around now.

"Let's get started! Help!" he blurted to Hammel, then scrambled toward Dunlap, Lucas, Parsons, anybody. "Get these men to follow me. We have to work along the ridge, away from these flames, toward higher cover."

A rock struck Slaughter's back. Another walloped his thigh. Ignoring the pain, he pointed toward a dry streambed that veered upward away from the fire. He shouted more instructions as rocks hailed all around him, and from above, he felt the scorching heat approach the ridge. "Get moving!"

It likely wasn't so much what he said as what they sensed. They couldn't stay here. They were shooting less. They glanced around. They stared down at the fire. The rocks were hurtling toward them, and the blaze in the lowland kept getting wider, brighter, stronger. There wasn't any sense in running toward it. They were forced to move along the angle of the razorback toward the dry streambed that Slaughter had noticed and that would lead them away from the fires up toward the rockwall.

"Let's do it!"

Frantic, they started. Slaughter didn't realize until later that the route they followed had been calculated for them, that they had been pushed in one direction and were headed for a trap. But no one else took the time to figure it either. All they knew was that they had to get away, and they were shouldering their knapsacks, grabbing rifles, stumbling across the boulders up the razorback toward the streambed and the rockwall, their silhouettes made vivid by the flames below them, easy targets as the rocks kept coming.

"Watch for anybody hurt! Make sure you bring them!"

Men were falling, moaning, others kneeling, staring at the blood on their hands and their clothes. Slaughter tugged a man to his feet and struggled up the razorback with him. Around him, others were limping, moaning, flinching.

They reached the streambed and kept going. Then the fire was a distance from them. Even so, the flames kept roaring, pushed by the wind, and the men didn't dare rest. Soon the blaze would come for them again. The rocks continued to pelt them as they stumbled higher, on occasion shooting, mostly fleeing, working upward, and the rockwall—lit by the moon and the blazing trees—was vivid, high above them as they struggled.

Time was telescoped. It seemed like twenty minutes, but it must have taken several hours for their panicked flight. The streambed sloped high up toward the rockwall, and the rocks kept striking them all the while they ran and stumbled, screaming. Then the flames were far behind them as they came rushing from the streambed onto flat ground. They ran up to the rockwall and stopped abruptly, puzzled, gasping, staring all around.

Finally they understood.

"Christ, they've trapped us."

Rocks swooped toward them from three sides. The cliff was behind them, and they bunched there, facing outward, shooting. One man and then another fell. The group consolidated, crowding closer, tighter.

Slaughter was the first to notice. Pausing to reload, he glanced to his left and saw the ancient wooden structure in the shadows that were half lit by the flames in the lowland.

"What's this thing here?"

"It's the railroad," someone said and chambered a fresh cartridge.

"Railroad?"

"When they mined the gold, they built a railroad. That's the trestle. It slopes toward the valley."

Slaughter almost couldn't hear him amid the rifle reports, amid the blasts from shotguns and handguns. He was almost blinded by the muzzle flashes. A rock struck his throat, and he felt as if he was being choked.

"We can climb it," someone said.

"Climb the trestle," others echoed.

Slumped on one knee, Slaughter fought to breathe, to overcome the swelling in his throat. A rock whizzed past his head while others clattered against the cliff behind him. He swayed to his feet, leaned against the cliff, and massaged his throat as the group surged toward the trestle. Lucas stopped to help him.

"I think I can manage," Slaughter gasped. His voice was hoarse, disturbing him as he stumbled to catch up to the men.

They all tried to climb it at once.

"No, it won't hold. A few men at a time," Hammel ordered.

But no one listened. They were clustered on the trestle, on the zig-zagging beams that supported it. One beam started creaking.

Slaughter, overwhelmed by anger now, charged close and jerked several men from the trestle. "You and you shoot to give us cover. *You* get off. The rest of you stay the hell back while these men climb."

His voice was raspy, distorted. They glared at him, and unexpectedly they obeyed. Kneeling among the beams, they shot toward the blazing darkness while above them other men climbed. Slaughter heard the scrape of their boots, the groan of old wood, the clatter of rocks striking near him. The flame-ravaged valley echoed from their shooting.

"You five men," Slaughter groaned. "Now it's your turn."

The pattern was established. Small units of men climbed in relays while the other men shot at unseen targets in the trees, guided by the trajectory of the hurtling rocks. Slaughter remained at the bottom, rasping orders, shooting, flinching from stones that periodically struck him. More men now were climbing, and again time was telescoped. The next thing Slaughter realized, Hammel was beside him.

"Now it's our turn."

Slaughter glanced around. He saw Hammel, Lucas, a few other men. He didn't know where Dunlap was, or Parsons, but he understood that this was the last of the group. He gripped his rifle, and he reached up toward a beam, and he was climbing. Once he almost lost the rifle, and he wished it had a strap, but there was no way to provide one now, and he kept climbing, reaching. He felt the old beams sag, the soft wood crumble in his hands, but the trestle was holding.

When he heard the scream, he looked down, and one man slipped. Falling, the man struck two beams and thudded in the darkness, where he didn't seem to move. Around the man, grotesque figures swirled. Can't look down, Slaughter told himself. I have to keep climbing. He was worried that it had been Lucas or Hammel who had fallen, but as he glanced toward the beams across from him, he saw Lucas and Hammel climbing. Still puzzled about where Dunlap and Parsons were, Slaughter strained and reached and kneed and stretched.

Peering over the top, he saw the group waiting. In the moonlight and the glow from the fires below, their expressions were unnervingly stark. Slaughter clutched for a handhold, crawled up from the final beam, and limped across the railroad ties toward solid rock. The trestle never should have held. He knew that. He never understood why it had. The fire that scoured this area of mountains eventually burned the trestle, so nobody had the chance to examine it in the daylight and understand the miracle of its construction. But meanwhile the wind intensified, funneling toward them from the lowland, surging up the draw that they were in, and pushed by it, they followed its urging. One thing favored them. Whatever had attacked them was below them. Granted, the figures were no doubt climbing the trestle, pursuing, but for the moment, Slaughter and his group were safe. They struggled up the narrow pass, the glint of snow on each peak flanking them. The wind howled at their backs. They worked onward, too exhausted to run.

"We have to find cover before they catch us," someone said.

"No," another man objected. "We have to keep going. If we reach the other entrance to the pass, we can get the hell away from here."

"That's stupid. They'll be waiting for us."

"They're behind us."

"Maybe."

They plodded forward without energy or reason.

Slaughter squinted back toward the burning lowland. As he turned ahead, the wind propelled him like a fist, and at last he saw Dunlap, Parsons, other men he recognized. But many others were missing. Some men moaned while others cursed. Still others were too weak even to murmur. They stumbled, limping, spread out through this narrow draw like refugees or soldiers in confused retreat. Then Slaughter heard the howling close behind him.

"They're up here now," he said. "They'll be coming."

"Look for cover."

But there wasn't any. There was just the narrow draw, the steep wind-scoured rocky slopes on each side leading toward the snow-capped peaks, and they kept moving.

Then they saw it.

"What?"

"The town. We've reached the town."

One of the men had a flashlight. He scanned its beam toward a dangling weathered sign that told them MOTHERLODE. Then other men fumbled for flashlights, turning them on. They saw listing shacks, tumbled sheds, crumbled walls, toppled roofs, sagging doorways. There were slogans on them in a language no one understood and no one ever would, stark cryptic signs and scrawls and symbols, and the streets were like a midden heap, the garbage from the mining town and from the culture that had been invented up here, a sprawling mass of junk and worn-out objects which as everyone approached turned out to be huge piles of bones, some human, others unidentifiable. The curses of the men combined with the roar of the wind and the howling that approached them.

"Okay, then, damn it, if they want a fight—!"

The flashlights lanced across the darkness. In the lowland, everything was burning. From the valley far across, the night sky was pierced by lightning. Thunder rumbled toward them. It was madness. The first man who reached in his pack to pull out a bottle filled with gasoline inspired all the others. Parsons had instructed them well. They'd come prepared.

The bottles were soft-drink empties, their twist-on caps sealing their dangerous contents. The men now unscrewed the caps. They pulled out handkerchiefs or tore off strips of clothing and stuffed them into the open bottlenecks. A frantic man lit his, braced himself, thrust his arm back, and threw the flaming bottle. Others watched as it flipped blazing through the darkness and struck a shack. The shatter of the breaking glass was followed by a whoosh, a surge of light, and the shack was suddenly in flames that shot skyward with stunning abruptness. Someone made a sound as if he watched fireworks. Another bottle had been lit, and after it arched toward the other slope, it struck a shack, exploded, and the street was flanked by flames now as the group huddled, gaping toward the trestle and what neared them: gimping, spastic, growling, frenzied, hairy figures, cloaked in furs, their mouths frothing, their limbs jerking. Lightning flashed in the valley. Ridges flamed in the lowlands. Winds fanned the burning shacks and spread destruction to their neighbors.

Slaughter shot and aimed and shot again as did the others near him. Burning bottles burst among the jerking figures. The things were moaning, howling, screaming. But they kept coming, relentlessly stumbling toward the gunfire. Nothing seemed to stop them. They had risen from the dead too many times. Confident of immortality, they were unafraid, ignoring the wounds that halted them a moment but didn't drop them. Some were in flames as they reached the group that shot them. The things struck with clubs. They howled. They slashed. They clawed. They kicked and bit.

Slaughter shot one, then another. As his rifle clicked on empty for the last time, he drew his handgun, aiming, shooting, aiming. Other flaming bottles burst before him. Men screamed as they fought hand-to-hand with the figures. Friends around him fell back. Those behind him tried to regroup. Half the town up here was burning, cryptic symbols gone forever, as Slaughter's handgun clicked on empty as well, and while he lurched back, attempting to reload, something struck him. It was big and solid, hairy. It was foul with stench and rot, and it was on him, slashing with its teeth and claws. He tried to push it off him, but its teeth sank into his wrist, and he was screaming.

"Jesus, no, don't bite me!"

But the thing braced its teeth and twisted, grinding, and the pain, the shock of fear was so intense that Slaughter didn't realize what he was doing. When he regained awareness, he saw how he had clubbed his handgun at the figure until fluid oozed from the figure's skull, and it was motionless on the ground beside him. Slaughter gasped, staring at his shredded wrist.

"I've got it!" he screamed. "I'm like them now! Christ, I've got it!"

That would be his most heroic moment, what in memory would be the apex of his life, the quick consideration that would save him. Thinking of the foulness creeping up his arm to reach his shoulder and his brain, thinking of the monster he would shortly be, he struck out with his handgun toward another monstrous figure, turned, saw Parsons, and ran. Parsons noticed him, Parsons who suddenly became rigid, the fear in his eyes more fierce than any emotion he'd ever displayed, for Parsons must have thought of Slaughter's anger toward him, must have assumed that Slaughter was already maddened and changed. Parsons raised his shotgun, firing blindly. Slaughter faltered as the pellets struck his side. But the image of the two kids in that grocery store returned to him, and he mustered the strength to keep running. As Parsons pumped a fresh shell into the shotgun's chamber, Slaughter reached him, knocked him flat, grabbed the shotgun, raised it to his shoulder, and he couldn't have accomplished this if he had not been large and tall the way he was, but with his great reach he could manage. Flames around him, buildings burning, lightning flashing, Slaughter pulled the trigger and blew his contaminated arm off.

ELEVEN

Dunlap huddled in the blackness of the tunnel. The sight of the gruesome battle had so unnerved him that he'd stumbled backward, tripped, and fallen. Raising his frightened gaze, he'd glimpsed the tunnel's murky entrance and raced to it for shelter, so afraid that his sphincter muscle weakened, making him void his bowels, the revolting stench humiliating him as he crouched and whimpered in the tunnel.

This at last was his great truth, the story he had worked for, and he couldn't bear to watch it. He was a loser, not because he drank too much so often or because he had that trouble with his wife or because the big investigations never came his way. He was a loser simply because he wasn't the man he thought he was. He had run in panic with the other men toward the cliff. He had been the first man to climb in a frenzy up the trestle. He had known reporters who in Vietnam had stood with soldiers in the shriek of battle. He had known other reporters who had clambered into burning buildings or had waded into flooding rivers or had argued with a gunman holding hostages.

Not him, though. He had always said that he just never had the chance, but now he knew he didn't *want* the chance. When the opportunity occurred, he'd persistently *avoided* the chance. Now he saw the battle raging closer to the tunnel, and in fright, the stench of his voided bowels much worse, he groped backward, farther along the tunnel, fleeing. He gripped at the timbers. He felt along the clammy walls, and then he understood that, while he had befouled himself and caused this obscene stench, another stench was in here too, and despite his revulsion, he didn't understand his compulsion to fumble toward it.

From the change in sound, he realized that he was in a chamber, and he had a flashlight in the pack that Slaughter had lent him. Bringing out the light, switching it on, he scanned the chamber.

He moaned.

No! He didn't want this. He didn't want to see it. Dear God, he had fled for sanctuary to their secret place of burial. On wooden pallets along the floor, he saw their bodies, fetid, ugly, lined in neat rows, clubs beside them, rotted meat, their arms crossed gently on their fur-skinned chests. The mass of them were maggot-ridden horrors. Others were more recent, and as he lurched hard against a slimy wall, he saw that one was moving, rising from its death-like sleep, groggy, drawing breath for energy.

Dunlap screamed as the creature turned toward him. It was frowning. In a moment, it was grinning. Sure, Dunlap thought, remembering the boy who had seemed dead and then returned to life. The virus. These things didn't know what death was. Some returned and others didn't, but they all in time were laid to rest here in the expectation that they eventually would rise again. Dunlap dimly sensed the paintings on the wall: the bear, the antelope, the deer. They leapt in rampant silent beauty, clubs and rocks drawn next to them as if the animals fled from the weapons about to strike them. And the creature was kneeling, grinning, frothing, snarling, gaining strength to spring as all the tension Dunlap had been feeling clamored for release. He screamed in fury, lashing forward, striking with his flashlight, breaking teeth. He struck again and then again, feeling cheekbones snap, eyes burst. He hit until he completely lost his strength, and what had crouched before him lay still and silent.

Dunlap wept. He sank to the floor and sobbed until he thought his mind would crack. Hitting the creature, he'd broken his flashlight. He was trapped in the darkness. From outside, he heard the battle, heard the shooting and the screaming. He was torn between his need to flee this room and his determination to avoid the battle.

But he couldn't stay here in the darkness. He heard noises. Another figure rising? He groped to his knees, then his feet, and fumbled toward the tunnel. Then he found it, and he shuffled down it, bumping against the walls.

But the tunnel went on too far. In horror, he understood that by now he should have seen the flames outside. Dear Christ, he'd gone in the wrong direction. He was in a different tunnel.

"No!" he told himself. "No!" He needed *light,* and then he thought about the camera. Slaughter had retrieved it from the helicopter. It dangled from a sling on Dunlap's neck. Desperate, he raised the camera and triggered its flash. At once, although briefly, he saw more paintings. A bear. An antelope. A deer. The bear who seemed to die in the winter and come back to life in the spring. The antelope and deer who, when the cunning of the hunt was ended, willingly gave up their lives to feed those who'd stalked them.

Symbols of a death cult, and as Dunlap triggered the camera's flash again, his edge of vision showed him something high on the wall that both terrified and attracted him. He knew what it was. He didn't want to see it. But he had to, and he aimed the camera. He pressed the button. The flash went off. A second's brightness, and a charcoal drawing of his nightmare appeared before him, crouched sideways, part man, part cat, part wide-antlered elk, with paws and a tail, its deep eyes turning past its shoulder, glaring at him.

Dunlap was stunned, immobile. No. He insisted to himself that he hadn't seen it. This had to be a trick of his imagination. So he shifted, and his hands shook, but he nonetheless managed to aim again and trigger the camera's flash, and this time he saw more of the chamber. Not just the drawing of his nightmare, but something below it. Quiller's car. The red Corvette. The throne room. Red room. And above the car, beside Dunlap's nightmare, was an even greater nightmare, the final obscene horror. Quiller. What had finally become of Quiller. Quiller was mounted on a cross upon the wall, his arms stretched out, his hands and feet nailed, his gaunt naked body sagging, maggots dripping, his hair and beard grotesquely long, having continued to grow after he died. They had crucified him with fervent belief in the final miracle, the expectation of his resurrection. Something cracked in Dunlap's mind. He finally discovered peace.

### TWELVE

The townspeople talked about it as if years from now the story would assume the aspect of a legend, how the final battle of 1970 had taken place years later, the traumas of the past expunged with fire, how the western section of the mountains had been razed, the trestle burned, the mining town obliterated. Only ten men lived beyond the battle. Slaughter, Parsons, Lucas, Dunlap, and six others. By all logic, Slaughter should have died from his self-mutilation, but he was strong, his frame large, his constitution robust, and although he was close to death when everything was finished, Lucas cauterized the stump of his arm, then bound it. He and Parsons carried Slaughter through the pass and down the other side where they struggled across the next valley and by afternoon managed to reach a road. Dunlap almost wasn't found, but one man checked the tunnel, used a flashlight to learn its horrifying secrets, and saw Dunlap, kneeling, wide-eyed, staring up in reverence at Quiller. Dunlap never spoke again. In town, they joked that he had found religion, but the joke was poor because it *wasn't* any joke, it was the truth, and Dunlap's eyes were filled with silent wonder ever after. Hammel had died in the battle, clubbed to death until his skull was split in two. Parsons left town shortly after returning to it, before the investigation started. Owens had already gone, and neither man came back.

One day in late September, Slaughter managed the strength to go into town. He still was weak and light-headed, but he was alive, and that was really all he wanted, that and his new purity, his courage. He drove in to see the medical examiner. Because he had only one arm, he had to drive an automatic, and he wasn't with the force now, Rettig ran that, so he didn't have a cruiser. He parked at the house, which he had never been to, fumbled to open his car door and got out, walking across the grass. He felt off balance from the change of weight because of his missing arm, and he moved slowly, glancing at the boxes and the suitcases stacked on the porch.

The medical examiner came out to face him.

"I heard you were leaving," Slaughter said.

"That's right."

"I hate to see you go."

"Well, it's like King John and his pears."

"His what?"

"His pears. They say he died from a surfeit of them."

And Slaughter only stared.

"You know, the Magna Carta."

"Yes, I know which John you mean."

"He slept once at a convent. He'd been screwing all the nuns, or so the story goes. The outraged monks put poison in his food, although his death was caused, they claimed, by getting sick from eating too many pears."

"I don't quite get the point."

"Well, it's like . . ." The medical examiner paused. "It's like I'm suffering from a surfeit of death. Too much death. You don't know how it was."

"I have a fair idea."

"No, you missed it. All the cleanup. All the bodies they brought in. From the commune. From here in town. I stayed this long because I thought I could forget it, but I can't. It's too much, too damned much altogether."

Slaughter glanced at the weed-choked grass. He took his time. "Well, I won't argue."

"There's no sense. I'm going to Chicago. Hell, I'm going

to be a doctor."

"That's what you are now."

"But only for the dead. I'm going to treat the living now. I never want to see another corpse again."

And Slaughter nodding, continuing to stare.

"Resurrection," the medical examiner told him.

### THIRTEEN

Slaughter drove back to where he now was living, not to his place but to Wheeler's ranch where Lucas now was the owner. Sometimes Marge came out to cook for them, but mostly just the three of them were out there. Slaughter helped to tend the stock as best he could when he wasn't tending to the needs of Dunlap. Everyone finally had gained what each had wanted. Lucas had a father. Slaughter had another chance to have a son. Dunlap had his story, and his mind was now at rest, though not his body. Slaughter cleaned it, fed it, cared for it. He wasn't quite sure why, except that this man had become a friend, and anyway nobody else would take this man. Dunlap's wife had finally divorced him.

Life was peaceful. The full moon on the summer solstice had intensified the brilliance of the prior night when Slaughter had lost his arm. The fire, though, had destroyed the commune, all its members, those that Slaughter's group had not already destroyed. The town had lived in terror, but the help from outside had arrived. The infected animals and cattle were exterminated. The valley was a wasteland that at last had started its revival. Part of what had helped had been the storm that followed with the wind and cleansed the valley after flames had purified the mountains.

One discovery had been important. After the figure who had staggered into town at last had died, samples of the creature's blood had been enough to produce a vaccine that would stop the infection from spreading. The virus was no longer a threat, and as Slaughter sat now on the porch, he noticed that the blanket he had placed on Dunlap's knees was sagging.

Slaughter stood from where he rested in a hammock. He walked over and used his remaining hand to arrange the blanket.

"There. That's better. There'll be a frost they say tonight. We don't want you to catch a cold."

Dunlap rocked and gazed in peace toward the rangeland.

"That's the stuff. You thirsty?" Slaughter asked.

Dunlap continued rocking.

"Have a drink."

Slaughter poured a glass of beer and tipped it up to Dunlap's lips. The reporter swallowed, drooling.

"There. That's just the answer."

Slaughter wiped Dunlap's lips and drank from the same glass. "Nice place, don't you think? Do you guess you're going to like it here?"

Dunlap kept rocking.

"Sure you are. It's lovely. Just the place for us."

Then Slaughter returned to the hammock where he lay back, sipping. Life was good now. He had earned it. As he glanced out toward the rangeland, he saw Lucas riding on his pinto, admiring the other horses. There were cattle on the range as well. When Marge arrived tonight, she would watch over Dunlap while the one-armed man and the son in need of a father would ride out to check the steers, and in the meantime, Slaughter leaned back, smiling, as the setting sun cast an alpenglow on Lucas who rode straight and strong, and a colt veered from its mother, and they gamboled in the sun.